Developing Teachers

Educational Change and Development Series

Re-schooling Society
David Hartley

The Gender Politics of Educational Change
Amanda Datnow

The Rules of School Reform
Max Angus

Whose School is it Anyway?
Kathryn Riley

Developing Teachers: The Challenges of Lifelong Learning
Chris Day

Change Forces: The Sequel
Michael Fullan

Developing Teachers: The Challenges of Lifelong Learning

Christopher Day

UK Falmer Press, 1 Gunpowder Square, London, EC4A 3DF
USA Falmer Press, 325 Chestnut Street, 8th Floor, Philadelphia, PA 19106

First published in 1999

A catalogue record for this book is available from the British Library

ISBN 0 7507 0748 8 cased
ISBN 0 7507 0747 x paper

Library of Congress Cataloging-in-Publication Data are available on request

Jacket design by Caroline Archer

Typeset in 10/12 pt Times by
Graphicraft Limited, Hong Kong

Printed in Great Britain by Biddles Ltd., Guildford and King's Lynn on paper which has a specified pH value on final paper manufacture of not less than 7.5 and is therefore 'acid free'.

Contents

List of Figures

Acknowledgments

To the many children, young people, and teachers whom I have taught and from whom I have learned over the years.

To Alison, Simon and Tim for allowing me the space to write.

To the colleagues who have read and produced feedback on the drafts of this book, especially John Elliott, Andy Hargreaves, David Hopkins, and Judyth Sachs.

To Michael Eraut for his special brand of critical friendship in this and other ventures over the years.

To Tricia King for transforming difficult manuscript into clean copy.

To the teachers, headteachers and teacher educators who continue to commit their knowledge, skill and enthusiasm, often against the odds, to the education of children and young people.

I am grateful to the following for permission to reproduce figures:

Dr N. Hatton for Figure 2.1: Hatton and Smith (1995) 'Facilitating reflection: Issues and research', *Forum of Education*, **50**, 1, April, pp. 49–65.

Swets and Zeitlinger for Figure 2.2: Handal (1991) 'Promoting the articulation of tacit knowledge through the counselling of practitioners', in Letiche, H.K., van der Wolf, J.C. and Plooij, F.X. (eds) *The Practitioner's Power of Choice in Staff Development and In-Service Training*, Amsterdam: Swets and Zeitlinger BV.

Professor R. Burgess and Dr D. Ebbutt for Figure 2.3: adapted from Ebbutt (1985) 'Educational action research: Some general concerns and specific quibbles', in Burgess, R. (ed.) *Issues in Educational Research: Qualitative Methods*, London: Falmer Press, pp. 152–176.

Teachers College, Columbia University for Figure 2.4: based on Cochran Smith and Lytle (1996) 'Communities for teacher research: Fringe or forefront?' adapted by permission of the publisher from McLaughlin, M.W. and Oberman, I. (eds) *Teacher Learning: New Policies, New Practices*, New York: Teachers College Press © 1996 by Teachers College, Columbia University. All rights reserved.

Professor Michael Eraut for Figure 3.1 from Eraut (1994) *Developing Professional Knowledge and Competence*, London: Falmer Press, p. 124; and Figure 3.2 from Eraut (1996) *Professional Knowledge in Teachers Education*, University of Juensu, Bulletin of the Faculty of Education, **64**, pp. 1–27.

Teachers College, Columbia University for Figure 3.3: Huberman (1995) Reprinted by permission of the publisher from GUSKEY, T.R. and HUBERMAN, M. (eds) *Professional Development in Education: New Paradigms and Practices*, New York: Teachers College Press © 1995 by Teachers College, Columbia University. All rights reserved.

Allyn and Bacon for Figure 3.4: Fessler and Christensen (1992) *The Teacher Career Cycle: Understanding and Guiding the Professional Development of Teachers*, R. Fessler and J. Christensen © 1992 Boston: Allyn and Bacon.

ASCD and Ken Leithwood for Figure 3.5: Leithwood (1990) 'The principal's role in teacher development,' in JOYCE, B. (ed.) *Changing School Culture through Staff Development*, ASCD Yearbook, p. 73.

Cassell for Figure 4.1: adapted from Hargreaves (1991) 'Cultures of teaching: A focus for change', in HARGREAVES, A. and FULLAN, M. (eds) *Understanding Teacher Development*, London: Cassell.

Dr L. Stoll and Open University Press for Figure 4.2: Stoll and Fink (1996) *Changing Our Schools*, Buckingham, Open University Press, p. 85.

Croom Helm for Figure 7.1: Bolam (1986) 'Conceptualizing In-service', in HOPKINS, D. (ed.) *In-Service Training and Educational Development: An International Survey*, Beckenhan: Croom Helm.

Professor D. Hopkins for Figure 7.2: adapted from Hopkins (1989) in JOYCE, B. and SHOWERS, B. (eds) 'Improving in-service training: The messages of research', *Educational Leadership*, **37**, 5, pp. 379–385.

Carfax Publishing Company for Figure 9.1: from Huberman (1995) 'Networks that alter teaching: Conceptualizing exchanges and experiments', *Teachers & Teaching: Theory and Practice*, **1**, 2, October, p. 193.

Preface

Chris Day has been a major contributor to research and thinking about teachers' professional development for nearly 20 years. In this important and timely book he updates and expands his thinking, putting his own experience of working with teachers in a wider context which encompasses other strands of research, particularly those focusing on teachers' life histories and teachers' daily work in classrooms. The result is a most comprehensive review of teachers' learning and the wide range of factors which affect it. He returns afresh and with renewed enthusiasm to the project of improving the quality of education through developing the professionality and capabilities of teachers. But he also asks the broader, deeper questions about teachers' learning. Are the goals worthwhile? Does it serve the pupils' interests? Are learning programmes properly negotiated, planned and resourced? What motivates teachers to engage in self-directed learning?

Apart from the perennial issue of funding, the two issues preoccupying policy makers for the compulsory period of schooling must be the quality of teaching, and the recruitment and retention of good teachers. Research has increasingly revealed that teaching is a complex process involving a range of activities and that its quality depends on appropriate adaptation of teacher capabilities to particular pupils and particular contexts. Moreover, analysis of post-war society would indicate increasingly rapid social and economic change in almost any location. Not only have the outcomes of schooling changed radically but so also has the behaviour of teachers and pupils. The quality of teaching clearly depends on teachers continuing to learn as teaching contexts, pupil behaviour and expectation of teachers change. Even if there was less change the challenge of adapting to the needs of individual pupils and seeking to improve the quality of one's teaching and associated professional activities would require continuing professional development. Thus the central questions of the book — *How, when and under what conditions do teachers learn?* — are of supreme importance.

Provided one has the requisite prior knowledge, motivation is the most critical factor in learning. Ideally both intrinsic motivation — the disposition to follow one's interests, acquire knowledge and become more capable — and extrinsic motivation — the confidence that the goals of learning are achievable and valuable — should be present. One of the great strengths of this book is that teachers' motivation to learn is treated as problematic. There are factors which encourage it and factors which discourage it, and these have to be constantly kept in mind. Moreover, some of the more discouraging factors may be the same aspects of the teacher's job and work context as those which make it difficult to recruit and retain good teachers.

One major contradiction in education policy which the book identifies arises from a double emphasis on basic schooling and lifetime learning. In order to become lifetime learners, young people will need to leave school motivated towards further learning and confident in their ability, with appropriate guidance, to set and achieve their own learning goals. But basic schooling is normally conceived in terms of following structured courses of study towards tightly specified achievement targets, with little opportunity to participate in goal setting or self-directed learning. Because these learning targets are easier for some to achieve than others, a significant proportion of each age group emerge without confidence in themselves as learners. Even those who are successful in the school context may find themselves ill-prepared for learning in other contexts, where there is less structured support for learning. It is difficult to believe that this discontinuity between the need to prepare young adults for lifetime learning and the demands and conditions of schooling will survive long into the next millennium.

This brings us to another central theme of the book. How can teachers' learning best be facilitated and supported by management? Day consistently argues that learning goals should be explicitly negotiated between teachers and management to meet the perceived needs of both parties; and that teacher's commitment of time and effort to major learning endeavours should be matched by management support within the limits of its resources. The imaginative initiation and support by management of collaborative learning arrangements is also needed to ensure that an appropriate range of learning opportunities is available for teachers. The purposes are (1) to establish a positive learning climate in schools; (2) to maintain a programme of change which enables them to continue to meet the needs of their pupils and; (3) to make teachers enthusiastic participants in a learning community.

Day warns also against an alternative strategy being increasingly adopted in many countries: the introduction of performance management systems based on tightly specified learning targets for pupils and teachers alike. This deprofessionalization of teaching will not only militate against the recruitment and retention of good teachers but will prevent teachers becoming any kind of role model for self-directed learning. Performance management has not been universally accepted by companies. Critics argue that temporary efficiency gains are counterbalanced by declining staff morale and lack of flexibility. It is rarely found in 'high skills' businesses which depend for their success on the knowledge creation capabilities of their employees because it stifles innovation and creativity. If we want pupils to develop these qualities, then they have to be fostered, developed and sustained in teachers.

What Day provides in this book is a comprehensive review of research in several countries into teachers' learning and continuing professional development, accompanied by a wide range of positive examples. These examples, however, are not marketed as success stories, in many the success is only partial. They illustrate some of the conclusions of the research review and they are analysed for the evidence they provide about the central questions of how, when and under what conditions teachers learn. His analysis is far removed from that of a remote expert prescribing what teachers should learn next and how they should do it, but rooted in a deep understanding of teachers' lives and careers. The daily experience of teaching and the norms and conditions of the school as a workplace are seen as critical factors affecting both the level of effort which teachers are prepared to invest in learning and the goals towards which that effort is directed.

This understanding of the teachers' context and predicament is accompanied, however, by a very challenging view of teacher professionalism. From the outset Day notes that the principal motivator for teachers is 'making a difference' in the lives of the pupils they teach; for this reason alone there is a strong professional obligation to regularly evaluate and inquire into the effect on pupils of their practice. But the privacy of their main work location, the classroom, and the normative influence of school culture constrain their professional approach to learning. Teachers, and indeed other professionals, develop frameworks of taken for granted assumptions which bring order and continuity to their work and enable them to cope with and survive the daily demands which pressure them. However these demands become increasingly difficult to challenge, so that teachers' learning is limited to what Argyris and Schon (1974) have called 'single loop learning', which attempts to respond to new situations and improve quality without changing their framework of assumptions. Indeed these assumptions become increasingly tacit as the disposition to review one's practice recedes. It is another example of a possible short-term gain in effectiveness being achieved at the expense of longer-term flexibility. In order to cope with change, and also with the inevitable decay of long-established routines, teachers have to engage in 'double loop learning' in which tacit assumptions are made explicit, challenged and reassessed.

Day argues that this more radical approach to learning and the evaluation of one's practice is extremely difficult to achieve on one's own. It requires groups of teachers working together, though even then the group may be too self-confirming and reluctant to challenge assumptions. Wider networks and partnerships with other schools and universities will almost certainly be needed — but not, he argues, at the expense of disempowering teachers or usurping their professional obligation to set their own learning goals in conjunction with their managers. Otherwise the motivation to engage in more challenging forms of learning will rapidly dissipate. He suggests that external resource people are most appropriately used as critical friends or collaborators. But he has not claimed any special privileges for teachers. There should be no diminution in their responsibility for the pupils whose learning they seek to foster, encourage and support. Nothing he suggests would seem unusual to the manager of a company who takes seriously the concept of a learning organization. Indeed his many examples provide much more practical advice on how to develop a learning organization than most of the trendy business school writers on the subject.

The principles which are advocated in this stimulating book support several different strategies. Chris Day wants to transform schools into learning communities for all their members; and they have to learn for themselves what strategies will work for them. His 'alternative prospectus' for improving education is about helping young people and teachers to develop and maintain the motivation to learn, both collectively and individually. In the long term, he argues, this will achieve more flexible and more enduring approaches to learning than setting targets which do not satisfy. He argues for strengthening teachers' responsibility and sense of efficacy, in order that they become more confident in, and more committed to, their own learning because that is the best way to develop those qualities in pupils. To restrict the learning of teachers and students alike to limited and prescribed pathways would be to deny what most analysts have agreed to be necessary for meeting the rapidly changing needs of individuals and society in the twenty-first century. Reading this book should make people think again about what kinds of teachers and schools they really want. It does not offer a prescription, but a constructive way to address this vitally important question.

Michael Eraut
University of Sussex
August 1998

Chapter 1

Being a Teacher, Developing as a Professional

> Teachers are at the heart of the educational process. The greater the importance attached to education as a whole — whether for cultural transmission, for social cohesion and justice, or for human resource development so critical in modern, technology-based economies — the higher is the priority that must be accorded to the teachers responsible for that education. (OECD, 1989)

This book presents an holistic view of the continuing professional development of teachers — the challenges and constraints which affect their ability to sustain commitment and build capacity so that the education and achievement of the children and young men and women with whose learning lives they are entrusted may be enhanced.

The meaning of teachers' development is located in their personal and professional lives and in the policy and school settings in which they work. The different chapters focus, therefore, upon teachers' contexts, purposes and lives, capacities for inquiry, development of expertise and competences, conditions of work — classrooms, cultures and leadership — appraisal, personal development planning and change, in-service teacher education, partnership models and networks for learning and improvement.

The nature of teaching demands that teachers engage in continuing career-long professional development, but particular needs and the ways in which they may be met will vary according to circumstance, personal and professional histories and current dispositions. Growth involves learning which is sometimes natural and evolutionary, sometimes opportunistic and sometimes the result of planning. Continuing professional development (CPD) as used in this book is inclusive of these different kinds of learning. Over the course of a career it would be reasonable to expect that teachers will have opportunities to participate in a range of informal and formal activities which will assist them in processes of review, renewal, enhancement of thinking and practice, and, importantly, commitment of the mind and heart; and that these will focus upon personal and professional purposes, individual and collective, inquiry-based and technical needs (Darling-Hammond, 1993; Hargreaves, D., 1994).

There are ten precepts upon which this book is based which are grounded in the researched realities of teachers and teaching, professional learning and development, and the contexts in which they take place.

1. Teachers are the schools' greatest asset. They stand at the interface of the transmission of knowledge, skills and values. Teachers will only be able to fulfil their educational purposes if they are both well prepared for the profession and able to maintain and improve their contributions to it through career-long learning. Support for their well being and professional development is, therefore, an integral and essential part of efforts to raise standards of teaching, learning and achievement.
2. One of the main tasks of all teachers is to inculcate in their students a disposition towards lifelong learning. They must, therefore, demonstrate their own commitment towards and enthusiasm for lifelong learning.
3. Continuing, career-long professional development is necessary for all teachers in order to keep pace with change and to review and renew their own knowledge, skills and visions for good teaching.
4. Teachers learn naturally over the course of a career. However, learning from experience alone will ultimately limit development.
5. Teachers' thinking and action will be the result of an interplay between their life histories, their current phase of development, classroom and school settings, and the broader social and political contexts in which they work.
6. Classrooms are peopled by students of different motivations and dispositions to learning, of different abilities and from different backgrounds. Teaching, therefore, is a complex process. Although organizational complexity may be reduced, e.g. through setting, successful teaching will always demand both intrapersonal and interpersonal skills, and personal and professional commitment. It is a synthesis of the head and the heart.
7. The way the curriculum is understood is linked to teachers' constructions of their personal and professional identities. Content and pedagogical knowledge cannot, therefore, be divorced from teachers' personal and professional needs and moral purposes. It follows that professional development must pay close attention to these.
8. Teachers cannot be developed (passively). They develop (actively). It is vital, therefore, that they are centrally involved in decisions concerning the direction and processes of their own learning.
9. Successful school development is dependent upon successful teacher development.
10. Planning and supporting career-long development is the joint responsibility of teachers, schools and government.

Professional development, then, is a serious business, central to maintaining and enhancing the quality of teachers and the leadership roles of principals. The concept of professional development which underpins this book represents what others have termed an 'expanded view of professional learning' (Lieberman, 1996). It therefore includes the largely private, unaided learning from experience through which most teachers learn to survive, become competent and develop in classrooms and schools; as well as informal development opportunities in school and the more formal 'accelerated' learning opportunities available through internally and externally generated in-service education and training activities. Lieberman (1996) provides a classified list of practices which encourage development which, 'moves teachers beyond simply hearing about new ideas or frameworks for understanding teaching practice, to being involved in the decisions about the substance, process, and organisational supports for learning in school, to finding broader support mechanisms — such as networks or partnerships — that provide opportunities and innovative norms from groups outside the school' (p. 187). She identifies three settings in which learning occurs: i) direct teaching (through, for example, conferences, courses, workshops, consultations); ii) learning in school (through, for example, peer coaching, critical friends, quality review, appraisal, action research, portfolio assessment, working on tasks together); and iii) learning out of school (through, for example, reform networks, school–university partnerships, professional development centres, subject networks and informal groups). A further setting in which much learning might be expected also to occur is: iv) learning in the classroom (through, for example, student response).

The significance of this classification is that it draws attention to the importance of informal learning which derives its purpose and direction from the goals of teachers' work; and illustrates the relatively small proportion of learning in the workplace that formal education and training contribute. This is not a judgment on the quality or significance of education and training targeted at key moments in individual professional and organizational development. Both learning in and out of the workplace are necessary. However, it suggests strongly that a learner-focused perspective is much more important than a training-focused perspective in the successful planning and management of the continuing professional development of teachers.

> . . . much learning at work derives its purpose and direction from the goals of . . . work. Achieving the goals often requires learning, which is normally accomplished by a combination of thinking, trying things out and talking to other people. Sometimes, however, people recognise a need for some additional knowledge or skill that seems essential for improving the quality of their work, expanding its range or taking on new duties . . . This sometimes involves undertaking some formal training, but almost always requires learning from experience and other people at work. (Eraut, Anderton, Cole and Senker, 1998, p. 1)

Such a learner-focused perspective will need to recognize the characteristics and roles of the individual learner, organizational culture, colleagues and leadership as factors which contribute to the quality of professional learning and development. Figure 1.1 provides an illustration of the ways in which they are interrelated.

Actively engaging in development throughout a 40-year teaching career is an ambitious undertaking. It means setting and maintaining high standards of teaching; interacting differentially with a range of students whose needs, motivations, circumstances and abilities will vary, yet for whom achievement expectations must be appropriate and challenging; being an active member of adult communities in and

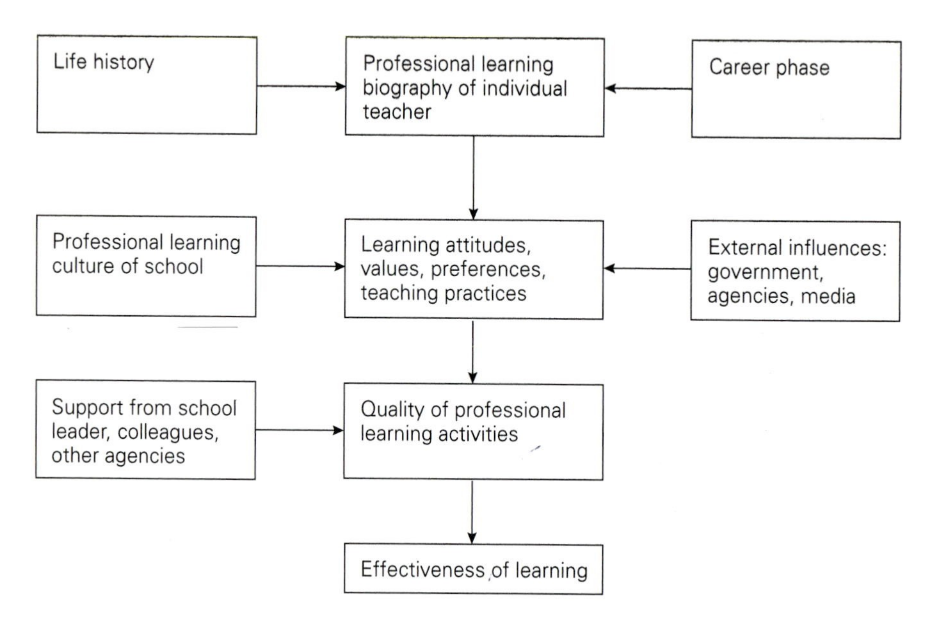

Figure 1.1 Factors contributing to the quality of professional learning

outside the school; responding to external change demands; and maintaining commitment, enthusiasm and self-confidence amidst the continuing turbulence of classroom and school life. These constitute the professional role of the teacher; and the central purpose of professional development is to enable teachers to fulfil that role in the changing contexts in which teachers work and learning takes place.

Most definitions of professional development emphasize its principal purposes as being the acquisition of subject or content knowledge and teaching skills (Hoyle, 1980; Joyce and Showers, 1980). The definition in this book includes these, but goes beyond them.

> *Professional development consists of all natural learning experiences and those conscious and planned activities which are intended to be of direct or indirect benefit to the individual, group or school and which contribute, through these, to the quality of education in the classroom. It is the process by which, alone and with others, teachers review, renew and extend their commitment as change agents to the moral purposes of teaching; and by which they acquire and develop critically the knowledge, skills and emotional intelligence essential to good professional thinking, planning and practice with children, young people and colleagues through each phase of their teaching lives.*

The definition reflects the complexity of the process. More importantly, though, it takes account of research into teacher learning and development which reveals the crucial importance to effective teaching of maintaining and building upon the desire of most teachers 'to make a difference in the lives of students' (Stiegelbauer, 1992).

Being a Professional

Changes over the last 25 years have challenged teachers' professional autonomy and brought the question of what it means to be a professional under increasing scrutiny. Hence the next part of the chapter sets the scene by exploring the notion of professionalism within the new accountability contexts in which teachers work and the interaction between these and the moral purposes of teaching.

A core traditional claim by teachers has been that they are 'professionals'. Implicit within this is the perception of a tradition that their training provides them with expert knowledge of subject, pedagogy and students and that their position as teacher accords a degree of autonomy. Whether or not teachers are professionals has been the subject of much writing over the years. Traditionally, 'professionals' are distinguished from other groups of workers because they have: i) a specialized knowledge base — *technical culture*; ii) commitment to meeting client needs — *service ethic*; iii) strong collective identity — *professional commitment*; and iv) collegial as against bureaucratic control over practice and professional standards — *professional autonomy* (Larsson, 1977; Talbert and McLaughlin, 1994). As teachers do not have control over professional standards (unlike, for example, doctors and lawyers), in this respect teaching has been regarded as a 'semi-profession' (Etzioni, 1969). However, historically the key area in which teachers are able to exercise autonomy has been their use of discretionary judgment in classroom decision-making. Teachers themselves, and those who are responsible for the quality of the system in which they work, have in the past talked of some whose development is restricted and others whose development is extended:

> By *restricted* professionality, I mean a professionality which is intuitive, classroom-focused, and based on experience rather than theory. The good restricted professional is sensitive to the development of individual pupils, an inventive teacher and a skilful class-manager. He is unencumbered with theory, is not given to comparing his work with that of others, tends not to perceive his classroom activities in a broader context, and values his classroom autonomy. The *extended professional*, on the other hand, is concerned with locating his classroom teaching in a broader educational context, comparing his work with that of other teachers, evaluating his own work systematically, and collaborating with other teachers. Unlike the restricted professional, he is interested in theory and current educational developments. Hence he reads educational books and journals, becomes involved in various professional activities and is concerned to further his own professional development through in-service work. He sees teaching as a rational activity amenable to improvement on the basis of research and development activities, particularly those involving extended study. (Hoyle, 1980, p. 49)

These terms no longer apply to the world in which teachers now live. Lawrence Stenhouse's (1975) notion of the critical characteristics of professionals' lives as demonstrating 'a capacity for autonomous professional development through systematic self-study, through the study of the work of other teachers and through questioning and testing of ideas by classroom research procedures . . .' (p. 144) is much closer to contemporary and future needs — as are his later statements on the need for self-study to be extended to encompass reflection on the conditions and policy contexts which affect the quality of teaching and learning.

Extensive research on how secondary school teachers identify their professionality has been carried out recently in England. Teachers differentiated between '*being a professional . . .*'

> Many referred to the importance of training and of the specialist knowledge, skills and qualifications that would be displayed by a 'professional', and also to the observance of particular standards. Another key fact . . . was the ability to exercise autonomy in decision-making . . . (and) . . . the degree of standing. . . . This included public respect and status . . . accompanying material rewards and favourable conditions of service. . . . Many believed that the position had deteriorated considerably in recent times. . . .

. . . and '*behaving as a professional*'. This involved:

> displaying . . . degrees of dedication and commitment, working long hours as a matter of course and accepting the open-ended nature of the task involved, which often impinged upon home and personal life. . . . it also entailed maximum effort to 'do the best you possibly can' and a constant quest for improved performance. At the same time it involved developing appropriate and caring relationships with students, which gave priority to their interests and well being, as well as dealing 'professionally' with colleagues, parents and other external agencies where appropriate. Finally, because of the complexities of the task of teaching and the obligation to meet varying individual needs, high levels of skill were necessary to respond intelligently to multiple demands in a complex and changing environment. . . . (Helsby, Knight, McCulloch, Saunders and Warburton, 1997, pp. 9–10)

How teachers behave as professionals is fundamental to the quality of classroom teaching and learning and is at the core of much research and writing which links purposeful, skilled caring with effective teaching.

> Good teaching is not just a matter of being efficient, developing competence, mastering technique, and possessing the right kind of knowledge. Good teaching also involves emotional work. It is infused with pleasure, passion, creativity, challenge, and joy (Hargreaves, 1995). It is in Fried's (1995) terms, a passionate vocation . . . educational reform effects too often elevate cognition above care as a priority for improvement. Care for persons, things, and even ideas, becomes marginalised as a result. . . . (Hargreaves, 1997b, p. 12)

However, caught in the midst of new worlds of reform, teachers in many countries have, like those in the English study (Helsby et al., 1997), cited ways in which their ability and motivation to behave as professionals have been negatively affected. There is a widespread perception of an erosion of autonomy. This is demonstrated by an intensification of their working lives, extended bureaucratic and contractual accountability, decreasing resources (including time and energy, the most precious resources of all) and increased managerialism. Alongside these, the bulk of formal professional development activities are designed, by and large, for short-term curriculum or problem-focused purposes. The wise adage of Lawrence Stenhouse (1975) that there can be no curriculum development without teacher development seems to have been replaced in England and elsewhere by the adage that there can be no curriculum implementation without training. Whilst there are some signs of movement away from this narrowly focused view of teaching and training as simple acts of delivery towards a view of teaching as a 'moral practice which does not exclude the technical dimension but places it in a broader context of educational values' (Elliott, 1991, p. 103), it still predominates in contexts where policies are formulated and resources allocated.

Acquiring the qualifications to become a teacher has always been a necessary but insufficient condition to succeed as a professional over a career span. Inevitably, subject knowledge will need to be regularly updated, teaching organization and methods and skills revisited as, on the one hand, information becomes more accessible through advances in technology, whilst, on the other, teaching pupils who are less socially compliant in conditions which are less conducive to promoting learning becomes more challenging. Various forms of external monitoring of standards and published test results at 'key stages' in pupils' school lives mean also that teachers as well as schools are increasingly being judged — whether formally or informally — on a narrow set of results in 'basic' areas of education, so that the temptation to teach only to the test in order to demonstrate basic competence will, for many teachers, become overwhelming. The maintenance of good teaching, however, demands that teachers revisit and review regularly the ways in which they are applying principles of differentiation, coherence, progression and continuity and balance not only in the 'what' and the 'how' of their teaching but also in the 'why' in terms of their core 'moral' purposes. Visions of themselves as educationalists with broader purposes are likely to dim without continuing professional development. In other words, teachers do not only have to be professional, they have to *behave professionally*.

Towards a New Professionalism

Teaching takes place in a world dominated by change, uncertainty and increasing complexity. Government publications in Europe, North America and the Antipodes stress the technological, economic and social challenges which schools (and therefore teachers) face. They are confronted, it is said, by a number of changes which lead to contradictory demands.

On the one hand:

- a commitment to education for all;
- an extension of the period of initial schooling;
- recognition of the growing importance of life-long education;
- more emphasis or general education for children and young people which prepares them for life rather than providing vocational skills for specific jobs;

- increasing emphasis on teamwork and co-operation;
- a consensus that general education should include attention to environmental issues, tolerance and mutual understanding.

On the other hand:

- growing inequalities, deepening social differences and a break-down in social cohesion;
- an increase in alienation among youth and dropping out of school;
- high levels of youth unemployment and charges that young people are ill-equipped to enter the world of work;
- a resurgence of inter-ethnic tensions, xenophobia and racism as well as the growing influence of religious sects and problems of drugs and gangs, with associated violence;
- increasing emphasis on competition and material values. (UNESCO, 1996, p. 2)

Alongside these demands, the total resources available for education have declined. This has manifested itself in different ways in different countries. For example, rises in class sizes, in some countries, have resulted in a decline in conditions of teaching and learning, and intensification of teachers' work (Day, Tolley, Hadfield, Watling and Parkins, 1996). Concerned with the need to raise standards of achievement, and improve their positions in the world economic league tables (whilst at the same time reducing unemployment), governments over the last 20 years have intervened more actively to improve the system of schooling. Financial self-reliance and ideological compliance have become the twin realities for many of today's schools and their teachers (Hargreaves, A., 1994, p. 5). Externally imposed curriculum and management innovations have often been poorly implemented without consultation, and they have resulted in periods of destabilization, increased workload and crises of professional identity for many teachers. As external monitoring and assessment systems increase through teacher appraisal, school inspection and external pupil assessment they perceive a loss of public confidence in their ability to provide a good service. Whilst governments have introduced changes in different ways at different paces, change is nevertheless not optional. It is, it is said, a part of the 'postmodern' condition which requires political, organizational, economic, social and personal flexibility and responsiveness (Hargreaves, A., 1994). Hargreaves describes the organizational metaphor of postmodernity as a 'moving mosaic' which,

> . . . can create increased personal empowerment, but its lack of permanence and stability can also create crises in interpersonal relationships, as these relationships have no anchors outside themselves, of tradition or obligation, to guarantee their security or continuance. . . . (Hargreaves, A., 1994, p. 9)

Stability of employment and status have been the hallmark of teaching which traditionally has been regarded as a job for life. Little wonder that the postmodern condition for many teachers represents more of a threat than a challenge, or that many are confused by the paradox of decentralized systems, i.e. local decision-making responsibilities, alongside increased public scrutiny and external accountability.

David Hargreaves identifies the shifts in culture, values and practices of teachers which have resulted from government reforms in England, but may be applied equally in many other countries of the world.

> At its core, the new professionalism involves a movement away from the teacher's traditional professional authority and autonomy towards new forms of relationships with colleagues, with students and with parents. These relationships are becoming closer as well as more intense and collaborative, involving more explicit negotiation of roles and responsibilities. . . . (Hargreaves, D., 1994, p. 424)

He describes the 'piecemeal' and 'fragmented' emergence of a 'new professionalism' and identifies trends in which teachers' work is becoming less isolated, their planning more collaborative, their teaching more outcome oriented and their relationships with students and parents more overtly contractual. Crucially, he identifies a *'a post-technocratic' model* of professional education in which professional development is approached from four interconnected premises:

- teachers are understood to have life-long professional needs and these will be met only if treated as in the case of any learner, in terms of continuity and progression;
- for continuity and progression to be realised, teachers' developmental needs must be assessed on a regular basis;
- schools devise a plan for development from which also flow needs for professional development if the school's development plan is to be implemented successfully;
- professional needs arising from personal sources (e.g. appraisal) have to be reconciled with school needs from institutional sources (e.g. a development plan).

In this model, all teachers are held to have rights to professional development, and opportunities must be distributed equitably (p. 430). David Hargreaves places two propositions 'at the heart of' the new professionalism.

> To improve schools, one must be prepared to invest in professional development; to improve teachers, their professional development must be set within the context of institutional development. (p. 436)

This model appears to move beyond Hoyle's (1980) earlier notions that teachers operate on 'restricted' or 'extended' professionality by implicity suggesting that teachers do not now have a choice. In a sense, this is self-evident. What is more controversial, however, is Hargreaves' claim that, 'structures which nourish the new professionalism thereby empower schools and teachers, not only by providing them with the commitment and energy to pursue improvements in teaching and learning, but also by increasing the school's capacity to undertake further development' (p. 435). Critics have argued that the new managerialist structures serve to deprofessionalize rather than empower, and that by no means all of teachers' development needs are able to be located in or arise from institutional contexts (Stronach and Maclure, 1996).

The Technicization of Teaching: Fallacy or Fact?

> Professional practice is predicated on the notion of qualified persons having the freedom to exercise their knowledge and skill in the interests of their clients in situations where routine solutions are inapplicable. In limiting the scope of the practitioner's autonomy through rules, procedures and close hierarchical control, bureaucracy is inimical to this view of professional tasks. (Hoyle, 1986, p. 81)

What for some is a root and branch attack upon teacher autonomy or teacher professionalism, for others is a change in its nature. At the heart of this paradox lie competing and contested definitions of what it means to be a professional. It is relatively uncontentious to identify changes in the conditions of work (e.g. through legislated change and increased bureaucratic accountability alongside decentralized decision-making); the work itself (e.g. through the development of more systematic pupil assessment, target setting and curriculum prescription); and its effects upon teachers (e.g. a longer working week). It is less easy, however, to agree on the consequences for the teaching community.

At a macro-analytical level there are those who regard the increasing powers used by governments to restructure schools and schooling by, for example, determining curriculum context, relocating school governance, introducing forms of national pupil assessment, teacher appraisal, school inspection systems and differentiated salary structures, as an extension of bureaucratic control which has served to 'deprofessionalize' teachers:

> When individuals cease to plan and control a large proportion of their own work, the skills essential to doing these tasks self reflectively and well, atrophy and are forgotten. (Apple, 1992, p. 22)

Some argue that increased bureaucratic control and intensification over the last 20 years have reduced individual teachers' areas of discretion in decision-making, have led to 'chronic and persisting' overload and have effectively resulted in deskilling (Harris, 1996). The establishment in the UK, for example, of competency-driven, school-based apprenticeship models of pre-service teacher training and alongside these systems of in-service teacher development which emphasize short-term training needs related to nationally defined priorities provides evidence in support of a theory of 'proletarianization'. In New Zealand, for example, a research project among primary school teachers revealed that they regularly worked a 60 hour week (including 6 hours over the weekend) (UNESCO, 1996); and, in England, infant school teachers worked over 50 hours a week on average, with 1 in 10 working in excess of 60 hours (Campbell and Neill, 1993). In both countries, significant proportions of time are spent on non-teaching tasks. In England, the National Curriculum has been described as 'a serial killer' in the demands it makes upon teachers (Campbell and Neill, 1994c), and there is widespread evidence of increased levels of stress and decreased morale. From this perspective, teachers are on the way to becoming 'technicians' whose job is to meet prespecified achievement targets and whose room to manoeuvre, to exercise discretion — a hallmark of an autonomous professional — is thus increasingly restricted. As externally imposed performance targets grow, as competency-driven models for pre-service and in-service teachers at different stages of career are developed, and as systems of re-accreditation at regular intervals are introduced — all in the name of maintaining and raising standards through increased professionalism — it is tempting to subscribe to the view that teachers are deluded, or blinkered, by the ideology of professionalism.

There can be no doubt that the circumstances in which teachers work and the demands made upon them are changing as communication technologies erode the role of teacher as exclusive holder of expert knowledge; as the social fabric of society becomes more fragmented, thus making the educative role of schools more complex; and as the need to compete economically in ever more competitive world markets leads inexorably to a market-oriented education service.

John Elliott (1993) characterizes the ideology as a 'social market' view in which:

- educational goals are treated as product specifications or targets . . .
- 'targets' or 'learning outcomes' must be prespecified and standardized . . .
- educational processes are technologies designed to achieve required outcomes . . .
- quality is defined by outcome . . .
- evidence of quality relates to effectiveness and efficiency . . .
- parents, employers (and students) are consumers . . .
- schools are units of production whose performance is regulated by consumer choice which itself relates to achievement scores. . . . (p. 54)

The impact of the changing economic, social and knowledge contexts upon the education service as a whole has caused a move, then, from the traditional post-war model of the autonomous professional. In particular, what students learn, what they must achieve as the outcome of learning and what standards apply are now explicitly the everyday business of government. Teachers, it seems, must conform to the social market model.

However, macro-oriented analyses such as those above cannot tell the whole story, for, by their nature, they do not investigate individual realities of teachers at local levels. It is unlikely that teachers 'misrecognize' what is happening to their work, as some would suggest (Robertson, 1996; Apple, 1989; Ozga, 1995). Can anyone seriously believe that teachers have not noticed the new metaphors of 'curriculum *delivery*', 'attainment *targets*', '*value for money*' and '*performance* appraisal'? Many teachers, far from being the passive 'victims' of reforms, are re-asserting their autonomy alongside the new accountabilities which are required of them. They are actively interpreting the restructuring of their work in accordance with their own professional judgments (Woods, 1994; Helsby, 1996; Troman, 1996a) in order to maintain their professional or substantive selves.

> Teaching is very much part of these teachers' substantive self. They have a strong sense of professionalism. They know how they want to teach and are not going to be dictated to. They consequently strongly resist the notion that they are being deprofessionalized. (Woods, 1994, p. 402)

There is still considerable room to manoeuvre (Bowe and Ball, 1992) and whilst teachers' choice in many areas is more restricted, their core professional task of taking decisions in the classroom based upon their view of what is in the best interest of the student remains.

Changes in the operational practice of 'professionalism' reflect the increasing complexities and contradictions of teachers' work in a postmodern world which means 'coming to terms with ambivalence, with the ambiguity of meanings and with the indeterminacy of the future', whilst at the same time, being cognizant that, 'acceptance of ambivalence can be life-enhancing, especially when contrasted to the driven world of certitudes that modernity used to foster . . .' (Sugrue, 1996, p. 202). Their work embodies both challenge and threat. They may be both autonomous and accountable to others, independent and collaborative, in control and not in control, teacher and child centred.

Jon Nixon and colleagues, in a review of the changing purposes of professionalism in the second part of the twentieth century, outline 'a new version of teacher professionality based upon the enabling of learning, the accommodation of difference, and the practice of agreement' (Nixon et al., 1997, p. 5). They propose that teachers, as part of a learning profession, will necessarily be involved in a 'continuing process of learning . . . about difference and about how difference may be accommodated' within four integrative modes of agreement-making:

- *Intra-professional: collegiality.* Teachers working together, sharing ideas and evaluating their collective practice in such a way as to achieve a coherent public presence . . . ;
- *Professional/student: negotiation.* Teachers negotiating learning tasks with students and seeking to involve them in school organisation issues and community education projects . . . ;
- *Inter-professional: co-ordination.* Teachers working intensively 'at the boundaries' liaising with other professionals and agencies and involving themselves in the local community . . . ;
- *Professional/parent: partnership.* Teachers working with parents as partners and recognizing them as complementary educators. (Nixon, Martin, McKeown and Ranson, 1997, p. 16)

They advocate *communicative action* which seeks to build agreements through shared understandings, but warn that the success of these, 'will depend upon the extent to which its agreement making processes aspire to be integrative and participative; the extent to which they recognise difference' (p. 25).

> From this perspective, teachers attain to professionalism through a commitment to establishing effective working relationships and alliances with those who stand outside the professional frame . . . Any claim teachers might make to professionalism within the new management of education should be based, then, not on a set of monopolistic practices, but on a commitment to breaking down the old professional monopolies and working with both students as agents of their own learning and parents as complementary educators. (p. 25)

Writing in the Australian reform context, Judyth Sachs (1997) argues similarly that reclaiming teacher professionalism requires, 'a recasting of professional and industrial issues and relationships between employers, unions and teachers, and other education stakeholders' (p. 264); and suggests that the new sets of relationships invest greater responsibilities in teachers to meet achievement targets. However, rather than becoming technicians whose role is merely to implement or deliver policy, which has as its central priorities increased productivity and economic as well as educational efficiency — a claim often made about recent reform (Ozga and Lawn, 1988; Popkewitz, 1996) — teachers have the opportunity, with others, to construct a model of professionalism which 'accommodates teaching's distinct aspects' (Sachs, 1997a, p. 269). Citing the work of two national examples of school-based initiatives, Sachs (1999) identifies *five core values* which constitute 'the fundamentals of a proactive and responsible approach to professionalism':

1. *Learning* in which teachers are seen to practice learning, individually with their colleagues and students.
2. *Participation* in which teachers see themselves as active agents in their own professional worlds.
3. *Collaboration* in which collegiality is exercised within and between internal and external communities.
4. *Co-operation* through which teachers develop a common language and technology for documenting and discussing practice and the outcomes.
5. *Activism* in which teachers engage publicly with issues that relate directly or indirectly to education and schooling, as part of their moral purposes. (Sachs, 1997b)

This brief analysis of 'professionalism' reveals an emerging consensus of the 'norms' which may apply to being and behaving as a professional within personal, organizational and broader political conditions which are not always conducive to teacher development. Equally important are the values frameworks which inform the work of teachers.

Teaching as a Moral Enterprise

> To assert one's leadership as a teacher, often against forces of administrative resistance, takes commitment to an educational ideal. It also requires the energy to combat one's own inertia caused by habit and overwork. And it requires a certain kind of courage to step outside of the small prescribed circle of traditional 'teacher tasks', to declare through their actions that they care about and take responsibility for more than the minimum, more than what goes on within the four walls of their classroom. (Barth, 1990, p. 131)

Teachers have always worked within a framework of accountability, identified as:

1. *Answerability* to one's clients, i.e. pupils and parents (moral accountability).
2. *Responsibility* to oneself and one's colleagues (professional responsibilities).
3. *Accountability* in the strict sense to one's employers or political masters (contractual accountability). (East Sussex Accountability Project, 1979, p. 27)

In recent years, government reforms worldwide have tended to highlight contractual accountability and to include within this parents and pupils who are presented more as customers than clients. The interpretation of answerability and accountability through a host of policy initiatives has caused attention to become focused upon a rather narrow range of desired 'basic' student achievement outputs which are able to be tested and compared. The logic is that teachers' work can be assessed in relation to their success in enabling students to achieve the desired results.[1] Their intrinsic importance is not being questioned. But concentration upon them has distracted attention from the care and commitment which needs to be in place if learners are to be motivated, challenged and supported. In some countries, the use of 'raw scores', which can be compared without recourse to local circumstances, emphasizes differences in school and teaching quality. Consideration of local factors (the 'value added' argument) seems to be a much fairer way of assessing achievement (Wilcox and Gray, 1996). However, even this fails to take into account the complexity of teaching and learning and other outcomes as well as outputs which result from teachers' work in classrooms; for teachers exercise in practice a potentially far broader influence upon students.

Though it may not appear as part of the explicit curriculum, there can be little doubt that teaching is a moral enterprise:

> To anyone who takes a close look at what goes on in classrooms it becomes quickly evident that our schools do much more than pass along requisite knowledge to the students attending them (or fail to do so, as the case may be). They also influence the way those students look upon themselves and others. They affect the way learning is valued and sought after and lay the foundations of lifelong habits of thought and actions. They shape opinion and develop taste, helping to form likings and aversions. They contribute to the growth of character and, in some instances, they may even be a factor in its corruption. (Jackson, Boostrom and Hansen, 1993, p. xii)

Although teachers' concern for children is grounded in relationships, 'in the connectedness of teachers and learners' (Elbaz, 1990, 1991 and 1992, p. 421), it goes beyond being responsive and caring for them to include a moral duty. Thus, Hugh Sockett (1993) argues:

> The generic teacher does not just get people to learn within an educational endeavour, for teaching is an interpersonal activity directed at shaping and influencing (not moulding), by means of a range of pedagogical skills, what people become as persons through whatever it is that is taught. . . . As a teacher is one who helps to shape what a person becomes, so the moral good of every learner is of fundamental importance in every teaching situation. . . . I am describing a view of teaching as primarily moral (i.e. dedicated to an individual's welfare rather than instrumental (e.g. for economic reasons) or non-educative (e.g. for custodial reasons)). (p. 13)

Sockett's concern is with the moral rights and duties of a professional role and he defines four dimensions: *community* (which provides a framework of relationships);

knowledge or expertise (with technique subservient to moral criteria); *accountability* (to individuals and the public); and *ideals*. He suggests that only by seeing the interplay between ideals of service, purposes and practices can the professional comprehend the moral role, and adds to these dimensions five major virtues intrinsic to teaching which are central to understanding its practice: *honesty*, *courage*, *care*, *fairness* and *practical wisdom*. Michael Eraut, too, argues convincingly that, 'it is the moral and professional accountability of teachers which should provide the main motivation for their continuing professional development'. He suggests further that being a professional practitioner implies:

> 1 A moral commitment to serve the interests of students by reflecting on their well-being and their progress and deciding how best it can be fostered or promoted.
> 2 A professional obligation to review periodically the nature and effectiveness of one's practice in order to improve the quality of one's management, pedagogy and decision-making.
> 3 A professional obligation to continue to develop one's practical knowledge both by personal reflection and through interaction with others. (Eraut, 1995, p. 232)

Teaching has an essentially moral purpose in the sense that it is always concerned with the betterment or good of pupils (Noddings, 1987, p. 23; Sockett, 1989a, 1989b, 1993; Elbaz, 1992). What is deemed 'good' will, of course, vary across cultures, religions and individuals. However, whether the teachers' definitions of 'good' arise from e.g. a humanistic, agnostic, atheistic, Muslim, Judaeistic, or Christian perspective, they will demand commitment and care which actively seeks to change the way students are.

Teachers are not only recipients of policy change initiated from outside their schools and classrooms, but also are themselves *initiators of change*. Moral purpose is a natural ally of 'change agentry':

> Stated more directly, moral purpose — or making a difference — concerns bringing about improvements. It is, in other words, a change theme . . . Moral purpose keeps teachers close to the need of children and youth; change agentry causes them to develop better strategies for accomplishing their moral goals. (Fullan, 1993a, p. 12)

Teacher change, a necessary outcome of effective professional development, is complex, unpredictable and dependent upon past experience (life and career history), willingness, abilities, social conditions and institutional support. There is a need for continuing research into this change agent role and its relationship to moral purposes held by teachers. This is particularly important at a time when in many countries there is a real challenge to both these core functions through unprecedented externally imposed reform which a multitude of research projects in different countries have shown will not necessarily result in teachers implementing the intended changes as planned (Carlgren, 1990; Sikes, 1992).

> It has taken time since the difficulties and pessimism of the 1970s and early 1980s for the perception to be widely shared that the success of educational reforms, no matter how well they are conceived in principle, will be only fortuitous if the teachers who are actually responsible are not made an explicit and pivotal plank of those reforms. An uncommitted and poorly motivated teaching body will have disastrous effects for even the best of intentions for change. (OECD, 1989)

Commitment to change implies that teachers have responsibilities and answerabilities which go beyond the transmission of knowledge, experience and skills. If this is the case, then they must be not only competent technicians, but also:

- knowledgeable, yet respectful of those who are ignorant . . .
- kind and considerate, yet demanding and stern as the situation requires . . .
- entirely free of prejudice and absolutely fair in their dealings with others . . .
- responsive to individual students' needs, without neglecting the class as a whole . . .
- able to maintain discipline and order, whilst allowing for spontaneity and caprice . . .
- optimistic and enthusiastic, even when harbouring private doubts and misgivings . . .
- able to deal with the unexpected and sometimes even with surly and abusive students without losing their composure and control . . .
- able to smile and appear cheerful on days when they are not quite up to par and would rather be somewhere else . . . (Jackson et al., 1993, p. 233)

It is not always easy to achieve the kinds of equilibrium required by those demands. For example, many teachers continue to work in overcrowded classrooms with scarce resources in which both students and teachers feel overwhelmed, discouraged and often disgusted. A survey of the opinions of 599 students and 200 teachers in New York public schools found that overcrowding was, 'having significantly negative effects on instruction and learning in the system', and that only about 50 per cent of the teachers looked forward to each working day in their school (Rivera-Batiz and Marti, 1995). There are many studies which draw attention to the prevalence of a perception of stress among teachers in various countries and which show that large classes are more likely to lead to staff disillusionment and burnout.[2] The demand to give attention is a factor that has been related to teacher exhaustion (Esteve, 1989) and, therefore, to stress and possible burnout. In short, one of the reasons why the imposition by some societies of rising class sizes, frequent external intervention which results in increased bureaucratic contractual accountability, and increasing management demands result in stress among teachers is the increased time and effort required by them to maintain the very qualities in teaching demanded by that same society. 'Burned-out' teachers give significantly less information and less praise to pupils, and interact less frequently with them (Mancini et al., 1984). This, in turn, is likely to result in an increase in behaviour problems which, in its turn, will create more stress — a clear case of a negative downward spiral of cause and effect.

A report of results of a major nationwide questionnaire-based study of stress among UK teachers (Travers and Cooper, 1996) indicated that 23 per cent of the sample reported having significant illness in the last year. The major illnesses reported are those which are generally viewed as highly stress related. In particular the study also showed that teachers suffer from higher levels of mental ill-health in most aspects when compared to other 'highly stressed' groups of workers. In addition, and perhaps most importantly, survey results indicated that of the teachers in the sample, 66.4 per cent had actively considered leaving the profession over the last five years, 28 per cent said that they were actively seeking alternative employment, and 13.3 per cent were currently seeking premature retirement. The researchers considered that the results of the survey were quite startling as:

- a very large number of teachers intended to leave; and
- a large proportion of these would-be 'escapees' were young.

Support for these findings was provided by the NCPTA (National Confederation of Parent Teacher Associations) survey (1996) which found that 46.6 per cent of primary schools and 42.1 per cent of secondary schools were of the opinion that staff morale was then worse than it had been at the time of the last survey (1991).

There are complications in sustaining the applications of moral purposes across a career span. There is evidence that commitment and care sooner or later may become frayed at the edges. Considerable variation in teachers' commitment to pupils and their own work in the classroom has been observed (Raudenbush, Rowan and Cheong, 1992; LeCompte and Dworkin, 1992). Citing research by scholars in England, America, Canada and Switzerland (Huberman, 1989; Sikes, Measor and Woods, 1985; Noddings, 1992; Goodson, 1992; Ball, 1987; Hargreaves and Earl, 1990), Andy Hargreaves (1993) concluded that 'many teachers in mid-to-late-career had become "disenchanted" or "defensive focusers"', no longer holding the good of their pupils as a high priority.

Because most teachers are committed morally in the ways Sockett and others have described, they may become initially frustrated and guilty when they fail to live up to their own and others' expectations. Andy Hargreaves cites the work of Alan Davies who highlighted two forms of 'the politics of guilt':

> - *persecutory guilt* that leads many teachers to concentrate on covering the required content, rather than ignoring it or subverting it to develop more interesting materials and approaches of their own . . . for fear of prejudicing the test scores by which one will ultimately be held accountable.
> - *depressive guilt* . . . when we realise we may be harming or neglecting those for whom we care [by being] . . . prevented from doing what is right or caring . . . by insoluble dilemmas or impossible constraints. (Hargreaves, A., 1994, pp. 143–4)

Teachers who have been involved as recipients of changes which have challenged their moral purposes may well react, at least temporarily, in these ways (although guilt can also have its roots in personal history and organizational culture).[3] This is an issue for public concern since it will impact upon the quality of their work and their sense of professionalism. Teachers and those responsible, with them, for ensuring regular opportunities during their career lives for appropriate professional development, need to revisit and renew moral purposes at regular intervals:

> . . . teachers must be seen and see themselves as occupying key roles in classrooms — not simply as technicians who know how to run good discussions or teach encoding skills to beginning readers but as persons whose view of life, which includes all that goes on in classrooms, promises to be as influential in the long run as any of their technical skills. It is this extended view of a teacher's responsibility that makes it appropriate to speak of teaching as a moral enterprise. (Jackson et al., 1993, p. 277)

Since professional development programmes must address the values, knowledge and skills of teachers as agents of student change with moral purposes, they must recognize their active, shaping role in the change process, and provide support appropriate to their individual needs as well as those of the professional community.[4] However, teachers' and schools' development will be enriched, also, if they take account of the views of other stakeholders, in particular those of the students.

Students' Views

> Rarely is there a suggestion that schools might usefully start the process of improvement by inviting their students to talk about what makes learning a positive or disappointing experience for them; what enhances or diminished their motivation and engagement . . . Taking account of the student perspective in planning for change could really make a difference. (Rudduck, Day and Wallace, 1997, p. 74)

Two recent studies from England and America provide evidence which clearly supports the proposals in this book that teachers must be provided with growth opportunities which go far beyond the instrumentalism which pervades much current practice if they are to be encouraged to meet student learning needs effectively.

In a study designed to provide insight into students' experience of their secondary schools in different regions of England over a four-year period (aged 12–16 years), the teachers most likely to increase commitment to learning were identified as those who:

- Enjoy teaching the subject . . .
- Enjoy teaching students . . .
- Make the lessons interesting and link them to life outside schools . . .
- Will have a laugh but know how to keep order . . .
- Are fair . . .
- Are easy for students to talk to . . .

- Don't shout . . .
- Don't go on about things (e.g. how much better other classes are, or how much better an older brother or sister was) . . .
- Explain things and go through things students don't understand without making them feel small . . .
- Don't give up on students. (Rudduck et al., 1997, p. 86)

This confirms earlier work on students' experience of schooling in which 'cheerfulness', 'good temper' and 'a sense of humour' were paramount (Taylor, 1962) and in which 'good' teachers were 'firm but fair', had a sound knowledge of their subject, were able to explain difficult points and be 'helpful' and 'encouraging' (Hargreaves, 1972; Nash, 1976; Gannaway, 1976); did not shout, let students talk to them, explained things clearly and were interested and enthusiastic (Makins, 1969; Davies, 1978).

Students' feelings about the environments in which they study and their teachers and experiences of teaching affect their interest, motivation and, ultimately, levels of achievement. Research over the years has consistently found that teaching of the highest technical competence counts for little if classmates are uncooperative or teachers unfair or uncaring (Fraser, 1991; Walberg, 1991).

> Though educators rightfully emphasise achievement, they should also think of motivating their students and awakening a love of learning for its own sake. Affectionately remembered classes sustain interest in learning in the workplace and over a lifetime . . . well-organised classrooms foster responsibility, humaneness, and mutual respect — the very social skills students need to participate productively in our civic society. (Rudduck et al., 1997, p. 46)

So, too, must professional development build upon teachers' 'passionate vocation' (Fried, 1995), nurturing and maintaining their motivation and enthusiasm not just to be a professional, but to behave as professionals over the span of their careers.

As for students in classrooms, so for teachers in schools, the quality of leadership plays an important part in enabling or discouraging learning. A study of the Teacher Quality of Work Life (TQWL) in eight restructured high schools in America which focused upon how teachers' work was altered in schools where 'significant change efforts had been underway for some time' (Louis, 1994), found that teachers talked of good change leadership as non-linear, non-rational and that leaders 'did not dwell on organisational development, nor use any of its accepted techniques' (p. 8). Rather:

> What comes through in these descriptions is the attention to values, both at the grand level ('caring for kids') and at the daily level (reinforcing small behaviours because they are involved in the daily life of the school). Surprisingly, teachers appreciated their principals as intellectuals, and saw this as a major feature of their success in changing the school. Without being overly idealistic, we were surprised

> to find that teachers in these schools (not all, but a surprising number) also operated as intellectuals to a greater degree than in more typical schools. Engaging in reflective discussions about educational issues and philosophies was not a daily occurrence, but was also not unheard of. (Louis, 1994, p. 8)

If teachers are to develop, then, attention must be paid to their thinking, moral purposes and skills as change agents, their pedagogical and management skills and the leadership and cultural contexts in which they work. Finally, if schools are to be part of the lifelong learning community they need to be concerned with the lifelong development of all their members. The kinds of structural reforms which have led to the 'self-managing' school (Caldwell and Spinks, 1988) do not necessarily lead to schools becoming learning communities.

> If we cannot design schools so that basic assumptions about teachers' work can be shared on a regular basis, can we expect schools to become self-designing in the long run? If schools are to become learning organisations they will require a profound change in the use of time so that teachers and administrators have the opportunity to work together to begin the real restructuring that will affect the paradigms surrounding the central tasks of the school: creating a system that will ensure a higher level of learning for all children. (Louis, 1994, p. 17)

Conclusion

The view of teachers' work which informs and underpins the thinking in this book is that teaching consists of complex sets of differentiated interpersonal interactions with students who may not always be motivated to learn in classroom settings. These involve difficult considerations of curriculum and the application of teaching strategies and skills which, ultimately, will depend for their success upon the quality of teachers' discretionary judgments. It is, therefore, important in schools which are effective, 'good' and engaged in continuous development that attention is paid to teachers' lives, their learning and development needs and working conditions as well as those of the students they teach. School cultures do not always encourage adult learning. Whilst it is important to recognize that ideas and practices should continue to be reviewed, refined and renewed in order to enhance students' knowledge, skills and capacities to learn, it is unlikely that this will occur successfully if the needs to maintain and develop care and commitment, enthusiasm and autonomy of the kind described in this chapter alongside the need to improve the professional capacities of teachers as 'agents' of learning and change are ignored.[5] The provision of time and opportunity as well as the dispositions and abilities of teachers to learn from and with one another inside the workplace and from others outside the school are key factors in continuing professional development. In the absence of these it is not unreasonable to predict that their capacities for development and abilities to model these capacities for students who will live and work in a world which is already characterized by change are likely to be diminished.

Notes

1. For a detailed critique see Elliott, J. (1996). He suggests, for example, that priority might be given to improving the quality of teaching and learning without 'maximising learning time, emphasising "academic" goals or focusing on "achievement". The classroom practices in these schools may express the beliefs that the quality of learning is more important than the amount of time pupils spend "on task", that the acquisition of systematically organized academic knowledge is not the main aim of education and that the latter requires teachers to focus on the quality of the teaching–learning process, rather than its outcomes since, if the former is right, then the pupils will take care of the latter' (p. 206).
2. Research on the effects of class size, on the quality of teaching and learning has been synthesized in Day, Tolley, Hadfield, Watling and Parkins (1996).
3. See Hargreaves, A. (1994) Chapter 7 for a detailed consideration of teachers' guilt.
4. See also Louis (1994); Goodlad, Soder and Sirotnik (1990); Sergiovanni (1995).
5. Writing in the context of innovation, Michael Huberman claims that if we settle for the 'teacher capacity' outcome only, 'we are, in subtle ways, distracting ourselves from the reasons for which we made the change in the first place', admitting, however, that we are unlikely to get pupil change without teacher change (Huberman, 1992).

Chapter 2

Teachers as Inquirers

> I cannot teach clearly unless I recognise my own ignorance, unless I identify what I do not know, what I have not mastered. (Freire, 1996, p. 2)

If behaving as a professional means a commitment to inquiry then it is necessary to examine what this involves for the teacher. Reflection lies at the heart of inquiry, but whilst this is a necessary condition it is not sufficient in itself. This chapter explores the possibilities, challenges and problems of extending knowledge about practice and understandings of the settings in which it takes place. It focuses on the purposes and processes of reflection through which critical thinking and emotional intelligence may be developed, and examines action research and narrative as means by which such qualities may be stimulated and sustained. The chapter identifies key challenges which must be met if teachers' full potential for learning through inquiry over a career is to be realized and if schools are to establish professional learning cultures to support this. It concludes by emphasizing the key part played in reflection, of cognition and emotion.

In the broadest sense, teachers who reflect in, on and about the action are engaging in inquiry which is aimed not only at understanding themselves better as teachers, but also at improving their teaching. In England, Lawrence Stenhouse defined the extended professionalism of 'teacher as researcher' as involving:

- the commitment to systematic questioning of one's own teaching as a basis for development;
- the commitment and the skills to study one's own teaching;
- the concern to question and to test theory in practice by the use of those skills;
- readiness to allow other teachers to observe your work — directly or through recordings — and to discuss it with them on an honest basis. (Stenhouse, 1975, p. 144)

In this vision, teaching is more than a craft. It is an educational science and pedagogical art in which practice, knowledge about practice and values are treated as problematic. 'Each classroom is a laboratory, each teacher a member of the scientific community' (Stenhouse, 1975, p. 142). Both teachers and students are researchers in an enterprise in which the purpose is access to knowledge, 'on terms that confer the power to use it' (cited in Rudduck, 1995, p. 7). Stenhouse's theme was emancipation:

> The essence of emancipation, as I conceive it, is the intellectual, moral and spiritual autonomy which we recognise when we eschew paternalism and the rule of authority and hold ourselves obliged to appeal to judgement. Emancipation rests not merely on the assertion of a right of the person to exercise intellectual, moral and spiritual judgement, but upon the passionate belief that the virtue of humanity is diminished in man when judgement is overruled by authority. (Stenhouse, 1979, p. 163)

Though there have been some criticisms that it is predominantly those who are ideologically committed to particular forms of emancipation i.e. so-called 'progressive' teaching approaches who are its principal advocates (Hammersley, 1993), these should not distract from the necessity for all teachers who wish to improve their practice to engage, routinely, in inquiry. The problem is that knowledge about practice which is explicit soon becomes implicit, embedded in the practice itself.

Extending Learning about Practice

Most new teachers very quickly develop practices which allow them to cope with the complexities of teaching and being a member of a school community. These include what Yinger (1979) has labelled as 'routines', i.e.

1. routine patterns of working;
2. rapid intuitive responses to classroom situations and events;
3. taken for granted assumptions which frame normal practice and discourse in the classroom, staffroom and other school settings.

Under normal conditions teachers' thinking and disposition towards development are limited by these perceptual and contextual constraints. In the staffroom setting, for example, talk about teaching is governed by tacit assumptions about the nature of talk about teaching; whereas in the classroom setting, teaching actions are governed by tacit assumptions about the nature of teaching actions. Teachers' explicit actions both as educationists and practitioners are, therefore, often based on implicit, unstated knowledge of the nature of practice in any given setting (Polanyi, 1967). Furthermore, not all teachers consistently employ practices which directly reflect their beliefs (Duffy, 1977) and there is as yet little empirical evidence concerning how teachers assess their plans and accomplishments and so revise them for the future. The sets of beliefs which guide them are often unconscious and their decisions intuitive (Clark and Yinger, 1977; Stenhouse, 1975). Since it is rare for these to be made explicit or tested, the possibilities for evaluating those values, expectations and assumptions which underpin their teaching are minimal.[1]

Argyris and Schön (1974) suggest that we can explain or predict a person's behaviour by attributing to them 'theories of action' which determine practice. A theory of action is defined as:

> . . . a theory of deliberate human behaviour which is for the agent a theory of control but which, when attributed to the agent, also serves to explain or predict his behaviour. (Argyris and Schön, 1974, p. 6)

Within each person's theory of action two components may be distinguished: 'espoused theories' and 'theories-in-use'. The former are those which justify or describe behaviour (what we say about what we do), the latter are what a person does, or how s/he operationalizes his/her espoused theories. Professional practice itself is made up of a number of interrelated theories of action that 'specify for the situations of the practice the actions that would, under the relevant assumptions, yield intended consequences' (p. 19). For example, a teacher may hold different espoused theories and theories-in-use about education in different settings (e.g. the classroom, the staffroom, colleagues in the department, friends, etc.). Teachers' behaviour or theories-in-use in these settings will often rest on unstated but tacitly understood assumptions. These may be privately held or part of a shared culture with others who work in the same social settings. Inconsistencies and contradictions may be evident to an outsider listening to teachers talking about their theories-in-use, or observing their practice without them being apparent to the teacher or teachers themselves.

Argyris and Schön (1974) characterize the normal world of learning as 'single loop', in which, '. . . we learn to maintain the field of constancy by learning to design actions that satisfy existing governing variables' (goals) (p. 6). In this sense, teaching practices are rules of action which allow both stable views of, for example, the classroom or the school to be maintained, and priority to be given to certain kinds of information while other kinds are ignored. They are *theories of control*. Whilst single loop learning is necessary as a means of maintaining continuity in the highly predictable activities that make up the bulk of our lives, it also limits the possibilities for change. It is argued that if we allow our theory of action to remain unexamined indefinitely, our minds will be closed to much valid information and the possibilities for change will thus be minimal. In effect, if we are content with maintaining our field of constancy we become 'prisoners of our programs' (p. 19) and only see what we want to see.

Teachers who are inquirers must from time to time investigate their theory of action. In order to do this they must first make explicit their espoused theories (what they say about teaching) and their theories-in-use (the behavioural world of the classroom). Only by evaluating the compatibilities or incompatibilities which exist within and between these two elements of their theory of action and the contexts in which these occur will teachers be enabled to increase their knowledge of teaching, its contexts and themselves as teachers. However, once their current theories of action have been made explicit a second problem is encountered, for they must devise strategies for new theories-in-use which are more compatible with their espoused theories. Having devised them, they must put them into practice and, like new skills, that practice must take place in a 'learning situation that permits a reinforcing cycle of feeling and performance to begin'. This is not always an easy task and without support may lead to compromise rather than development.

For example, teachers faced with a difficult situation in which their theories-in-use do not allow them to achieve what they want may either change their theories-in-use in order to achieve their espoused theories or continue to use them even though they are no longer perceived to be compatible with their espoused theories. They may thus choose not to get what they say they want. Their theories-in-use in this instance become pragmatic responses to difficult teaching situations. Argyris and Schön (1974) give examples of the repertoire of devices used to protect or maintain current theories-in-use in the face of emerging dilemmas with regard to effectiveness:

> (a) We keep our espoused theory in one place and our theory-in-use in another. We continue to speak in the language of one theory while acting in the language of another.
> (b) We become selectively inattentive to the information that points to dilemmas (i.e. we ignore it).
> (c) We suppress offensive data.
> (d) We change jobs, or sack someone.
> (e) We make a self-sealing, self-fulfilling prophecy by using authority to elicit the desired behaviour from others, and cause the rest to be suppressed.
> (f) We change our espoused theory but not our theory-in-use.
> (g) We make marginal changes to our theory-in-use. (pp. 32–3)

Pragmatic responses such as these occur partly because teachers lack the time, energy, support systems and expertise to move from the implicit and intuitive to the explicit systematic reflection necessary to develop their thinking about practice. The basic dilemmas are of effectiveness, constancy, and the difficulties of self-confrontation and change.

A second complementary kind of learning is suggested, characterized as 'double loop learning'. This involves allowing things which had previously been taken for granted to be seen as problematic, and opening oneself to external perspectives and, through this, new sources of evidence. Seeing oneself as others (both adults and students) see one is a crucial means of gaining a better understanding of one's behavioural world and one's effect upon it.

The problem with moving towards 'double loop learning' is that attention is drawn to myriads of additional variables of information which are normally 'filtered out' by teachers through the development, for example, of routines and decision habits in order to keep mental effort at a reasonable level (Eraut, 1978). They may no longer respond only intuitively to situations, but are forced, through confrontation with self, into critical, rational and emotional responses.

> [In self study] we may be entering into processes by which we deconstruct some basic, historically rooted views of ourselves. In such processes our existing images of the professional self will be challenged, questioned, re-thought and re-shaped in some degree. These processes are necessary if change and development are to occur and if self study is to lead to new learning. We cannot escape them, nor the discomfort they may bring if we value our commitment to professional development. (Dadds, 1993, p. 288)

Moreover, if teachers depart from their niche in the social and organizational structures of the school into which they have been socialized by engaging in systematic inquiry, they risk taking on at least temporarily a 'burden of incompetence' where the approved certainties they have striven to construct since their own days as beginning teachers are laid to one side. This is not a process to be undertaken every day, nor without assistance, but certainly one which should be considered at key development phases by all teachers.

In effect, then, inquiring into one's own practice raises two problems. The first is concerned with self-confrontation and the extent to which an individual can engage in this, and the second related problem concerns the extent to which the consequences of self-confrontation can be accommodated in thought and action by the teacher without assistance. If teachers are to extend their knowledge about practice over a career (and thus gain the possibility of increasing their professional effectiveness), they will need to engage alone and with others in different kinds of reflection on both their own thinking, the values which underpin this and the contexts in which they work. To do this they will need intellectual and affective support. They will need to be both individual and collaborative inquirers.

Reflection, Inquiry and Critical Thinking

So called 'appreciative systems', of reflection in and on action according to Schön, enable teachers to reinterpret and reframe their work:

> Reframing describes the familiar process in which an event over which we have puzzled for some time suddenly is 'seen' differently and in a way that suggests new approaches to the puzzle. The significance of reframing is that it sets the puzzle differently, and it frequently does so in a fashion that is not logical and almost beyond our conscious control. (Munby and Russell, 1990, p. 116)

Over the last three decades a growing body of theoretical literature and case studies of practice have sought to emphasize the importance of critical reflection to teachers' development. The contexts for and varieties of reflection have been the subject of much writing. Schön's (1983) term, 'reflective practitioner' has acquired popularity with teachers because it seems to link their espoused commitment to critical thinking with their experience of largely uncritical practice. To be a 'reflective practitioner' has thus become synonymous with 'good' practice. According to Schön (1983, 1987) reflective practitioners reflect 'in' and 'on' action. *Reflection-in-action* refers to the process of decision-making by teachers whilst actively engaged in teaching. *Reflection-on-action* occurs outside of the practice which is the subject of reflection. The focus is on but not bounded by the action whereas reflection-in-action is necessarily context bound. His views, like those of Stenhouse, characterize the interrelationship between theory and practice in terms of knowledge as embedded in rather than existing outside the action. They celebrate teachers' artistry and critique models of 'technical rationality' which separate theories of teaching (generated in universities by academics) from its practice (implemented by teachers in schools). In a very real sense, Schön's work legitimized teaching as a knowledge-based, intellectual activity in which teachers are not only capable of deconstructing but also reconstructing experience:

> Competent professional practitioners often have the capacity to generate new knowing-in-action through reflection-in-action. The sources of knowing-in-action include this reflection-in-action and are not limited to research produced by university-based professional schools. (Schön, 1987, p. 40)

Reflection-in-action

The three principal features of reflection-in-action, according to Schön, are:

1. Reflection is at least in some measure conscious, although it need not occur in the medium of words. We consider both the unexpected event and the knowing-in-action that led up to it, asking ourselves, as it were, 'What is this?', and, at the same time, 'How have I been thinking about it?'. Our thought turns back on the surprising phenomenon and, at the same time, back on itself.
2. Reflection-in-action has a critical function, questioning the assumptional structure of knowing-in-action. We think critically about the thinking that got us into this fix or this opportunity; and we may, in the process, restructure strategies of action, understandings of phenomena, or ways of framing problems.
3. Reflection gives rise to on-the-spot experiment. We think up and try out new actions intended to explore the newly observed phenomena, test our tentative understandings of them, or affirm the moves we have invented to change things for the better . . . What distinguishes reflection-in-action from other kinds of reflection is its immediate significance for action. (1987, pp. 28–9)

The application of Schön's conception of reflection-in-action to classroom teaching has been criticized on the grounds that it takes no account of the social conditions of workplace learning (Smylie, 1995), that reflection might also be initiated in other ways (e.g. curiosity, escape from boredom), and that it fails to take into account the importance of the time variable upon understanding professional behaviour (Eraut, 1994). The time available for reflection will vary enormously depending upon size of class, teaching strategies, composition and behaviour of class, and purpose of lesson. The depth of reflection will also depend upon energy levels, disposition of the teacher and ability to analyse not only the practice but also the context in which the practice is occurring — all within an extremely short timescale. Even longer in-class times for reflection (e.g. when students are engaged in individual reading or writing or self-directed group work) would not provide time for deliberative reflection. In reflecting-in-action it is likely that teachers will draw upon existing frameworks to solve rather than define problems. Reflection in this context does not lead to development, rather it reinforces experience without re-evaluating. Furthermore, because reflection-in-action is intuitive it is by no means certain that problematic situations in classrooms will result in reflection which enables the teacher to interpret and respond appropriately. Neither experience nor intuition are infallible.

Reflection-in-action focuses upon the identification and rapid solution of immediately pressing problems, thus reinforcing rather than breaking free of the notion of teacher as an artisan, and teaching as 'bricolage' which:

> . . . envisions the teacher as creating or repairing learning activities of different kinds with a distinctive style or signature. He or she adapts on the spot the instructional materials . . . as a function of the time of day, the degree of pupil attentiveness, the peculiar skill deficiency emerging in the course of the activity . . . in doing this, the teacher relies heavily on concrete bits of practice that have proved successful in the past but must be reconfigured as a function of the specific situation in the classroom, in order to make them work. (Huberman, 1993a, p. 15)

It can, it seems, have benefits, but these are unlikely to result in critical reappraisal or change. What Schön terms a 'reflective conversation with the situation', Levi Strauss in writing about primitive thinking 20 years before, described more accurately as 'engaging in a dialogue with the situation' (1962, cited in Huberman, 1993a, p. 16), in which continuous readjustment, but not change, occurs. The process is unlikely to result in the articulation and critique of tacit understandings and routines which teachers develop and which can make them prisoners of their own technique, nor in reflective teaching as a form of educational theorizing (Elliott, 1991).

Reflection-on-action

Reflection-on-action occurs both before and after the action. Ideally, it is a more systematic, considered process of deliberation enabling analysis, reconstruction and reframing in order to plan for further teaching and learning. Unlike reflection-in-action, it opens up possibilities for talking with others about teaching. It seems to fit well into the kinds of collective planning activities which are being directly or indirectly encouraged through reforms in, for example, England, Australia, Sweden, the USA and Norway. Unlike reflection-in-action it is not necessarily carried out in isolation from other professionals, though in practice time constraints ensure that much of it is.

Reflection about Action

Behaving as professionals clearly involves reflection not only in and on, but also about the action. This represents a broader, critical stance which involves inquiry into the moral, ethical, political and instrumental issues embedded in teachers' everyday thinking and practice. Reflection of this kind is a means for professionals to exercise both responsibility and accountability for the decisions that they make in their teaching and maintain broader understandings of the interrelationships between teaching purposes and practices and the policy contexts in which these occur.

Over the years, various writers have provided classifications of different kinds of reflection related to different purposes. Many of these are derived from discourses which occur outside the classroom and seek to focus attention on the effects of external influences upon teachers and learners from a particular value stance. For example, Gore and Zeichner (1991) and Zeichner (1993) suggest that being a reflective practitioner must involve reflection upon issues of ethics and social justice (as being related to key values in teaching); whilst others suggest that attention must be given to the social and political forces which distort and limit teachers' educational conduct (Carr and Kemmis, 1986, pp. 31–2). Wellington and Austin (1996) emphasize the importance of transpersonal reflection which focuses upon the questioning of educational content, means and ends in the context of inner self-development. Zeichner and Liston (1996) identify five different traditions of reflective practice which indicate 'a particular emphasis in the content of teacher thinking':

- *Academic* in which reflection is concentrated on content, and how it is taught.
- *Social Efficiency* which stresses the thoughtful application of teaching strategies that have been suggested by research on teaching. There are two strands in this: i) technical (attempt to pursue predetermined ends); ii) deliberative (emphasizes the pre-eminence of teacher judgment of teaching situation, whilst taking account of other information sources).
- *Developmentalist* which focuses upon teaching which is sensitive to and builds on students' backgrounds, interests, thinking, and patterns of growth.
- *Social Reconstructionist* in which reflection 'is viewed as a political act that either contributes towards or hinders the realization of a more just and humane society'.
- *Generic* which encourages teachers to reflect about their teaching in general, without much attention to how they reflect, what should be the focus of the reflection, and the extent to which reflection should involve examination of social and institutional contexts in which they work. (based on Zeichner and Liston, 1996, pp. 51–62)

Hatton and Smith (1995) writing in the context of pre-service teacher education, propose a developmental sequence related to concerns in an attempt to relate different kinds of reflection to contexts (see Figure 2.1). Whilst it has as yet no empirical basis, their table does provide a useful summary and begins to probe possible relationships between technical rationality, reflection-on-action and reflection-in-action. However, it does seem to be over optimistic about the ability of teachers to apply 1–4 to their work in classrooms and seems to ignore critiques of reflection-in-action as outlined in this chapter, discontinuities in the learning lives of teachers and the limitations of learning from experience.

One of the few authoritative pieces of empirical research on reflection with serving teachers took place in Norwegian secondary schools. The researchers, Handal and

Reflection Type	Nature of Reflection	Possible Context
Reflection-in-action (Schön, 1983, 1987) addressing IMPACT concerns about some experience in the profession	5 **Contextualization of multiple viewpoints** drawing on any of the possibilities 1–4 below applied to situations as they are actually taking place	Dealing with on-the-spot professional problems as they arise, (thinking can be recalled and then shared with others later)
Reflection-on-action (Schön, 1983; Smith & Lovat, 1990; Smith & Hatton, 1992, 1993) addressing TASK and IMPACT concerns in the later states of a preservice program	4 **Critical** (social reconstructionist), seeing as problematic, according to ethical criteria, the goals and practices of one's profession	Thinking about the effects upon others of one's actions, taking account of social, political and/or cultural forces (can be shared)
	3 **Dialogue** (deliberative, cognitive, narrative), weighing competing claims and viewpoints, and then exploring alternative solutions	Hearing one's own voice (alone or with another) exploring alternative ways to solve problems in a professional situation
	2 **Descriptive** (social efficiency, developmental, personalistic), seeking what is seen as 'best possible' practice	Analysing one's performance in the professional role (probably alone), giving reasons for actions taken
Technical rationality (Schön, 1983; Shulman, 1988; van Manen, 1977) addressing SELF and TASK concerns early in a program which prepares individuals for entry into a profession	1 **Technical** (decision-making about immediate behaviours or skills), drawn from a given research/theory base, but always interpreted in light of personal worries and previous experience	Beginning to examine (usually with peers) one's use of essential skills for generic competencies as often applied in controlled, small scale settings

Figure 2.1 Types of reflection related to concerns (Hatton and Smith, 1995, p. 59)

Lauvas (1987), were essentially pessimistic about serving teachers' opportunities to move beyond practical reflection. They identified in Norway, as in England, a 'triple pressure' on schools and teachers to develop a more collective strategy of work through: the establishment of collective tasks; the provision of collective time to solve them; and the ideological pressure on teachers to work together (often in 'contrived' collegiality). Confronted with this task, they suggested that it was no longer sufficient to make curricular decisions on the basis of a largely implicit personal practical theory of teaching. Teachers also needed to formulate and develop their own personal practical theories; to have the capacity to do this and to share them with others; and to have the opportunities to do so.

In exploring how these might be achieved, they split the concept of 'reflective practice' into three hierarchical levels, as shown in Figure 2.2. They found that

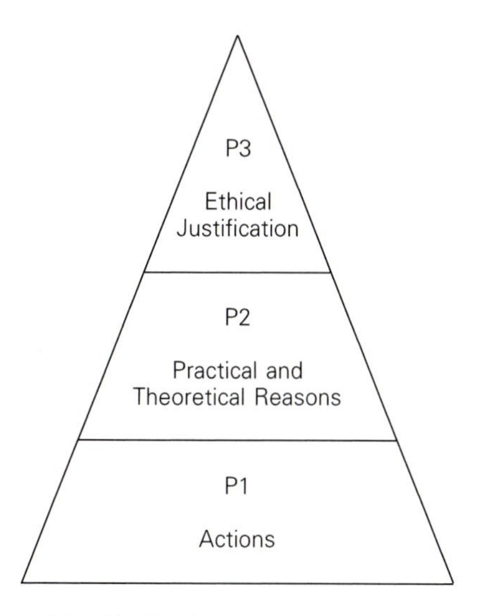

Figure 2.2 Practical theory (Handal, 1991)

teachers in Norway were used to talking about their work and deciding what to do, when to do it, and how to do it, i.e. planning at the level of action (P1), but rarely explicitly referring to reasons for this (P2) or the justification, the moral and ethical basis of their actions (P3). In finding this they were not making a critical moral judgment, but speculated that the reasons and justifications at levels P2 and P3 were not highly in demand in the 'busyness' culture of schools. Citing Carr and Kemmis's (1986) action research cycle of planning — acting, observing and reflecting — they suggested, on the basis of their evidence, that the normal conditions for school-based action research may well be such that an incomplete 'self-reflective' spiral is encouraged. In most situations teachers spend most of their time planning and acting (constructing practice) at the P1 level and less on observation and reflection (deconstructing practice) at levels P2 and P3. Change, where it occurs, is mainly at the P1 level of action. The fundamental attitude of 'treating what counts as knowledge as problematic' (Carr and Kemmis, 1986, p. 85) or studying critically one's own practice was not yet, they concluded, established.

The use of 'levels' of reflection does imply the existence of a particular value stance, and so it may be more useful to consider the different kinds of reflection as being related to purpose, and P1, 2 and 3 as actions which involve different degrees of complexity of thought.

These and other classifications are useful to the extent that they enable teachers and teacher educators to interrogate aspects of their values, purposes and practices and the personal, institutional and policy contexts which influence these.

It is important, however, to place learning through reflection at the centre of teachers' critical thinking and development. Developing as a professional means paying attention to all aspects of practice.

> When we become critical thinkers we develop an awareness of the assumptions under which we, and others, think and act. We seem to pay attention to the context in which our actions and ideas are generated. We become sceptical of quick fix solutions, of single answers to problems, and of claims to universal truth. We also become open to alternative ways of looking at, and behaving in, the world . . . When we think critically, we come to our judgements, choices and decisions for ourselves, instead of letting others do this on our behalf. We refuse to relinquish the responsibility for making the choices that determine our individual and collective futures to those who presume to know what is in our best interests. We become actively engaged in creating our personal and social worlds. In short we take the reality of democracy seriously. (Brookfield, 1987, pp. ix, x)

Brookfield identifies four aspects of critical thinking:

1. *Identifying and challenging assumptions.* Testing the taken-for-granted nature of assumptions and generalisations against our own experiences and understanding. Questioning and challenging passively accepted traditions and habitual patterns.
2. *Challenging the importance of context.* Developing awareness of the importance of relating our thinking to the context in which it is set. Practices, structures and actions are never context-free.
3. *Imagining and exploring alternatives.* Thinking beyond the obvious and the immediately logical. Adopting different perspectives and standpoints. Thinking laterally and imaginatively.
4. *Developing reflective scepticism.* Being wary of claims to universal truth or ultimate explanations. Because others think differently than we do, does not mean that they are right. (Brookfield, 1987, pp. 7–9, cited in Whitaker, 1997, pp. 152–3)

The Heart of the Teaching Act

It is self-evident, and for this reason perhaps rarely acknowledged, that teachers' actions in classrooms are both rational and non-rational. They are contingent upon a variety of factors, e.g. personal beliefs and values, lesson purposes, classroom conditions, resources, pupil behaviour, numbers of pupils. Their ability to exercise critical thinking which takes account of these is, therefore, central to their professional role in the classroom. The application of this thinking depends, importantly, upon their ability to exercise *pedagogical tact*, *connoisseurship*, and *emotional intelligence*.

van Manen proposes a concept of pedagogical tact which attempts to capture the 'improvisational pedagogical–didactical skill of instantly knowing, from moment to moment, how to deal with students in interactive teaching–learning situations' (van Manen, 1995, p. 41). Its application involves and invokes, simultaneously, perceptiveness, insight and feeling. Teachers who exercise pedagogical tact cannot be said, therefore, to be engaging in acts which are solely rational or cognitive. van Manen's 'pedagogical tact' closely resembles intuition. However, the application of intuition is likely to be context specific and, unless audited by self or others, uncertain and fallible. Pedagogical tact is not far removed from Eisner's notion of 'connoisseurship', a term which, although originally developed by Eisner as a method of 'outsider' evaluation, may also be used to describe teachers who are not only able to distinguish between what is significant about one set of teaching and learning practices and another, and to recognize and appreciate different facets of their teaching and students' learning, but also, as critics, to disclose 'the qualities of events or objects that connoisseurship perceives' (Eisner, 1979, p. 197).

The quality of teachers' pedagogical tact and connoisseurship will relate not only to their experience and expertise, or the conditions under which they work, but also to their 'emotional intelligence' (Goleman, 1995). Daniel Goleman, in a survey of research, identified a key set of characteristics or 'domains' which make up emotional intelligence which teachers need to perform their jobs successfully over a career: 'the ability to motivate oneself and persist in the face of frustrations; to control impulse and delay gratification, to regulate one's moods and keep distress from swamping the ability to think; to empathise and to hope' (1995, p. 34). He refers to the work of psychologists who have taken a broad view of intelligence which goes beyond the cognitive or academic (Gardner and Hatch, 1989; Sternberg 1985; Salovey and Mayer, 1990). Four of these domains of emotional intelligence may be applied directly to the intelligences or basic competences needed by teachers in their management of classrooms:

1 *Knowing one's emotions.* Self awareness is the keystone of emotional intelligence.
2 *Managing emotions.* Handling feelings so they are appropriate is an ability that builds on self-awareness.
3 *Recognising emotions in others.* Empathy . . . is the fundamental 'people skill'.
4 *Handling Relationships.* . . . skill in managing emotions in others . . . social competence. These abilities underpin popularity, leadership and interpersonal effectiveness. (Goleman, 1995, pp. 43–4)

Many writers on reflection tend to ignore or downplay the importance of attending to emotional development. Yet they do so at their peril. Writing about teaching and educational change, Andy Hargreaves finds that emotions:

> . . . are usually acknowledged and talked about only insofar as they help administrators and reformers 'manage' and offset teachers' resistance to change, or help them set the climate or mood in which the 'really important' business of cognitive learning or strategic planning can take place. (Hargreaves, 1998, p. 2)

To ignore the place of emotion in reflection, in, on and about teaching and learning is to fail to appreciate its potential for positively or negatively affecting the quality of the classroom experience for both teachers and learners.

In working lives characterized by busyness the constant challenge is to find the means of sustaining such critical thinking and emotional intelligence. Two such means which may be used at particular times for particular purposes and over limited periods are action research and narrative.

Action Research

Action research has been defined as 'the study of a social situation, involving the participants themselves as researchers, with a view to improving the quality of action within it' (Somekh, 1988, p. 164). It is characterized by systematic inquiry that is 'collective, collaborative, self-reflective, critical. The goals of such research are the understanding of practice and the articulation of a rationale or philosophy of practice in order to improve that practice' (McCutcheon and Jung, 1990, p. 148). Thus it enables teachers to adopt the discipline of becoming researchers, whilst still maintaining their commitment to improve their practice.

Action research may be carried out at different levels of complexity, thus making it as attractive to the 'learner researcher' as to the more experienced connoisseur. Witness, for example, this definition:

> Action research is a form of self-reflective enquiry undertaken by participants in social (including educational) situations in order to improve the rationality and justice of (a) their own social or educational practices, (b) their understanding of these practices and (c) the situations in which these practices are carried out. (Carr and Kemmis, 1986, p. 162)

This kind of thinking about the purposes and processes of teaching through action research may include a critical examination of the relationship between school culture and professional development. The implication here is that research into action may not only be a means of improving practice by the development of a particular value stance towards it, but also a means of generating theories of action which will include a critical consideration of the part played by the school environment in conditioning or moderating that action.

> Action research which is educational, encourages the researcher to go **beyond** the constraints imposed by schools and to act for the reconstruction of educational systems. The quality development process (in schools in England) directs its proponents to work **within** the constraints to improve the existing system in whatever manner is thought to be the most effective. (O'Hanlon, 1996, p. 87)

This still relatively young discipline requires also a quite different 'mindset' by those who engage in it from that required in most other research endeavours. In summary, it requires:

1. equitable relationships between participants;
2. the assistance of critical friends with an ability to engage in collaboration which is not always comfortable;
3. an understanding of change processes as both rational and non-rational;
4. a willingness to reflect upon and move from single to double loop learning;
5. a belief that authentic settings are best researched by those practitioners experiencing them direct, but that outsider viewpoints may enrich these through challenge and support;

6 an acceptance that those affected by planned changes have the primary responsibility for deciding on courses of action which seem likely to lead to improvement, and for evaluating the results of strategies tried out in practice; and
7 a supportive organizational culture.

Action research relies both on the desire of teachers to engage in reflection as a means of development and the willingness of the school in which they work to provide appropriate support. It requires also that those from outside the school who participate in collaborative action research with those inside schools engage in a synthesis of research activity with human correspondence. The former has often been over-emphasized at the expense of the latter.

It has been argued, however, that action research is not a natural process because systematic, collaborative and critical inquiry do not feature strongly in teachers' natural approaches to reflecting on and improving their practice as they work daily under pressures of immediacy and complexity (Jackson, 1968; Doyle, 1977).

> The assumption that external intervention is a necessity for teachers to organise themselves into enlightenment fails to acknowledge that many teachers do already have a professional, reflective and critical approach to their practice yet still do not take up an action research process. Another explanation for the reluctance of teachers to use action research approaches may lie in the action research process itself. It could be suggested that action research is an artificial process being imposed on teachers. Teachers' reluctance to take on action research may arise because action research, although appearing on the surface to be a natural part of what is considered good teaching, usually does not fit with the processes that reflective, inquiring teachers use. (Johnston, 1994, p. 43)

Johnston presents three areas of action research; (i) 'systematic problem solving', (ii) 'collaboration', and (iii) 'critique and justification' as problematic for teachers because they do not readily 'fit' teachers' normal everyday working lives. She goes on to suggest alternative ways of exploring practice which are less constraining. Narrative inquiry (Connelly and Clandinin, 1990; Noddings and Witherell, 1991) in which teachers learn by both hearing and telling stories is presented as 'a particularly natural way in which teachers come to know themselves and their practice' (Johnston, 1994, p. 46).

Broadening the Scope of Inquiry: The Use of Narrative

> ... the ways in which teachers achieve, maintain and develop their identity, their sense of self, in and through a career, are of vital significance in understanding the actions and commitments of teachers in their work. (Ball and Goodson, 1985, p. 18)

Listening to teachers' voices, narratives and stories (knowledge from the inside) and learning about life histories has long been a vital part of researchers' and teacher educators' work in reaching for an understanding of professional values, knowledge and practice (Brown and McIntyre, 1986; Day, 1981; Elbaz, 1983, 1990; Butt and Raymond, 1987; Yinger, 1987; Clandinin and Connelly, 1984a, 1984b, 1987, 1995). The exploration of personal and professional life histories can act as a window through which teachers can track the origins of the beliefs, values and perspectives which influence and inform their current theories and practices of teaching and 'being' a teacher. Reflecting upon their past experiences and the contexts in which these have occurred, often, 'becomes an occasion to change direction, to redouble efforts, to surpass themselves' (Ayers, 1990, p. 273).

Many researchers have emphasized the importance of personal and professional biography in understanding teachers and their teaching, and as a basis for furthering their professional development (Nias, 1989; Connelly and Clandinin, 1988; Elbaz, 1991; Gudmundsdottir, 1990; Carlgren and Lindblad, 1991; Tripp, 1993; Butt, 1994; Holly, 1989). They argue that narrative, autobiographical approaches which are contextually grounded provide the best means for teachers to reflect upon or give 'voice' to their experiences (Elbaz, 1990). Some focus upon critical incidents (Tripp, 1993) defined as, 'key events in an individual's life, and around which pivotal decisions revolve'.[2] These provoke the individual into selecting particular kinds of actions, which lead in particular directions (Sikes et al., 1985, p. 57). Others emphasize broader, more consciously constructed narrative inquiry approaches through extended interviewing, diaries and journals, and the use of 'metaphors' and 'images' (Lakoff and Johnston, 1980; Clandinin and Connelly, 1984b; Clandinin, 1986). Common to all these approaches are the beliefs that practical teaching competences are a necessary but not sufficient basis for the development of professional expertise; that it is the personal face of professional life that makes it possible to understand the professional knowledge landscape (Connelly and Clandinin, 1995, p. 153); that teachers have a store of 'personal practical knowledge' which is shaped by past experiences; and that making this explicit is a means by which teachers can take control of their development.

A focus upon personal and professional life histories places teachers at the centre of the development agenda. For many years, Clandinin and Connelly have worked closely with teachers in Canada in exploring their lives as educational wholes rather than as regarding life, learning, teaching and education as distinct, encouraging teachers to draw upon their professional knowledge 'landscapes' from inside and outside classrooms and schools.

> What is missing in the classroom is a place for teachers to tell and retell their stories of teaching. The classroom can become a place for endless, repetitive, living out of stories without possibility for awakenings and transformations . . . (But) . . . the possibilities for reflective awakenings and transformations are limited when one is alone. Teachers need others in order to engage in conversations where stories can be told, reflected back, heard in different ways, retold, and relived in new ways in the safety and secrecy of the classroom. (Connelly and Clandinin, 1995, p. 13)

They have identified three 'desires' of teachers which relate to their professional development: the desire to tell stories of practice; the desire for relationships in the telling of the stories; and the desire to think again, and reflect on practice and its past, present and future contexts. However, they acknowledge that professional work contexts for teachers do not always encourage teachers to be 'knowers who can teach each other' (Connelly and Clandinin, 1995, p. 126).

The personal and social difficulties of engaging in narrative inquiry accounts of this kind should not be underestimated as writers 'recount, interconnect and make meaning of their past experiences . . . [which] . . . often contain stories within stories, accounts that people sometimes prefer to forget or to place in the unreachable recesses of their minds' (Knowles, 1993, p. 75). Understanding stories and making sense of experience is a complex business which is both cognitively and emotionally demanding. Although narrative inquiry provides a means for teachers to reclaim the agenda of their own development, as with action research, trusted critical friends are needed to provide support and challenge in the process. Like action research, it also has its limitations, since it is at the level of investigating practice by talking about it without the benefits of observing it.

Ten Challenges of Inquiry

Challenge 1. The Limits of Learning Alone

It can be argued that while teachers need to be reflective in the classroom in order first to survive and then to be at least competent in their classroom management, ultimately reflecting in and on action will result in bounded learning if carried out in isolation. In other words, there is a limit to what can be learnt from examining one's own practice whilst being simultaneously engaged in that practice. Reflection-on-action, while offering more possibilities for development, will usually be unsystematic with checks against realities constrained by the limitations of the single perspective on the action provided by the teacher, selective memory and time. Even where teachers meet in order to share and analyse practice for assessment and planning purposes, usually the dialogue will be based upon talk about practice rather than the practice itself. I have criticized Schön's notion of reflective practice elsewhere for his lack of attention to how teachers may reflect together on a regular basis about their work (Day, 1993b). Clearly, analysis and planning which occurs in a collaborative environment holds the possibilities for greater learning (Osterman and Kottkamp, 1993). However, 'double loop' learning of this kind requires colleagues to trust each other and feel confident in their own ability to disclose and receive feedback. Even then, it is not certain that teachers working together will move far beyond 'comfortable' forms of collaboration.[3]

Challenge 2. The Capacity to Reflect

Neither the processes of reflection nor its outcomes are entirely rational. The capacity to reflect will be affected by situational constraints (e.g. work overload, innovation), personal limitations (e.g. phase of development, knowledge or skill level) and emotional well-being (e.g. self-confidence, esteem, response to negative criticism). As a result of working with student teachers of mathematics in the Netherlands and following them over a 10-year period, Korthagen and Wubbels (1995) found that:

> Emotions and attitudes play a crucial role . . . [Though] the stimulus to engage in reflection is almost always rooted in a need to get a better grasp of the situation . . . when fear of the situation becomes too great, as often happens during the 'transition shock' . . . (the first years of being a teacher), . . . reflection may disappear altogether. (p. 70)

They identified a 'latency period' of about one year, after which those graduates who had experienced their reflection-oriented pre-service programme could be differentiated from those in their subject matter oriented group as having a more adequate self-perception, better interpersonal relationships with students and a higher degree of job satisfaction. Many teachers work within 'non or miseducative environments' (Cole, 1997, p. 13). Writing in the context of recent systemic reforms in the province of Ontario, Canada, in which, 'perhaps the most persistent and poignant [example] of teacher helplessness is within the context of formalised professional development' (p. 16), Ardra Cole describes most initiatives as being still, 'for the most part, conceptualised, designed and delivered **for** teachers, not **by** them' (p. 17). In investigating impediments to reflective practice through analysis of the current conditions in schools, she argues that 'the conditions under which teachers work have generated feelings and psychological states that militate against reflective practice and professional growth' (p. 7). By working conditions she is referring to, 'external structures imposed by schools and school systems, the profession, government and the public at large'. By psychological states, she refers to perceptions which interfere with 'optimum productivity and practice' (p. 13).

Jersild's (1995) work in exploring the effects of anxiety, fear, loneliness, helplessness, meaning and meaninglessness and hostility in relation to understanding self is particularly relevant here. He argues that these emotions are prevalent in teachers' lives in schools and classrooms and must, therefore, be addressed as part of teachers' professional education. Ardra Cole has extended Jersild's analysis of the relationship between self-understanding and education to the classroom and school settings in which teachers work, arguing convincingly that, 'until these issues are addressed teachers will not be able freely and meaningfully to engage in the kind of reflective practice and professional development that brings meaning to their own lives and the lives of their students' (Cole, 1997, p. 14).

Challenge 3. Technician or Reflective Practitioner?

Simply to advocate reflection in, on and about action as a means of learning provides no indication of the depth, scope or purpose of the process. Distinctions between teachers as technicians and teachers as reflective practitioners (e.g. Zeichner and Liston, 1996) are not always helpful. Good teachers will be technically competent and reflect upon broader issues of purpose, process, content and outcome. It is when technical competence ceases to involve reflection that the quality of teaching is likely to suffer.[4] Such 'technicians' identify a problem in the classroom as 'given' and plan strategies to solve the problem without questioning their own goals, values or moral responsibilities and accountabilities, or the broader assumptions which might, for example, contribute to the school setting, shape of the curriculum or the attitudes and behaviour of the students. Unless a more critically reflective stance is adopted, analysis and understanding will be restricted to unarticulated values, assumptions and conditions (Wellington and Austin, 1996). However, it must be recognized that pressures now being experienced by teachers in many countries to meet pre-specified achievement standards have reduced the potential for genuine teacher development through 'inquiry' by causing:

> 1 a means-end thinking which limits the substance of teachers' reflections to technical questions of teaching techniques and internal classroom organization and a neglect of questions or curriculum and education purposes;
> 2 neglect of the social and institutional context in which teaching takes place. (Gore and Zeichner, 1995, p. 204)

These practices, it is claimed, help create a situation 'where there is merely the illusion of teacher development'. Citing Israel Scheffler, Zeichner and Liston (1996) argue that if teachers want to avoid the bureaucratic and technical conceptions of their role that have historically been given to them then they must seek to maintain a broad vision about their work and not just look inwardly at their own practices:

> Teachers cannot restrict their attention to the classroom alone, leaving the larger setting and purposes of schooling to be determined by others. They must take active responsibility for the goals to which they are committed, and for the social setting in which these goals may prosper. If they are not to be mere agents of others, of the state, of the military, of the media, of the experts and bureaucrats, they need to determine their own agency through a critical and continual evaluation of the purposes, the consequences, and the social context of their calling. (Scheffler, 1968, p. 11, cited in Zeichner and Liston, 1996, p. 19)

Those who are responsible for policy whether in school or out may well view teacher inquiry as a technical means of improving the efficiency of, for example, curriculum delivery or classroom control rather than as a means of emancipation through knowledge. Thus it may be supported at the 'technical rational' rather than 'critical reflective' level. Teacher inquiry which is part of a broader professional development agenda should be focused in this way from time to time. However, where it is the sole concern, as has been suggested in criticisms of some systemic school improvement efforts in England (Elliott, 1996) then it becomes, in effect, a means of control masquerading as enlightenment.

Challenge 4. Comfortable or Confrontational?

Processes of reflection, central to learning, may not in themselves lead to confrontation of thinking and practices nor take account of broad institutional and social contexts necessary as precursors to decisions about change when carried out by the teacher alone (Day, 1993b). Collaborative work with Michael, a secondary school teacher, provides an example of how confrontation resulting from engagement in reflective processes is not always 'comfortable'. Michael had wanted to examine his teaching practices in order to identify whether they reflected his 'espoused theories'. This examination took place over time during two 'sequences' of lessons with the help of a trusted colleague from outside the school and involved classroom observations, stimulated recall and the interviewing of teacher and students over a period of a year (Day, 1997b). During this time, he was beset with intra-departmental conflict relating to his own role in the future, to the way in which he perceived he was being treated by his Head of Department and the school in general, and his workload.

Despite his wish to do so, Michael found it difficult to modify his 'charismatic' teaching style where he was at the centre of the teaching–learning process, dominating its content, pacing and procedures for ideological reasons. Sustaining attempts at change was made more difficult both by stress which he felt as a result of events which were occurring outside the classroom and his difficulties in managing conflicts within the 'educative', 'professional' and 'ideological' selves of his espoused theory. As a *professional ideologue* Michael believed in the importance of the teacher transmitting a 'relevant' body of knowledge to students which was value laden. As an *educator* he believed in the importance of encouraging students to be 'self-searching'. The two values are not intrinsically inconsistent and indeed may be complementary. However, it would appear upon reflection that whilst both were considered when planning the second sequence of lessons, they were irreconcilable in action. The teaching of the second sequence of lessons took place against a set of aspirations determined by Michael himself. The revelation that these were irreconcilable proved to be a most uncomfortable experience. What was revealed to Michael during and as a result of the collaborative research process was that his commitment to a teaching approach to which students and content must accommodate themselves, and to his need for dominance in the classroom conflicted with his ideological goal of 'emancipating' students. In this example, the dominance of the *personal* and *ideological* selves was a constraining factor on change. It was the process of collaborative action research which challenged and clarified this. Relatively little attention has been given also (outside the action research movement) to what engaging in reflective processes which are both rational and non-rational will mean for the teacher. It is clear that there are parts of ourselves which we might prefer to remain private from ourselves and others. Alone these are rather easier to hide, but as part of a group much more difficult — unless there is a tacit agreement concerning 'boundaries' and thus a kind of *collaboration by collusion*.

Challenge 5. Engaging with the Possibilities of Change

In order to develop and sustain their critical thinking through reflection, teachers will need to engage in processes of metacognition and systematic collection, description, synthesis, interpretation and evaluation of data. The quality and authenticity of the data will depend upon their abilities to engage in reflective analytic conversations with themselves and others as well as their capacities to do so. Yet if teachers are to engage in critical forms of teaching, and move beyond the 'P1' planning level described earlier in this chapter, they will need not only to be concerned with describing what they do and informing themselves and others of the meaning of that description. They will need also to confront their practice (How did I come to be like this?) and reconstruct it so that they might do things differently (Day, 1985; Smyth, 1991). In short, they will need to be prepared to engage with possibilities of change. Whilst change involves cognition, it is not only a cognitive process. It involves emotion. Teachers who are reflective inquirers need to recognize that inquiry is likely to raise issues of change and that this will involve a confrontation of inconsistencies within and between existing core values, espoused theories and theories in use. This will not always be comfortable.

Challenge 6. Exploring the Continuum

The sixth challenge is for teachers to take a broader view of the ways in which they can learn through inquiry into their practices and the contexts which influence these over a career. In 1985, David Ebbutt published a paper in which he described different kinds of what he called 'Insider Activity', what Schön (1983) calls reflection in and on the action. This described teachers' working lives in school and, in relation to these, the kinds of research into practice in which they engaged. The paper did much to provide a map for those wishing to engage in further exploration of contexts for reflection. Reflective and non-reflective practitioners are not two fundamentally irreconcilable groups. Rather, they are teacher inquirers who are at different points on a continuum (see Figure 2.3). The continuum spans unsystematic, intuitive inquiry to inquiry through systematic research, defined by Stenhouse as 'systematic inquiry made public' (Stenhouse, 1975), and manifested particularly through action research. It may be that teachers will be working in different modes during different phases of their careers and for different purposes. Ebbutt's developmental classification of a range of insider research related activity has the virtue of being based upon the observed reality of teachers' working lives. In contextualizing the teacher as researcher within a realistic continuum of practice, he provides the means by which movement may be planned to occur between 'Usual Teaching Mode' where isolated single loop learning predominates and conscious reflection is sporadic; 'Teacher Self-monitoring' where data on classroom practice is regularly if informally collected, sometimes with the help of a critical friend colleague, and reflections are incorporated into practice; and three progressively more rigorous

TEACHER AS INQUIRER				
Usual Teaching Mode	Teacher Self-Monitoring	*Teacher-inquirer* Self-evaluation: limited action research mode	*Teacher-inquirer* Self-evaluation: limited action research mode	*Teacher-researcher* Traditional research mode
Works in isolation of own classroom *and* Reflects on own practice from time to time, may implement action steps *and* No use of external consultant *and* No systematic data collection *and* No written report *but* Incorporates reflections regularly into practice	Works in isolation of own classroom *and* Regularly reflects on own practice. May implement action steps *and* May use external consultant or a critical friend *and* Informally collects some data *and* Informally analyses data *but* No written report *but* Tries to incorporate reflections regularly into practice	Works in isolation of own classroom *and* Regularly reflects on own practice. Systematically implements action steps *and* May request help from a consultant or a critical friend *and* Systematically collects data *and* Systematically analyses data and generates hypotheses *and* Writes report open to public critique *and* Systematically incorporates reflections and subsequently changes practice	Works in isolation of own classroom as part of a coherent group who meet regularly *and* Systematically reflects about own practice and systematically implements action steps *and* Almost certainly uses consultant or critical friend *and* Systematically collects data *and* Systematically perhaps as a group analyse(s) data and generate(s) hypotheses *and* Write separate and joint reports open to public critique *and* Systematically incorporates reflections and changes practice. Also work towards improvement by testing hypotheses at institutional level	Works in isolation of own classroom *and* Reflects about aspects of practice. Selects hypotheses from formal theory *and* May request help from consultant or supervisor *and* Systematically collects data *and* Systematically analyses data to verify or falsify hypotheses *and* Written report, open to critique *and* Hopes to contribute to development of formal theory

Figure 2.3 A continuum of teacher inquiry (adapted from Ebbutt, 1985)

'teacher-researcher' modes of inquiry which lead to change at personal and school levels and development of theory from practice.

Challenge 7. Time

It has been argued that the mind works at three different speeds:

i) *Rapid thought* — this 'unconscious' level of working is the most common in the classroom, where teachers must often react instantaneously to a multitude of demands. It involves reflection in action.
ii) *Deliberative thought* — this involves 'figuring matters out, weighing up the pros and cons, constructing arguments and solving problems' (Claxton, 1997, p. 2). This is similar to reflection on action.
iii) *Contemplative thought* — this 'is often less purposeful and clear-cut, more playful . . . In this mode we are ruminating or mulling things over . . . What is going on in the mind may be quite fragmentary'. (Claxton, 1997, p. 2)

It is this last way of thinking that is in danger of being lost in the intensification of teachers' working lives through the rise of 'technopoly' (Postman, 1992) in which contemplation is regarded as a luxury. Technopoly is based upon:

> . . . the beliefs that the primary, if not the only goal of human labour and thought is efficiency; that technical calculation is in all respects superior to human judgement; that in fact human judgement cannot be trusted, because it is plagued by laxity, ambiguity, and unnecessary complexity; that subjectivity is an obstacle to clear thinking; that what cannot be measured either does not exist or is of no value; and that the affairs of citizens are best guided and conducted by 'experts'. (Postman, 1992, cited in Claxton, 1997, p. 2)

According to Claxton, the 'newly formed hybrid discipline of "cognitive science", an alliance of neuro-science, philosophy, artificial intelligence and experimental psychology, is revealing that the unconscious realism of the human mind will successfully accomplish a number of unusual, interesting and important tasks **if they are given the time**' (Claxton, 1997, pp. 3–4).

Because historically teachers' work has been regarded as 'contact time' with students, they have had few built-in opportunities or expectations placed upon them, for example, to collect data, share practice with colleagues, or collectively reflect in depth 'on' and 'about' their teaching and its contexts. They have little control over time. Andy Hargreaves (1994) discusses three dimensions of time in teaching: the micropolitical, relating to the distribution of time in relation to status; the phenomenological, relating to the way the use of time is constructed in schools; and the sociopolitical, relating to the claims on teachers' 'discretionary' time made by administrators.

Whilst time is always at a premium in teaching where conditions of service effectively define it as contact time, this is not the case universally. In Norway and

Sweden, for example, time is built into the working day which could be used for deliberative thought, perhaps in recognition that making sense of complex, ill-defined and ambiguous situations is a key determinant of quality teaching and that providing time for reflection which is more contemplative is an essential part of teacher development.

Challenge 8. Critical Friendship Support

Potentially, action research and narrative offer teachers tremendous opportunities to engage in professional development of an holistic kind through the systematic investigation of self and practice either over extended periods or through an intensive, relatively short timespan. The methods that are available do not need to demand the use of advanced research techniques. In other words, the level of engagement can fit the purpose. If reflection on practice is to probe current realities in a challenging way, however, there will also need to be practical and moral support from within and without the school in terms of that most valuable of all commodities, time, and the commitment of a 'critical friend'.

Critical friendships are *based upon practical partnerships entered into voluntarily, presuppose a relationship between equals and are rooted in a common task of shared concern.* The role of a critical friend is to provide support and challenge within a trusting relationship. It is different from the 'mentor' relationship in which one person (the mentor) holds a superior position by virtue of his/her experience, knowledge and skills. The critical friend is recognized as having knowledge, experience and skills which are complementary.

Challenge 9. Teachers' Voices

> What is missing from the knowledge base for teaching are the voices of teachers themselves. (Cochran-Smith and Lytle, 1996, p. 93)

There are criticisms that some of those engaged in studying teachers' thinking and action (an inevitable part of action research though not confined to it) attach importance to the narrative of teachers' stories without always locating them in broader social and political contexts, and that action research, now 'colonized' by many who support educational reform, is being used to serve the 'academic knowledge' interests of teacher educators rather than teachers. Criticisms have also been levelled at the myriad of published collaborative research reports which seem to imply (i) that the researchers (usually drawn from higher education) and the teacher-researchers (usually drawn from schools) must share the same (usually humanistic, radical or progressive-liberal) educational ideologies (Burbules, 1985); and (ii) that the reported direction of change in thinking and practice is almost always towards the 'social justice' end of the political continuum (characterized by emancipatory social action research espoused by, for example Carr and Kemmis, 1986; Zeichner, 1993). There are dangers, therefore, in assuming that the teachers' voices, once liberated, will provide authentic accounts. Andy Hargreaves (1997a) supports the promotion of teachers' voices through research but, like Elliott (1994), questions those advocates who 'selectively appropriate' those voices which are consonant with the value positions and educational ideologies which they themselves hold so that the effect is to present them as 'the voices' which are representative of teachers as a whole. Authentic portrayals of teaching should contain other voices, e.g. students, in addition to those of teachers, so that they may be interpreted 'with reference to the contexts of teachers' lives and work that help give them meaning' (Hargreaves, 1997a, p. 16).[5]

Challenge 10. Building Professional Learning Cultures: Making Time to Reflect

Although reflective practice and action research can occur in environments which are alien to adult learning, it is clear that they will be more effective in those that promote cultures of inquiry for students and teachers. With Stenhouse, I believe that:

> . . . long-term improvement of education through the utilization of research and development hinges on the creation of different expectations in the system . . . The different expectations will be generated only as schools come to see themselves as research and development institutions rather than clients of research and development agencies . . . It is not enough that teachers' work should be studied; they need to study it for themselves. (Stenhouse, 1976, pp. 222–3 and 143, cited in Grundy, 1994, pp. 35–6)

Shirley Grundy presents a challenge to the school to play its part in teacher development. She argues that it is, 'not sufficient for education systems to "pass the buck" for educational improvement to teachers and construe the school as simply the location of teachers' work' and that, 'just as professional autonomy needs to be reconceptualised in terms of the professional community of the school, so also we need to understand that responsibility for the quality of education is also a matter for the school, not just for the individual teacher' (Grundy, 1994, p. 25). Structural reforms which have created opportunities for collaboration and inquiry, by themselves are insufficient means of realizing the potential of professional development.

Cochran-Smith and Lytle (1996) argue for the building and sustaining of 'intellectual communities of teacher-researchers, or networks of individuals who enter with other teachers into a collective search for meaning in their work lives' (p. 93) and who use their research for the purpose of changing their teaching and their working conditions where appropriate. They develop an analytical framework which focuses upon the main qualitative and quantitative problem areas in work of this kind — organizing time, using talk, constructing texts and interpreting the tasks of teaching and schooling.

Setting up and developing collaborative work over time requires 'sustained interactivity' (Huberman, 1993b) and this requires that teachers engage in discussions in their schools about the use of each of these dimensions of time for their learning.

Organizing time	Constructing texts
Leading transitions	Critical friendships, confrontation and change
Interpreting the tasks of teaching and schooling	Educational knowledge and knowledge about education

Adapted by permission of the publisher from McLaughlin, M.W. and Oberman, I. (eds) Teacher Learning: New Policies, New Practices (New York: Teachers College Press, © 1996 by Teachers College, Columbia University. All rights reserved.), Figure 9.1 (p. 99).

Figure 2.4 Communities for teacher inquiry and development: A framework for analysis (based on Cochran-Smith and Lytle, 1996, p. 99)

Talk is the means by which teachers deconstruct, test out and reconstruct their beliefs and 'espoused theories' of education (Argyris and Schön, 1976). Most 'co-construction', whether it takes place through anecdote, ideas, information and material swapping, or the sharing of problems, issues and opinions will need to challenge teachers to move beyond exchange to critique; and the success of this depends upon the level of individual trust and institutional support. Critique, as we have seen, involves both disclosure and feedback. The way communities use talk as a means of probing meanings and uncovering diversity is crucial to their growth. In addition, *texts* need to be 'readerly'. They may be fragments from lessons taught, teaching journals, students' work or teachers' work plans, which together constitute the experienced worlds of the teachers — their staffrooms, classrooms, schools and the inner worlds of values and beliefs. Finally, *interpreting the tasks of teaching and schooling* demands that teachers examine the consistencies and inconsistencies within and between their 'espoused theories' of teaching and learning and their 'theories-in-action', and that they set these in the context of an appreciation of the challenges and constraints of the system as a whole: the demands of externally generated policies, expectations of the community, the school, parents and students, and the learning cultures of the classrooms and schools in which they teach.

Making time for sustained reflection and dialogue is a primary challenge in building professional learning cultures. Figure 2.4 provides a framework for planning which takes account of difficulties of 'confronting' the personal, professional and organizational contexts which influence teaching and learning. It acknowledges also the importance to learning of combining educational knowledge based on practical experience of teaching with knowledge about education, based on research knowledge; and recognizes the need for leaders and critical friends who will facilitate, coordinate and sustain transitions in the development lives of learning communities.

Learning communities require the discipline of learning to start with dialogue 'while traditional organizations require management systems that control people's behaviour, learning organizations invest in improving the quality of thinking, the capacity for reflection and team learning, and the ability to develop shared visions and shared understandings . . .' (Senge, 1990, p. 287). In such cultures, reflection in, on and about the action will occur routinely rather than be reserved for the formal appraisal process or the staff development day.

Conclusion

Being an adult learner means reflecting upon purposes and practices and the values and social contexts in which those are expressed. Disclosure and feedback, central to reflection, are processes of learning which will challenge not only the emotional and cognitive competencies of teachers but also the personal and professional values which underpin these and which lie at the heart of professional practice. If teachers are to continue to develop then they need to engage in different kinds of reflection, action research and narrative over their careers and be supported in meeting the challenges of doing so. It should always be remembered, though, that reflection on teaching is not simply a cognitive process. Like teaching itself, it demands emotional commitment. It will involve the head and the heart. Perhaps the greatest challenge for individuals and organizations is to ensure that both of these are nurtured in systems designed to improve the quality of teaching and learning for teachers as well as students.

Notes

1 The Ford T project in the 1970s provides one example of work which was designed to elicit teachers' practical theories (Elliott, 1976). In England, Wilfred Carr has written a great deal about teachers' implicit theories.

2 In a detailed examination of the use of critical incidents in teaching as a means of developing professional judgment, David Tripp, an Australian, suggests that four kinds of judgment are necessary to professional teaching:
   i) *Practical judgment* which is the basis of every action taken in the conduct of teaching, and the majority of which is made instantly.
   ii) *Diagnostic judgment* which involves using profession-specific knowledge and academic expertise to recognize, describe, understand and explain and interpret practical judgments.
   iii) *Reflective judgment* which concerns more personal and moral judgments involving the identification, description, exploration and justification of the judgments made and values implicit and espoused in practical (teaching) decisions and their explanations.
   iv) *Critical judgment* which, through formal investigation, involves challenge to and evaluation of the judgments and values reveal reflection in action.

   However, he goes on to state that, 'contrary to the logic of the way in which I have presented them, personal experience suggests that these kinds of judgment are not necessarily successively dependent' (Tripp, 1993, p. 140).

3 There are a growing number of accounts of collaborative reflection on action, many of these published in *Educational Action Research: An International Journal* (Triangle Press).

4 Distinctions between teachers as technicians and as reflective practitioners have been debated for many years in the context of teacher autonomy and notions of 'emancipation', e.g. Carr and Kemmis (1986); Grimmett and Erickson (1988).

5 See also Ebbutt, D. (1985) and Elliott, J. (1983) accounts of the TIQL Project (Longmans/Schools Council), in which all data was the property of the participating teachers who also wrote up the research.

Chapter 3

Understanding Teachers' Development: Experience, Expertise and Competence

Continuing calls for raising standards of student learning and achievement have now focused national policies upon the quality of teachers and their teaching in classrooms. Efforts have been made to ensure that all teachers undertake regular in-service training so that they remain up to date with curriculum content knowledge, continue to develop their classroom organization and teaching and assessment strategies, and, where appropriate, their leadership roles. Yet it is still the case that most teachers work in isolation from their colleagues for most of the time; opportunities for the development of practice based upon observation and critique of that practice remain limited; and, despite the best efforts of many school leaders to promote collegial cultures, these are almost always at the level of planning or talking about teaching rather than at the level of examining practice itself. In this context, Barth's observation of the 'perilous place' of learning in the life of teachers is not, perhaps, surprising:

> . . . the voracious learners are the beginning, first year teachers who care desperately to learn their new craft. The learning curve remains high for three or four years at which time the life of the teacher becomes highly routinized and repetitive. The learning curve flattens. Next September, the same as last September. After perhaps ten years, many observers report that teachers, now beleaguered and depleted, become **resistant** to learning. The learning curve turns downward. With twenty-five years of life in schools, many educators are described as 'burned out'. No learning curve . . . It appears that life in school is toxic to adult learning. The longer one resides there, the less the learning. Astonishing. (Barth, 1996, pp. 28–9)

Research suggests that care and commitment sooner or later may become 'frayed at the edges'. Farber (1991), in a study of teacher burnout, identified the effects of a lack of attention to teacher need such that 'career development' is often accompanied by a 'sense of inconsequentiality'. Although many teachers begin their careers, 'with a sense that their work is socially meaningful and will yield great satisfactions', this is lost as, 'the inevitable difficulties of teaching . . . interact with personal issues and vulnerabilities, as well as social pressure and values, to engender a sense of frustration and force a reassessment of the possibilities of the job and the investment one wants to make in it' (Farber, 1991, p. 36).

Many 'short-burst' training opportunities do not fulfil the longer term motivational and intellectual needs of teachers themselves. They fail to connect with the essential moral purposes that are at the heart of their professionalism or to address directly the needs of teachers seeking to improve the quality of pupils' learning in changing circumstances. Teachers' emotional commitments and connections to students, both positive and negative, energize and articulate everything they do. Teaching involves immense amounts of emotional labour:

> This kind of labour calls for a co-ordination of mind and feeling, and it sometimes draws on a source of self that we honor as deep and integral to our personality. (Hochschild, 1983, p. 7, cited in Hargreaves, 1997b, p. 16)

Such emotional commitments are part of teachers' substantive, professional selves. Kelchtermans (1993) found that there were six components of the substantive selves of primary school teachers in Belgium: self-image, self-esteem, job motivation, job satisfaction, task perception and future perspective; whilst an American study identified 7 themes which teachers associated with their professional selves — willingness to go beyond the call of duty, effective communication, personal satisfaction from teaching, relationships with colleagues, satisfaction with particular students' successes, the students' perspectives, and learning through reflection on practice (Nelson, 1993). These components of the substantive self of the teacher are essential features of teachers' lives. Teacher development, then, must take account of these and the psychological and social settings which can encourage or discourage learning — for example, the teachers' own personal life histories, their professional learning experiences, expertise and school professional learning cultures which provide the day-to-day contexts for their work.

If we are truly to engage in the learning project for teachers as well as students, then interventions into their working lives over a career must be based upon an understanding of them. This chapter examines three themes necessary to such an understanding:

1 Teacher experience and expertise;
2 Professional knowledge, competence and capability; and
3 Teachers' development phases.

Teachers' Experience and Expertise

At any given stage in their lives and careers, teachers will be at a particular phase in their personal and professional development.[1] Because professionals' learning on the job is situated in a broader developmental framework, it is important to recognize the positive or negative influences which may be associated with these. There are a number of theories of expertise which describe and explain differences between teachers. The commonly accepted view is that teachers learn to teach by experience, but what is meant by 'experience'? Whilst there are different models relating to cognition (Dewey, 1938), intuition (Dreyfus and Dreyfus, 1986) and concerns (Fuller, 1970) these are different facets of a more complex reality relating to both expertise, capability and personal and professional biography.

Level 1 Novice
- Rigid adherence to taught rules or plans
- Little situational perception
- No discretionary judgement

Level 2 Advanced Beginner
- Guidelines for action based on attributes or aspects (aspects are global characteristics of situations recognizable only after some prior experience)
- Situational perception still limited
- All attributes and aspects are treated separately and given equal importance

Level 3 Competent
- Coping with crowdedness
- Now sees actions at least partially in terms of longer term goals
- Conscious deliberate planning
- Standardized and routinized procedures

Level 4 Proficient
- See situations holistically rather than in terms of aspects
- See what is most important in a situation
- Perceives deviations from the normal pattern
- Decision-making less laboured
- Uses maxims for guidance, whose meaning varies according to the situation

Level 5 Expert
- No longer relies on rules, guidelines or maxims
- Intuitive grasp of situations based on deep tacit understanding
- Analytic approaches used only in novel situation or when problems occur
- Vision of what is possible

Figure 3.1 Summary of Dreyfus' Model of Skills Acquisition (from Eraut, 1994, p. 124)

There is much literature which conceptualizes professionals in training and in-service as moving through a number of skill development stages. Fuller's (1970) 'concerns based' developmental model of pre-service teachers indicated six phases in which pre-service students moved from concerns about self, professional expectations and acceptance, own teaching adequacy, relationships with pupils, concerns about pupils' learning what is taught, concerns about pupils' learning needs, to concerns about teachers' own contributions to pupil change. Not all 'novice' teachers are likely to have reached the sixth phase when they enter teaching, however, and professional socialization in school will inevitably affect disposition with regard to the direction and extent of further development.

One of the most influential models for the development of expertise is that of Dreyfus and Dreyfus (1986).[2] They identify a number of levels of skill development as the professional moves from being a 'novice' through to 'advanced beginner', 'competent', 'proficient' and 'expert'. The Dreyfus and Dreyfus model, like the work of van Manen, Eisner and others, recognizes that 'perception and understanding are based in our capacity for picking up not rules, but flexible styles of behaviour' (1986, p. 5) within a given situation. Its main features are summarized in Figure 3.1.

The temptation to adopt and apply this model is seductive. Despite its emphasis upon perception, understanding and intuition it appears to have a logical progression and is based upon learning from experience. Note the way in which Dreyfus and Dreyfus (1977) describe the transition that may occur towards becoming an expert performer as:

> The performer is no longer aware of features and rules, and his/her performance becomes fluid and flexible and highly proficient. The chess player develops a feel for the game; the language learner becomes more fluent; the pilot stops feeling that he/she is flying the plane and simply feels that he/she is flying. (p. 12)

Yet this ignores the complexity and dynamic of classroom life, the discontinuities of learning and the importance of continuing regular opportunities for deliberative reflection 'on' and 'about' experience as ways of locating and extending understandings of the meaning of experience in broader contexts.

> . . . experience is incoherent . . . it doesn't come in neat packages of pre-determined meetings. This is not to say that it is meaningless, but simply that meaning is often multiple, at times contradictory, and although temporarily fixable always has an undecidability, and excess of meaning. (Usher, p. 172, 1993)

Research by Feiman-Nemser (1990) and Korthagen and Wubbels (1995) also confirms that developing experience and becoming an expert is fraught with complications. Elliott (1993) argues for a much more interactionist view of development. This takes into account the need for professionals to prepare for and respond to changing personal, professional, organizational and policy contexts and is much more in tune with the notions of continuing professional development espoused in this book. He suggests that the 'levels' should be treated as overlapping, interactive phases, and that these might relate to expectations of teachers as inquirers in all phases of their working lives — inquirers who at different times, for different reasons, may regress or progress. *Phase 1* would incorporate Novice and Advanced Beginner and would in development terms, focus upon promoting the notion of teacher self-evaluation. *Phase 2* — Advanced Beginner to Competent — would focus upon teachers as 'reflective practitioners', reflecting upon the problematics of situations. *Phase 3* — Competent to Proficient — would focus upon developing teachers' ability to self-evaluate actions and decisions. *Phase 4* — Proficiency to Expertise — acknowledges the difficulties for conscious deliberation caused by the development of experience and intuition. It may be necessary here to engage in 'double loop' learning in order to test what Eraut (1994) calls the fallibility of expertise. Teachers will move backwards and forwards between phases during their working lives for all kinds of reasons to do with personal history, psychological and social factors. Taking on a new role, changing schools, teaching a new age group or a new syllabus will almost inevitably result in development disruption, at least temporarily; and becoming an expert does not mean that learning ends — hence the importance of maintaining the ability to be a lifelong inquirer. Elliott argues for action research as a:

> ... process by which the structure of abilities that define competent professional practice are most fully realised in those practitioners who aspire to develop their skills a stage beyond that of the advanced beginner. (Elliott, 1991, p. 134)

Whilst the Dreyfus and Dreyfus model is useful as a means for conceptualizing growth which is not merely dependent upon rationality, it implies an over-reliance upon learning from direct experience. It is a model of skill development in which situational understanding plays an important role, but not contextual understanding. It seems also to ignore other kinds of experience, i.e. learning from the observed experience of others or from 'vicarious' experience such as in case studies (Elliott, 1996); and it appears to assume that the end point of development is becoming an expert — with the (mistaken) implication that an expert is always infallible.[3]

It is clear, however, that differences do exist between 'novice', 'experienced' and 'expert' teachers. The 'poor fit' which many novice teachers feel between what they have learned about teaching and its application to practice is a well-known phenomenon, despite continuing attempts to address the issue through various forms of apprenticeship models and school–university partnership schemes. Experienced teachers, also, despite their abilities in managing the immediacy and busyness that characterize the press of classroom life, are often imprisoned by it. Indeed, it may be that we do not learn from experience, but that experience, 'has to be arrested, examined, analysed, considered and negotiated in order to shift it to knowledge' (Aitchinson and Graham, in Boud et al., 1993). Although learning from experience results 'when preconceived notions and expectations are challenged, refined, or disconfirmed by the actual situation' (Benner, 1984, p. 3), learning from direct experience of practice alone indicates at best limited growth. The development of routines, the presence of tacit knowledge and the resistance to disclosure and feedback act to control rather than free teachers from the burden of unexamined, accumulated practice. Learning from practice itself, then, will result in experience but without opportunities to reflect in different ways 'on' and 'about' action. Even experience may be ignored and will not necessarily result in the development of expertise.

> The belief that all genuine education comes about through experience does not mean that all experiences are genuinely or equally educative. Experience and education cannot be directly equated to each other. For some experiences are miseducative. Any experience is miseducative that has the effect of arresting or distorting the growth of further experience. (Dewey, 1938, p. 25)

Sternberg and Horvath (1995) have developed the notion of a 'prototype' view of expert teaching, in which the characteristics which separate the 'expert' from the 'experienced' regardless of 'age', or 'stage', are:

- **Domain knowledge** Experts bring knowledge to bear more effectively on problems. They have more integrated knowledge, planning structures, knowledge of social and political contexts in which teaching occurs. They know, then, how to apply their teaching knowledge to particular contexts. They also have 'tacit' knowledge which allows them to adapt to practical constraints in the field of teaching. Routinized skill enables the prototype expert to 'reinvest' cognitive resources in problem reformulation and problem solving . . . to selectively encode, combine, and compare information to arrive at insightful solutions to problems in teaching.

- **Efficiency** Experts can do what novices do in a shorter period of time (or can do more than novices do in an equivalent period of time) with apparently less effort. Experts typically spend a greater proportion of their solution time trying to understand the problem to be solved . . . The ability to automize well-learned routines is clearly related to the expert's capacity to be reflective.
- **Insight** Experts do not simply solve the problem at hand; they often redefine the problem and . . . reach ingenious and insightful solutions that somehow do not occur to others . . . applying all the information acquired in another context to the problem at hand.

An expert can be defined as one who works on the leading edge of his or her knowledge and skill. Thus, an expert seeks progressively to complicate the model of the problem to be solved, whereas an experienced non-expert seeks to reduce the problem to fit available methods.

Expert teachers are those who retain their ability to be self-conscious about their teaching and are constantly aware of the learning possibilities inherent in each teaching episode and individual interaction. Exploring an epistemology of reflective practice, van Manen (1995) writes of a 'phenomenology of tactful action [which] may reveal several styles of intuitive practice: from acting in a largely self-forgetful manner to a kind of running inner speech that the interior eye of the ego maintains with the self' (p. 41). It is when the teacher, 'tests and refines propositions, hypotheses, and principle-based expectations in actual practice situations' (Benner, 1984, p. 3) that growth occurs. But it is sustained reflection on and about those which will prevent expertise becoming detrimental to growth.

Professional Knowledge, Competence and Capability

Knowledge

The purpose of continuing professional development is to maintain and extend teachers' professional knowledge, defined as, 'the knowledge possessed by professionals which enables them to perform professional tasks, roles and duties with quality' (Eraut, 1996, p. 1). Eraut argues that the domains of teachers' professional knowledge can be mapped along two dimensions (see Figure 3.2). The vertical dimension describes the different contexts in which knowledge is used; and the horizontal dimension indicates the different kinds of knowledge. Teachers' ability to understand and interpret events in their classroom requires situational knowledge which itself will be based upon experiences in similar situations. Societal knowledge relates to the responsibility of teachers to 'look beyond the specific to the more general purposes of education' — vital in order to relate what the student is learning to the broader context which gives it meaning. Eraut argues that whilst

Context of Use	**Area of Knowledge**			
	Subject Matter Knowledge	Education Knowledge	Situated Knowledge	Societal Knowledge
Classroom Knowledge				
Classroom-related Knowledge				
Management Knowledge				
Other Professional Roles				

Figure 3.2 The domain of teachers' professional knowledge (Eraut, 1996, p. 25)

'process knowledge' ('knowing how') is at the heart of professional work, in order for this work to have quality it is necessary to combine it with 'knowing that' (Ryle, 1949) — i.e. the kinds of 'propositional knowledge' derived from reflection upon direct experience and that learnt from other knowledge holders, as represented by the experiences and research of other colleagues.[4]

Competence

The roots of competency are to be found in 'scientific management' (Taylor, 1911) and the 'cult of efficiency' (Callahan, 1962), and, in relation to teachers, to the perceived and now discredited direct link made by politicians, media and the public in many countries between worsening economic competitiveness and a relative decline in standards of student achievement. 'Back to basics' calls to schools in many countries have been accompanied by increased public accountability measures; and these invariably include the use of competency-based assessments. Competence is not problematic itself as an educational aim, but **becomes** problematic

> . . . when either or both of two conditions are fulfilled: firstly, when competence becomes a dominant aim, so diminishing other worthwhile aims; or, secondly, when competence is construed over-narrowly. (Barnett, 1994, p. 159)

Over time, the temptation for managers to judge teachers exclusively against sets of competences, rather than using them as benchmarks, may become as overwhelming as it is for teachers to judge pupil progress only against their results in tests which focus upon a relatively narrow range of achievements. It is important, then, that the limitations of competences as the sole means of both judging teachers' work and of planning their development are recognized. The following section focuses, therefore, on these.

> One cannot reduce judgements about the educational quality of the transactions between teachers and students to measures of their instrumental effectiveness in producing pre-specified and standardised outputs. (Eraut, 1991, p. 124)

Over the last decade, governments have introduced occupational standards at a variety of levels as a means of providing national benchmarks against which achievement and expertise may be judged and accredited. In good teaching, the application of wisdom, insight, experience, content knowledge, and pedagogical and organizational strategies varies according to the context of the problem. Because of this, it is impossible to provide universal authentic definitions of effective teaching beyond baseline generalities. This is the problem in attempting to use the same competences as a means of assessment for everyone. The application of particular kinds of competence reveals the expectations that 'employers' have of 'employees' at different levels and in relation to different roles and tasks. For this reason, there has been much criticism, for example, of behavioural competences which focus upon technical skills related to job and task analysis as 'atomizing' and thus oversimplifying teaching acts. Can we really understand teachers' work without understanding their understandings of it? In the absence of this, a sense of teachers as thinking, discriminatory individuals is omitted from the judgment. It is hard to imagine 'pedagogical tact' (van Manen, 1995) or 'discretionary judgment' being assessed as part of a list of competences when both represent applied integration of a number of skills, understandings and qualities to particular settings in particular circumstances. Because teaching is so context dependent, there are problems in generalizing both scope and quality without taking into account factors such as class behaviour, composition and size, which affect performance. Furthermore, they may be criticized also on the grounds that today's competency needs are not necessarily those of tomorrow.

It is worth remembering that competences for teaching have usually been developed by management for the purposes of controlling access to the profession and monitoring the performance of teachers. The result is a widespread perception that:

> Power and authority . . . is being taken away from the teacher. Now, everything is mandated to you. You have no freedom to venture out; you want to be creative with the kids, and you want to do things. You don't want to be so routinised . . . especially with the little ones . . . But you're accountable for so much, so many things and within such a framework . . . you just have to keep going. (cited in Kohn and Kottkamp, 1993, p. 140)

This quote from an American elementary school teacher illustrates a felt reduction in the ability to use discretionary judgment which resonates in teachers across many countries.

Nevertheless, employers, students and parents are justifiably concerned with the outcomes of schooling and teachers are accountable to them. Parents, the public, employers and teachers themselves have a right to participate in determining what can be 'reasonably' expected of teachers both generally and in given sets of circumstances. Benchmark competences are, therefore, as important for teachers as they are for any other profession. However, it is important to recognize their limitation in the different worlds of schools and classrooms.

> The practice and research of teacher development . . . should address the technical competence of teaching, the place of moral purpose in teaching, potential awareness, acuity, and adeptness among teachers, and teachers' emotional attachments to and engagement with their work. None of these dimensions alone can capture all that is important. What really matters is the interaction among and integration between them. Focusing on technical competence in isolation can make teacher development into a narrow, utilitarian exercise that does not question the purposes and parameters of what teachers do. (Hargreaves, A., 1995, p. 26)

Beginning teachers are expected to develop and there is scope for serving teachers to be less or more competent according to both personal and situational factors. Competences in teaching, therefore, describe both a minimum standard which has been achieved and imply a potential for further development. Viewed in this way they have some value when used as a means of benchmarking observable aspects of teachers' practice in a particular role or in relation to a particular set of tasks at a particular time. Even then, valid assessment will be complicated by contextual factors in the same way that measurements of student achievements have to take into account 'value added' factors (Gray and Wilcox, 1995).

Drawing upon Pearson's (1984) distinction between 'habitual skill knowledge' and 'intelligent skill knowledge', Elliott (1991, p. 122) agues that the technical know-how of the former is 'a necessary but not sufficient condition of competence'. The latter involves 'the exercise of capabilities for discernment, discrimination and intelligent action . . .' (Elliott, 1991, p. 122). These occur in the context of three kinds of knowledge which inform the work of the teacher: knowledge of self; knowledge of situation; knowledge of student. Each of these kinds of knowledge interact to influence the pedagogy and curriculum constructed and erected with each student (Webb and Blond, 1995, p. 612). Relational knowing — the interaction of student and teacher knowledge — is crucial to successful teaching.

Elliott (1991) argues that 'what is at stake' in competency-based assessment are the ways in which quite separate views of teaching, i.e. teaching as a 'technology' and teaching as a 'moral practice' (p. 124), are applied. Being competent in both is part of a professional's practice, but if the former prevails, then teaching will, in effect, be downgraded. At the end of the day, the abiding problem with externally devised and applied competency systems is that

> Too little specificity can lead to lack of clarity, poor communication and diminished credibility. Too much specificity leads to cumbersome standards, which take too long to read, and to possible abuse of the system by people taking short cuts. (Eraut, 1994, p. 212)

Conceptions of competence are insufficient for the purposes of development without 'a view of human beings located neither in operations and technique, nor in intellectual paradigms and disciplinary competence but in the total world experience of human beings' (Barnett, 1994, p. 178). This view corresponds both with those who promote an holistic view of teachers and those who see growth as being rooted within a framework of moral and professional accountability.

Capability

The achievement and further development of broadly defined competences which are part of the challenge of good teaching *and* being a good teacher are not only the responsibility of each individual but also that of the employing organization. Continuing professional development is a joint responsibility. Whilst the accountability of individual teachers includes:

- a moral commitment to serve the interests of clients;
- a professional obligation to self-monitor and to review periodically the effectiveness of one's practice;
- a professional obligation to expand one's repertoire, to reflect on one's experience and to develop one's expertise;
- an obligation that is professional as well as contractual to contribute to the quality of one's organisation; and
- an obligation to reflect upon and contribute to discussions about the changing role of one's profession in wider society,

the complementary distinguishing features of a quality organization are that it:

- sustains an appropriate climate;
- serves the interests of its clients;
- supports and develops its staff;
- continually seeks to improve its policy and practice; and
- reviews, evaluates and controls its affairs on the basis of valid information about its quality, impact and effect. (Eraut, 1994, pp. 236–7)

Writing in the context of the development of professionals who perform multiple roles in complex settings, Eraut suggests a conceptual framework and set of definitions of competence appropriate to the concerns of the health and caring professions, their stakeholders and their clients. He identifies three common approaches to the definition of competence: i) public usage; ii) politically negotiated and socially situated; iii) individually situated. He suggests that while the first two can be combined, the third creates only confusion. He therefore calls it '*capability*'. Thus competence is defined as 'the ability to perform the tasks and roles required to the expected standard', recognizing that deciding precisely *whose* 'requirements and expectations are to be taken into account' remains a problematic issue. Whilst capability is defined as 'everything a person can think or do', it is also important to remember that, 'competence does not necessarily lead to the expected level of performance', for this will be affected by disposition, capacity and context.

Eraut's research reveals that most professions assess both performance (through observation or inspection of products) and capability (through a wide range of written assignments). He sees this combination as enabling account to be taken of the 'interaction between individuals' continually developing capabilities and the organisation of professional work in response to changing needs and priorities'. He sees the relationship as being at three levels:

> 1 Current competence is by definition part of a person's capability. Such competence is normally inferred from evidence of job performance.
> 2 The range of current competence is most easily extended when further learning can build on areas of additional capability. But this potential has to be recognised both by the professionals involved and by their employers.
> 3 Part of a professional's capability involves being able to develop or transform one's practice over time, to create new knowledge through one's practice as well as learning from others. (Eraut, 1998, p. 12)

He proposes that the purpose of professional education and training should be to *develop professional capability* which includes competence in a range of tasks, roles and jobs but goes beyond these, recognizing that professional learning and development must be ongoing, and take account of changing individual and social contexts.

Teachers' Development Phases

Teachers' Career Development

> . . . a large part of development is neither externally programmed nor personally engineered but rather discontinuous, that is, lacking in continuity and order, and sometimes downright random. (Huberman, 1995b, p. 195)

In England (Ball and Goodson, 1985; Sikes et al., 1985; Nias, 1989), the United States (Lightfoot, 1983), Australia (Ingvarson and Greenway, 1984; Maclean, 1992), Canada (Butt, 1984) and Switzerland (Huberman, 1989), a number of key phases have been identified through which many teachers are perceived to move in their careers. Bolam (1990, p. 153) identified five 'job' stages: the preparatory stage; the appointment stage; the induction stage; the in-service stage (i.e. 3–5 years, 6–10 years, 11 years in post); the transitional stage (i.e. promotion, re-employment, retirement). He reminds us that needs of individuals will vary according to these and other factors such as age, gender, school type. Kremer-Hayon and Fessler (1991) posited nine career-cycle stages: Pre-service; Induction; Competency; Building; Enthusiasm and Growth; Career Frustration; Stability and Stagnation; Career Wind-Down; Career Exit.

The most authoritative studies of teachers' career experiences and the most influential determinants within and outside the institution on them are those of Swiss Secondary School teachers by Michael Huberman (1989, 1995c), of English teachers by Sikes et al. (1985) and of American teachers by Fessler and Christensen (1992). Their work suggests that teachers pass through five broad phases:

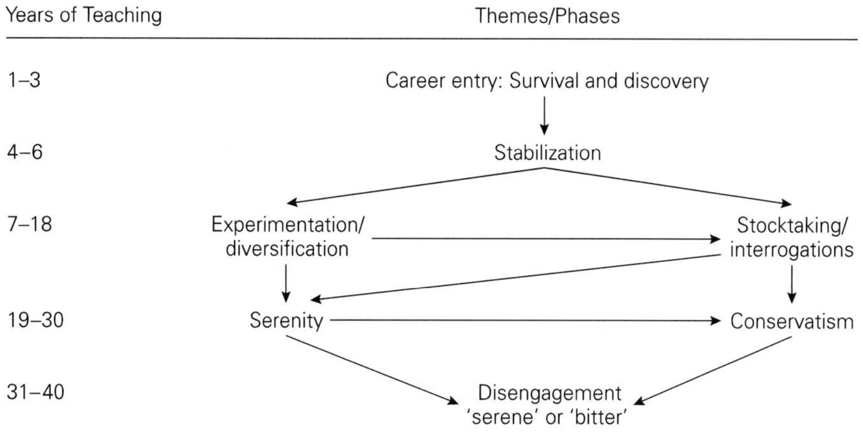

Reprinted by permission of the publisher from Guskey, J.R. and Huberman, M. (Eds), Professional Development in Education: New Paradigms and Practices (New York: Teachers College Press, © 1995 by Teachers College, Columbia University. All rights reserved).
Figure 9.1 (p. 204).

Figure 3.3 Modal sequences of the teacher career cycle: A schematic model (Huberman, 1995)

1 Launching a career: initial commitment (easy or painful beginnings).
2 Stabilization: find commitment (consolidation, emancipation, integration into peer group).
3 New challenges, new concerns (experimentation, responsibility, consternation).
4 Reaching a professional plateau (sense of mortality, stop striving for promotion, enjoy or stagnate).
5 The final phase (increased concern with pupil learning and increasing pursuit of outside interests; disenchantment; contraction of professional activity and interest).

Huberman developed an empirically-based schematic model of the teaching career cycle (see Figure 3.3). Yet even this conceptualization does not adequately account for the different levels of learning, development and the accompanying support needs.

Launching a career: A two-way struggle

This period will be crucial in establishing novice teachers' definitions of teaching and their particular visions of how to behave as professionals. Their 'beginnings' will be easy or painful, dependent not only upon their ability to deal with classroom organization and management problems, curriculum and pedagogical content knowledge, but also upon the influence of the school and staffroom cultures. These first few years of teaching have been described as a two-way struggle in which teachers try to create their own social reality by attempting to make their work match their personal vision of how it should be, whilst at the same time being subjected to the powerful socializing forces of the school. Lacey (1977) charted three phases through which the novice teacher moves — the 'honeymoon', the 'crisis', and 'failure' or 'getting by' (implying coping or teaching for survival). Whilst each of these phases will affect the way in which teachers think about teaching, it is their ability to deal with the 'crisis' that will affect their capacity for change. There is, fairly quickly, a 'crisis' because there is likely to be a mismatch between the aspirations of the individual and the culture of the institution. Lacey's argument is that the intersections of 'biography' and the 'social situation' leaves the beginning teacher with three possible responses:

1 *strategic compliance*, in which the individual complies with the authority figure's definition of the situation and the constraints of the situation but retains private reservations about them;
2 *internalized adjustment*, in which the individual complies with the constraints and believes that the constraints of the situation are for the best;
3 *strategic redefinition* of the situation, which implies that change can be brought about by individuals who do not possess the formal power to do so. (Lacey, 1977, p. 72)

If teachers strategically comply they can survive, but may harbour doubts which one day may re-emerge in the positive form of strategic redefinition. Teachers may internally adjust, in which case they will certainly survive and resolve their inner doubts by having effectively suppressed them. If teachers are very competent and do succeed in convincing figures in authority of their competence then, by having gained approval, they may effect a measure of change through the extension of their powers to use discretionary judgment even without formal authority roles. However, if teachers cannot live with their doubts or successfully adjust, and lack the ability as performers to redefine strategically, they may fail or simply 'get by'.

Lacey's analysis is plausible, but lacks any intimation of how, over time, the socialized teacher may shift from one position to another. It is difficult to believe that, once undertaken, one of these strategies represents the whole story. (Lacey acknowledged the great paucity of research data which could shed light upon the process of teacher socialization and there remains even today a lack of empirical data from longitudinal studies.) Moreover, 'strategic redefinitions' by teachers would appear to be rare. It is much more likely that the young teacher 'begins to push the blame for failures away from himself . . .', and onto the system, the head, other teachers — or even pupils — thus placing himself in the role of victim (Lacey, 1977, p. 84).

New teachers who compromise and adapt to school culture do so, in a sense, unconsciously. They become socialized into the norms which govern the culture. An American study noted the subtle ways in which one new teacher was socialized to her job, taking part in the very practices she once rejected:

> In just a few months, she accepts the demands of the school organization and its prevailing rationale for student failure. (Fuchs, 1973, p. 82)

In so far as assumptions about (a) school and (b) classroom practice remain unquestioned and unproblematic, these are likely to act as limitations on teachers' capacities to evaluate their work and hence increase their professional expertise. In this process of socialization, teachers develop a series of implicit expectations and norms of thinking and behaving. They

> . . . are acutely aware of some of these expectations, particularly those emphasised in transactions with people outside the school, but less aware of others. Some professional norms are so internalised that they only become apparent when somebody questions them or some unusual incident draws attention to them. (Eraut, Barton and Canning, 1978, p. 3)

Thus any process of development must involve making these tacit assumptions explicit.

Stabilization: New challenges, new concerns

Following the initial 'beginner' and 'advanced' beginner period, a sense of teaching 'mastery' is likely to have been established by most teachers. No longer novices, they are now accepted as experienced colleagues in the staffroom — feeling relatively secure in their knowledge of teaching practice and subject matter and comfortable with their identity as members of the particular school community. This sense of growing maturity is likely to be accompanied by some consolidation, refinement and extension of teaching repertoires and, possibly, involvement in a broader range of in-school and out-of-school educational developments as their vision of 'being a professional' evolves and broadens. The link to Dreyfus' 'competence' and 'proficient' phases is difficult to resist as teachers celebrate their hard won status in classroom, school and community.

This is a key phase which may lead initially to a *plateauing* of knowledge, skill and commitment but, ultimately, to stagnation and thus decline (Newman, 1979; Watts, 1980). According to Huberman's model, the stabilization phase is relatively brief. It is, therefore, crucial that those in school leadership roles support what Cooper (1982) claims teachers need as they arrive towards the middle phase of their careers:

> . . . new stimulation, new ideas . . . deeper commitments, new challenges . . . to become engaged in projects of scope and significance. (p. 81)

Reaching a professional plateau: Reorientation or continued development

It is likely that 'trajectories in the middle phases of the career cycle (7–18 years) are more diverse than earlier or later ones' (Huberman, 1995b, pp. 197–8). This diversity will relate to career advancement, school culture and the way in which teachers respond to the now well-established annually repeated cycle of students and colleagues which provides security but may, paradoxically, lack the variety, challenge and discovery of earlier years. It is a time when many teachers are likely to seek new challenges, either by taking new responsibilities in the same school or by moving schools for the purposes of promotion. It is a time, also, when responsibilities outside the school may begin to grow, whether it be ageing parents, growing families, or deepening relationships. Whilst the workplace may remain the epicentre of their lives, other demands may create tensions as they compete for time. Some teachers may begin to *reorientate* themselves, scaling down the time they give to their profession outside working hours. There may be a tension between this and increasing workloads. International research into teacher workload indicates that for most teachers the working week is between 55 and 70 hours (UNESCO, 1996).

This phase may also witness mid-life crises and the beginnings of increasing levels of disenchantment caused by lack of promotion or role change, or diminishing levels of energy and enthusiasm. On the other hand, the phase may lead to a 're-energizing' (Vonk, 1989), in terms of classroom teaching, together with a 'mellowing characterised by less drive but also less restlessness, a lesser need to control others or to drive oneself, a greater tolerance for one's limits or weaknesses, a greater acceptance of the "inevitability" of one's life course' (Huberman, 1995b, p. 200). It is during this phase, also, when some teachers may seek opportunities to re-examine the basis upon which their assumptions and beliefs about teaching are founded, to question the purposes and contexts of their work, to review and renew their intellectual commitments through further study either by participating in school, local education authority or district networks or participating in further degree work.[5]

The Final Phase

The final 10–15 years of a career is, theoretically, the phase of greatest expertise in teaching, albeit accompanied by the potential for increased personal health and family concerns. Yet it may also be the time of greatest 'conservatism'. Teachers in this phase complain more about the behaviour, commitment and values of students 'these days' (Peterson, 1964; Prick, 1986; Day and Bakioglu, 1996), and are sceptical about the virtues of change. This is not surprising, given the huge investment of time, effort and expertise these teachers are likely to have made already in their work. They are unlikely to be looking toward further promotion and may either be serenely moving towards a 'satisfactory' career end, or having to survive, dissatisfied, in an alien climate. These teachers may feel marginalized within the institution and embittered towards those whom they see as responsible for the condition of education, schooling and the declining standards of the students they must teach. They may work hard in their core acts of teaching, but this may not be accompanied by the levels of enthusiasm, emotional and intellectual commitment necessary for achieving excellence.

Fessler and Christensen (1992) have proposed a 'working model' based upon analysis of the literature on teachers' career stages and extensive interviews with

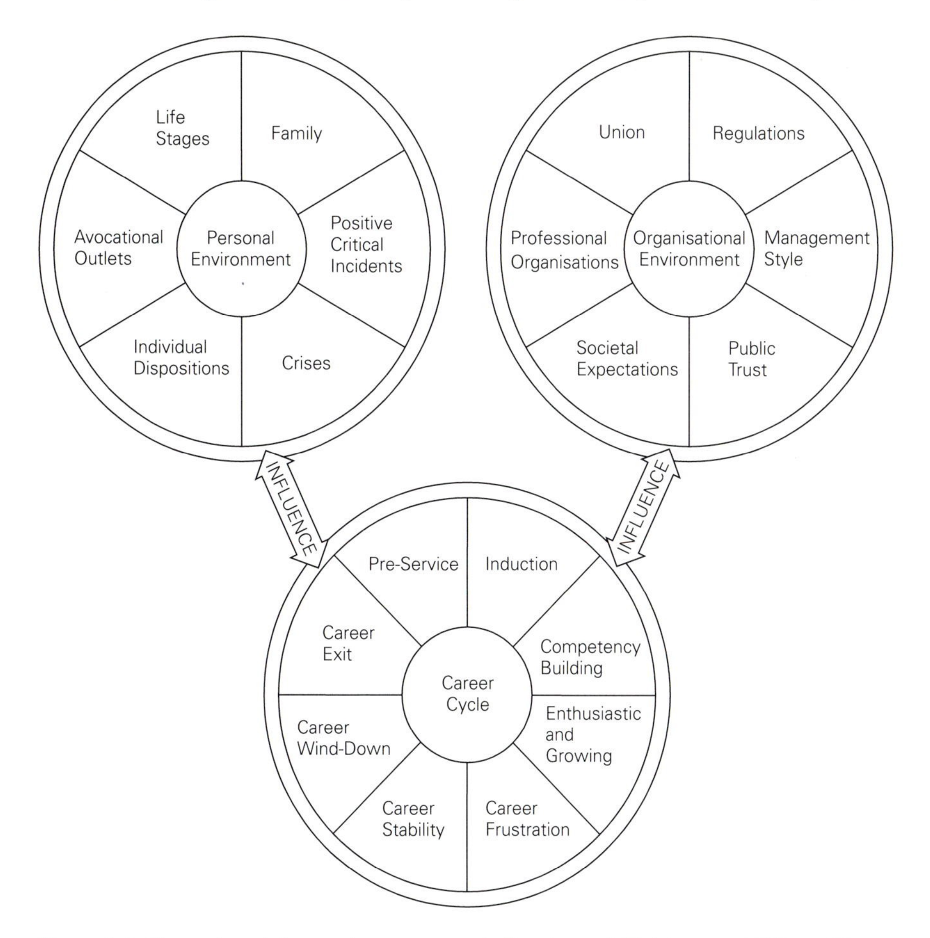

Figure 3.4 Dynamics of the teacher career cycle (Fessler and Christensen, 1992, p. 36)

teachers which may be used in planning for teacher development. The model (see Figure 3.4) identifies three broad categories of influence upon teacher development — career cycle, personal environment and organizational environment. The influences are represented as wheels and each wheel is subdivided.

The model postulates a 'dynamic ebb and flow . . . with teachers moving in and out of stages in response to environmental influences from both the personal and organisational dimensions' (Fessler, 1995, p. 187). Fessler proposes personalized support systems for teachers at various stages of their careers. Significantly, in line with educational researchers who focus upon life history, action research, teachers' narrative, leadership and change, he recognizes: (i) the need to acknowledge that professional development is centrally concerned with teachers' personal needs as well as student and system needs; (ii) the social learning dynamic between self and colleagues in the organization which is necessary throughout teachers' development lives; and (iii) the need for reflection on practice.

Cognitive-developmental Factors

Research into the growth of expertise and career phases adds significantly to the opportunities to plan for development which is relevant to teachers' needs; but such planning must also take account of their cognitive development. One piece of research which set out to find out why teachers chose to become involved in staff development found that there was not only a correlation with life period and career cycle, but also with cognitive-developmental stage (Oja, 1989). Teachers participating in an Action Research on Change in Schools (ARCS) project in America, were asked about: (i) their life histories; (ii) stability and transition in their lives; (iii) the relative importance of personal development and career goals; and (iv) current 'critical' or key issues. Oja and her colleagues concluded that:

1 Age alone does not provide sufficient information upon which to determine a teacher's career cycle, life period, or developmental stage.
2 Working on a longer term project is attractive to teachers who are in a variety of life periods from age 30, i.e. Crisis — settling down — becoming one's own person — mid-life transition — restabilization after the 40s transition and 50s transition.
3 Age, life period, and years of teaching experience can help explain key issues in a teacher's life and career, but they are not enough to explain *how* a teacher will participate in a chosen staff development activity. This will be based on cognitive-developmental stages which are not necessarily related to age or career cycle.
4 Staff development programmes need to provide environments deliberately designed to allow for adult development in:
    - *Moral/Ethical Development* Development toward principled moral judgments, away from unquestioned conformity to peer, social and legal norms *toward* self-evaluated standards within a world view framework.
    - *Ego Maturity* The development of more complex, differentiated, and integrated understanding of self and others.
    - *Conceptual Growth* The development of higher conceptual levels, away from thinking in terms of simple stereotypes and cliches *toward* recognition of individual differences in attitudes, interests, and abilities and toward increased toleration for paradox, contradiction and ambiguity.

The work of the project, then, recognized the importance of attending to the intellectual and emotional development needs of teachers. 'Ego maturity' relates to the importance of maintaining knowledge of self and others which is central to good teaching; 'moral/ethical development' suggests a need for reflection which places teaching and learning within broader contexts than increasing technical expertise; and 'conceptual growth' demonstrates clear links with Sternberg's and Horvath's (op. cit.) notion of expertise in teaching.

Critical Learning Phases

Whilst idiographic and longitudinal studies have found that adults pass through different developmental phases, it is clear that they do so in different ways at different times according to different circumstances. Some suggest that these are in response to predictable events (Levinson, Darrow, Klein, Levinson and McKee, 1978), whilst others focus, as we have seen, upon career (Huberman, 1989), cognitive development (Oja, 1989) and life-cycle factors (Ball and Goodson, 1985). Other research points to the importance of critical events in teachers' life and career histories and current phase of development (Denicolo and Pope, 1990; Eraut, 1991; Gudmundsdottir, 1990; Leithwood, 1990; Sikes et al., 1985; Oja, 1989; Ball and Goodson, 1985; Goodson, 1992; Huberman, 1989; Shulman, 1987).

Research in England, for example, suggests that '. . . cycles of accelerated development . . . whether prompted by internal or external factors, are likely to occur at any point in an individual's life' (Nolder, 1992). Nolder's empirical research over four years with secondary school teachers revealed that there were certain conditions which provide for development 'spurts'. These have been variously described as 'critical incidents', 'dilemmas', 'landmark' or key events in an individual's life, around which pivotal decisions revolve. They provoke the individual into 'selecting particular kinds of actions, which lead in particular directions' (Sikes et al., 1985, p. 57). These critical phases in teachers' professional biographies represent, 'the culmination of a decision-making process, crystallising the individual's thinking, rather than being responsible . . . [of themselves] . . . for that decision' (Sikes et al., 1985, p. 58). Individuals might be stuck at one level in some areas while more advanced in others (Watts, 1981). In supporting *continuing* professional development it is crucial to the interests of both individual teachers and schools to identify and relate to these key phases and stages of transition.

In a study of teachers' professional development in schools in England, teachers were asked to write brief autobiographies focusing upon events, experiences and people who had significantly affected their attitudes to their own professional learning. It was reasoned that there would be a connection between their own values, learning preferences and practices, and past experiences and influences, both negative and positive. It was further hypothesized that a connection might be made also between their life and career stages and their perceived learning needs (Day, 1993c). Whilst for some teachers learning was clearly an evolutionary, gradual, cumulative process, many talked of crucial landmark stages of their life and/or career development. For example, Teacher A who was looking for more responsibility, had, 'learned more recently than in the past . . . as a result of working with one particular teacher'; Teacher B's vision of mathematics teaching had been totally changed in one afternoon when he listened to an inspirational lecture; and Teacher C's 'whole approach to ownership' had been changed as a result of experiences on a long higher degree course.

Teachers reflected upon the need for planned professional development at particular *key stages* in their careers:

On changing role

Teacher D had found herself in a situation when taking up a subject leadership post where she

> . . . hadn't got enough theoretical knowledge to justify or explain what I'm doing. I knew what I was doing, but I just couldn't explain it . . . Up until the last four years all my teaching was from instinct.

Teacher E emphasized the need of supporting role rather than personal learning needs:

> In the early stages it was very much what was in-service going to do for me personally and nobody else . . . and then moving on to helping me develop my first responsibility as a curriculum leader. Now the way I have to look at it is again personal for me as a teacher but also me as a management leader . . . So it's changed from being self-centred to school centred. Is it going to be of any benefit to me and will I be able to pass anything on to either the head or other senior curriculum leaders or to other members of staff who are coming to me for help and advice?

After several years of teaching, in order to take stock

> . . . if I now went back to College and took time *out* of teaching — and I feel this more often, that I *need* time *out* of teaching in a school . . . a re-think, a re-train. That would be useful if at certain stages you get time out of the pressures of the classroom. That would be *very* useful. Especially now, when I feel in dreadful need of a change . . . It's very hard to change while you're doing the job, or to put it all together. (Teacher E)

To gain a broader perspective

Teacher F was concerned with the need, at certain stages of their career, to gain a broader perspective, to 'step back and look at the whole' learning which could not be accommodated in the 'norms' of school life, to avoid becoming 'entrenched':

> Step back . . . get out . . . talk to other people about their experiences . . . see a wider view . . . because you lose perspective . . . become very entrenched in your own little box . . . your own ways and ideas . . . this school.

To provide self confidence

Teacher G pointed out the danger of taking too much on board in the first five years of teaching:

> . . . because there's enough to cope with practically in a classroom, getting used to the job and how you're going to work, and I think any courses that help you achieve that and establish yourself, that's what you need in the first five years.

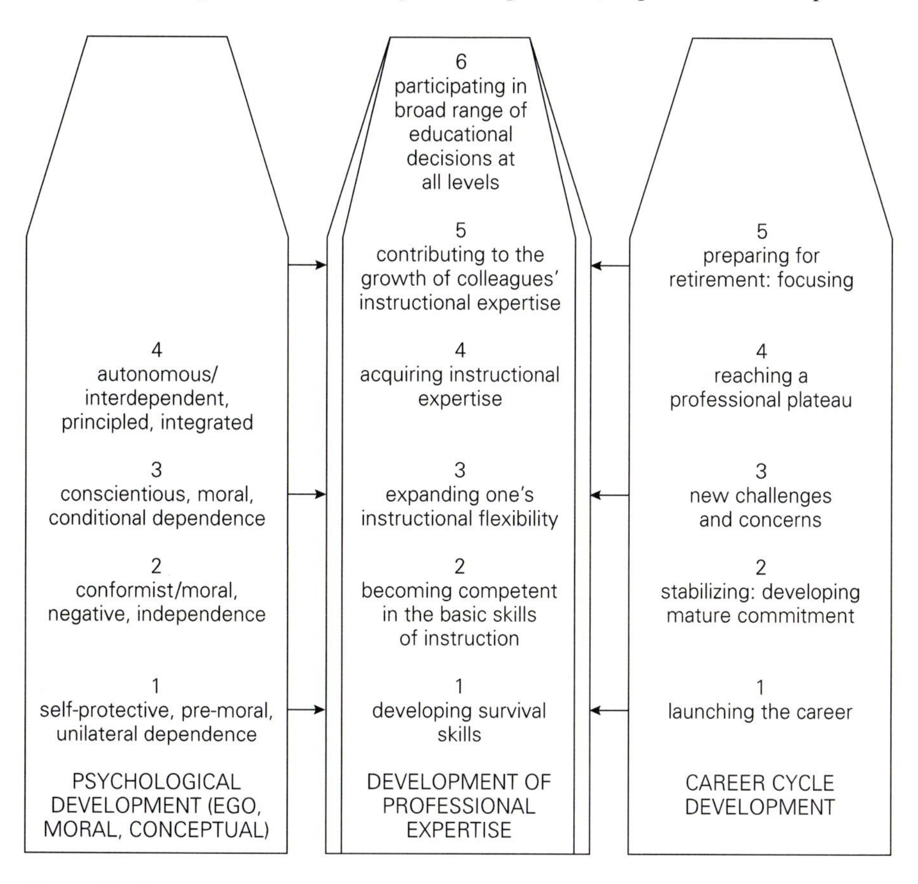

Figure 3.5 Interrelated dimensions of teacher development (Leithwood, 1990)

In Canada, Ken Leithwood related teachers' psychological and career cycle development to the growth of professional expertise which, he claims, can be influenced directly by school principals (see Figure 3.5). In exemplifying the way that the interrelated dimensions of teachers' development lives identified by researchers might be used for teacher development, he identified a direct relationship between reaching a professional plateau and stages 5 and 6 of development of professional expertise — which are similar to those developed by Dreyfus and Dreyfus (1986) — suggesting that:

> A significant part of the explanation for teachers perceiving themselves to be at a plateau is the failure, in many schools and school systems, to permit teachers greater scope to know and relate to multiple classrooms — to see and work with other teachers and their classrooms. Such challenges respond to the teacher's readiness to accept more responsibility and allow the school and school system to benefit from their accumulated expertise. Teachers who have experienced such challenges seem likely to enter their final career cycle stage either still in an expansionary frame of mind or at least as 'positive focusers'. (Leithwood, 1990, p. 81)

Whilst this multi-dimensional model, like that of Fessler, may be used to inform the planning of teachers' career-long professional development, it does not take account of their needs for self-confidence, the influence of emotional as well as cognitive factors, and the conditions in which they work.

Conclusion

Conceptualizations of professional development as a linear continuum, though superficially attractive and plausible, are both over-simplistic and impractical since they are not based on a 'teacher-as-person' perspective but on a systems, managerial perspective of 'teacher-as-employee'. An adherence to them might tend to oversimplify or skew provision towards meeting the needs of the system whilst ignoring, at their peril, the needs of the teacher within it. Models of teacher development which assume particular needs at particular linear career 'stages', whether these refer to roles and responsibilities or years of service, need then to take into account both the historical and organizational contexts and cultures in which teachers' work is located and their phases of cognitive and emotional development. They must also recognize that some teachers may not have a 'staged, continuous sequence of life experiences . . . and that we are talking about a process filled with plateaus, discontinuities, regression, spurts and dead ends' (Huberman, 1995b, p. 196). There are persuasive arguments for targeting particular learning opportunities — formal and informal — at teachers at 'landmark' phases of intellectual, experience, career or role development. Such teachers are most likely to be in high states of readiness to reflect systematically on their thinking and practice — and on the contexts in which they occur. They may wish to prepare for a new role; refresh themselves by more in-depth learning about their pedagogic or subject knowledge; or gain a greater sense of vision or direction for their careers. However, in all of these circumstances, success or failure will be influenced also by other factors. The next chapter explores the classroom, school and leadership conditions in which teachers work and which inevitably impact on their ambitions, abilities and opportunities to be lifelong learners.

Notes

1 It is important to recognize that the teacher–student relationship, like that of the nurse–patient, 'is not a uniform, professionalised blueprint but rather a kaleidoscope of intimacy and distance in some of the most dramatic, poignant and mundane movements of life' (Benner, 1984, p. xxii). There will, therefore, be 'good' and 'bad' days in the real worlds of teaching and learning. I am, therefore, discussing broad phases rather than everyday experience, though the one impacts upon the other.
2 For a critical review of these and other models of expertise, see Eraut, 1994, Chapter 7.
3 Eraut (1994) provides a detailed analysis of Dreyfus and Dreyfus (1986), and Benner (1984) provides the most detailed account of its use in the world of nursing.

4 The problem with some of the more popular models of in-service training is that they focus primarily upon 'knowing what' and 'knowing how' and thus ultimately restrict the development of professionalism whilst purporting to extend it. Joyce and Showers' (1988) matrix is a good example, in which 'modelling', 'coaching' and 'mentoring' are the preferred modes of learning. Even Kolb's cycle of observation, experience, evaluation fails to take account of the need for development link between cognitive, emotional, social and personal development in the journey towards expertise in teaching.
5 For a detailed consideration of this and other phases see Huberman (1995c).

Chapter 4

Teachers' Conditions of Work: Classrooms, Cultures and Leadership

This chapter highlights the importance to good teaching of self-confidence, professional learning cultures and committed leadership. It focuses upon the broad policy contexts within which teachers work; conditions for teaching and learning in the classroom; the effects of school culture; the role of the principal in professional development; and leadership development itself.

Conditions of Work in Schools

> If we want all students to actually learn in the way that new standards suggest and today's complex society demands, we will need to develop teaching that goes far beyond dispensing information, giving a test, and giving a grade. We will need to understand how to teach in ways that respond to students' diverse approaches to learning, that are structured to take advantage of students' unique starting points, and that carefully scaffold work aimed at more proficient performances. We will also need to understand what schools must do to organize themselves to support such teaching and learning . . . 21st-century schools must shift from a selective mode — 'characterized by minimal variation in the conditions for learning' in which 'a narrow range of instructional options and a limited number of ways to succeed are available' — to an adaptive mode in which 'the educational environment can provide for a range of opportunities for success'. (Darling-Hammond, 1996b, p. 7)

The intention of reform has been to raise standards of achievement among students. This requires increased commitment and teaching expertise from teachers and more dynamic, complex, interventionist leadership by headteachers and others in order to ensure that schools continue to develop. Paradoxically, however, most reforms have failed to give parallel attention to workplace conditions, leaving many teachers feeling deskilled, bewildered, angry and demoralized. They have a reduced sense of self-efficacy, defined as, 'beliefs in one's capabilities to organize and execute the courses of action required to manage prospective situations' (Bandura, 1997, p. 2). If governments are serious about raising standards of achievement and thus standards of teaching, then it is important to understand how the conditions for teaching, central to both job effectiveness and satisfaction, affect teachers.

The theme of the 45th Session of UNESCO's International Conference on Education in 1996 was the role of teachers in a changing world and its findings point to the importance of the conditions of teaching in enhancing the quality of teachers' work. It observed a 'dissociation between the recognition of the teachers' importance and the absence of any real measure taken in their favour, whether . . . from the financial point of view, from that of the level of involvement in management or of the improvement of the initial or in-service training processes' (Tedesco, 1997, p. 24); and it cited evidence that structural adjustment policies in many developing countries had led to a decline in expenditure and significant deterioration in the working conditions of teachers:

> This deterioration produced, in its turn, a series of well-known phenomena: demoralisation, abandonment of the profession, absenteeism, the search for other occupations and, finally, a negative impact on the quality of education offered. (Tedesco, 1997, p. 24)

In recent decades, morale among teachers has declined in many countries. In England, for example, there is a situation in which test and examination scores are improving, independent school inspection reports from OFSTED show improved teaching, but teachers and students are becoming increasingly disaffected. The National Commission on Education reported a survey of teachers in England and Wales which showed that only 9 per cent of qualified teachers (not including heads or deputy heads) were 'very satisfied' with their current posts, whereas 37 per cent were not satisfied or not at all satisfied (NCE, 1993). The 26 country Third International Maths and Science Study (TIMSS) revealed that one third of England's primary school teachers and more than 40 per cent of English secondary school teachers wanted to leave teaching. Additionally:

> Only 19% of English primary school teachers felt that society appreciated their work, compared with 57% in Canada. And while a third of English primary teachers wanted to leave teaching, only 19% of Dutch and 24% of Canadian teachers stated that they needed a career change. Whilst 27% of English secondary school Maths teachers felt that their work was appreciated, this compared unfavourably with the Germans (49%), Canadians (52%) and Swiss (84%). (reported in *TES*, 13 June 1997)

The reasons for low teacher morale, self-confidence and self-efficacy in many countries can be attributed to changes in occupational and organizational working conditions which have had the universal consequence of intensifying work in schools, increasing on- and off-site workloads and reducing trust in the discretionary judgment of teachers. Teachers with low self-efficacy are likely to exhibit low motivation in class and school settings, more likely to prefer routine rather than experiment and be less receptive to new teaching practices.

The ways in which working conditions have been changed by governments differ. Below are three brief examples of changes in conditions of work in different countries which have been perceived to affect adversely conditions for development.

Australia: Decentralization and Collaboration

In a national study, which researched the 'underlife' (Ball, 1994, p. 19) of the relationship between teacher, context and policy, Grundy and Bonser explored the 'new work order' of school development planning, accountability, financial planning, shared decision-making, participatory management, student learning, school development and teamwork which are features of school-based management in Australian schools. Although they found a strong advocacy of collaborative work practices and participative decision-making in, for example, school development planning, 'the differences between the responses of teachers and principals in their report of the extent of participation raises a question about both the extent and the quality of the participation' (Grundy and Bonser, 1997, p. 23). Decentralization, it appeared, had not necessarily resulted in reduced hierarchy or collaborative cultures which are known to promote collegiality (Stenhouse, 1975; Rosenholtz, 1989; Lieberman, 1990; Little 1982, 1992). Rather, administratively regulated, implementation oriented forms of 'contrived collegiality' (Hargreaves, 1994, pp. 192–6) were equally apparent.

Norway: New Work Time Arrangements

In Norway, new work time arrangements for teachers in the 1990s were renegotiated alongside structural and curriculum reform. With the new agreement, teachers' work was divided into three components: i) teaching hours; ii) organized collaborative work with colleagues, e.g. meetings, etc. (190 hours per year); and iii) teaching preparation. Klette (1998) studied the effects of imposed collaboration upon 2400 teachers in primary and secondary schools in Norway. She found that schools used the 190 hours mainly for joint staff meetings and smaller, subject-specific group meetings. Teachers valued the former less than the latter, regardless of the type of school. However:

> One of the most challenging findings . . . is the extensive and comprehensive discontent with the existing working time agreement practice on the one hand, combined with a feeling of powerlessness and apathy among the teachers on the other. (Klette, 1998, p. 18)

The issue that emerges here concerns the perception by teachers of diminished rather than increased control of their immediate work situation.

England: Increasing Managerialism

Another interesting example concerns recent changes in England, because of the speed, intensity and volume of the reform of school governance, curriculum and assessment and employment conditions which have radically affected teachers' working lives. In an authoritative study of the professional culture of secondary school teachers, which explored how changes had impacted upon teachers' sense of professionalism, Helsby (1997) identified the growth of a 'new managerialism' in which the increasing power of headteachers was seen as a threat to the professionalism of classroom teachers:

> Most of the comments about increased managerial powers were negative, suggesting considerable frustration amongst classroom teachers and ultimately a loss of commitment. . . . Professional confidence is too often diminished by top–down forms of accountability and inspection and by increasing managerialism, whilst the intensification of working life and resource constraints place severe limits upon the possibility of finding time for reflection and planning. Collaboration with colleagues is limited by time constraints, by the growing insularity of schools and departments and by the competitiveness engendered by published league tables of assessment and examination results in a market-oriented education system. (Helsby, 1997, pp. 9 and 10)

Burgess (1988), Ball (1987) and Bowe and Ball (1992) have pointed to the widening role gap between teachers and headteachers as structural reform has increased the management functions of heads, moving them towards a 'chief executive' role (Hughes, 1985; Grace, 1995) and giving less time for them to perform their 'leading professional' roles (Pollard, Broadfoot, Cross, Osborn and Abbot, 1994). Exceptions to this are to be found mainly in primary schools (Acker, 1990; Woods, 1993).

The capacity to learn, then, will not only relate to personal contexts but also to social contexts. If self-esteem is low, or the social context 'unfriendly' then it is likely that this capacity will be minimized. These three examples demonstrate how reform efforts have failed to take account of research over the years which has indicated that critical reflection alongside autonomy and choice, a sense of shared purposes, and positive interpersonal relationships within collaborative cultures enhance adult learning (Argyris and Schön, 1976; Marsick and Watkins, 1990; Knowles, 1984).

Conditions in the Classroom

Research worldwide about (i) the quality of teaching and learning in smaller classes and (ii) teachers', students' and other stakeholders' experiences and perceptions of the effects of larger class size[1] confirms the significance of class size to effective classroom teaching. It is a major influencing factor because it can affect the composition and thus range of aptitudes and attitudes of students, their ability to concentrate on task, and the provision of sustained interaction and differentiated attention from the teacher. Hopkins, West and Beresford (1998) suggest that six conditions need to apply in the classroom itself for teachers to facilitate the learning of all students:

1 *Authentic Relationships* — being the quality, openness and congruence of relationships existing in the classroom.
2 *Rules and Boundaries* — being the pattern of expectations set by the teacher and school of student performance and behaviour within the classroom.
3 *Planning, Resources and Preparation* — being the access of teachers to a range of pertinent teaching materials and the ability to plan and differentiate these materials for a range of students.
4 *Teacher's Repertoire* — being the range of teaching styles and models internalised and available to a teacher dependent on student, context, curriculum and desired outcome.
5 *Pedagogic Relationship* — being the ability of teachers to form professional relationships within and outside the classroom that focus on the study and improvement of practice.
6 *Reflection on Teaching* — being the capacity of the individual teacher to reflect his/her own practice, and to put to the test of practice, specifications of teaching from other sources. (p. 123)

Large classes mitigate against these, for they lead to increased teachers' workloads, more complex management and learning environments for teachers and students, and more problematic pedagogical relationships.

The Quality of Teaching and Learning in Smaller Classes

> Those aspects of teaching which research has shown best promote pupil achievement are all present in greater amounts in the smaller classes. Pupils are challenged more often, they get longer periods with the teacher, more time is spent on the task than on routine management and pupils in such classes also receive greater amounts of feedback on their work. Classroom studies both here and in USA over two decades have repeatedly shown that these are the most important features of teaching in promoting effective student learning. (Galton, Hargreaves and Pell, 1996, p. 24)

In America, meta-analyses of 76 studies revealed that, 'There is little doubt that, other things being equal, more is learned in smaller classes' (Glass and Smith, 1978, p. v). Slavin's (1989) 'best evidence' synthesis came to similar conclusions. He concluded that although the effects of substantial reductions on student achievement tend to be small, there are significant effects on other variables such as teacher and student morale. He acknowledged that class size reductions:

- help to attract and retain good teachers;
- make teachers more receptive to innovation;
- improve school tone and morale;
- contribute to the feeling that school is a supportive, caring place.

Other 'cluster analyses' research on 100 class size research studies concluded that:

- the most positive effects of small classes on pupil learning occur in classes of 22 or fewer with students aged 5–8 years;

- smaller classes can positively affect the academic achievement of economically disadvantaged and ethnic minority students;
- little increase in pupil achievement can be expected from reducing class size if teachers continue to use the same instructional methods that they use for larger classes. (Robinson, 1990, p. 82)

The most authoritative longitudinal empirical study of 7,000 pupils in Tennessee (reported in Mosteller, 1995; Johnson, 1990; Achilles et al., 1993a, 1993b) confirms these findings, adding that pupils placed in small kindergarten classes have significantly higher self-concept and motivation scores. Criticisms of this intervention project have focused upon its cost effectiveness rather than its results (Slavin, 1994). Indeed, the same critic also said:

> As a parent I want my child to be in the smallest possible class. As a teacher, I want to teach the smallest class I can. Nearly every teacher and parent in the world feels the same way. As a taxpayer, I would be more than happy to pay higher taxes to reduce class sizes. (Slavin, 1990, p. 6)

Other evaluation studies have identified the advantages of small classes:

- quicker completion of basic instruction, allowing more time to complete additional material;
- use of supplementary texts and enrichment activities;
- more in-depth instruction for children to engage in first-hand learning activities;
- increased use of learning resources;
- improved individualisation of instruction as reflected in increased monitoring of student behaviour, more immediate individualised re-teaching and enrichment, more frequent interactions with each child, a better match between each child's ability and the learning opportunities provided, and a more detailed knowledge of the learning needs of individual pupils. (Word et al., 1990, p. 14)

These findings have been reinforced by recent small-scale research in an English context. Galton and colleagues (1996) found that teachers in larger classes spend more time in 'critical control' as a percentage of all routine, less time in 'sustained interaction' with individual pupils, and less time in 'feedback' as a percentage of task supervision. These three areas of teachers' work are central to the provision of quality learning opportunities.

It is clear, then, that decreases in class sizes at all ages can and do lead to increased learning gains; have favourable effects upon student attitude, self-image and motivation; have positive effects upon disadvantaged and ethnic minority pupils; and positive effects on the morale, motivation and retention of teachers.

The management of pupil behaviour, too, is easier in smaller classes (Bain and Achilles, 1986; Klein, 1985; Cooper, 1989), where pupils:

- appear to be more absorbed in what they are doing;
- attend more, participate, and spend more time on task;
- interrupt less frequently.

One consequence of increases in class size is an increase in pupil misbehaviour (Bain and Achilles, 1986; Bennett, 1994; Fernandez and Timpane, 1995). Additionally, independent studies (e.g. HMSO, 1994) confirm that increases in class size lead to increases in the number of hours teachers have to work. A number of correlative studies indicate also the association between larger class sizes and increased teacher stress and burnout (e.g. Travers and Cooper, 1996). In relation to the opportunities teachers have for supporting the learning needs of all pupils, the effects of class size are only too obvious:

> There is one more child involved in the regular routine of classroom activities . . . One more set of materials to be prepared . . . there is one more piece of work to read, mark, think about and discuss with the child . . . There is one more child to assess (national curriculum assessments) and one more report to write to parents and discuss with them . . . There is one more child to share in that small amount of time which can be spent focusing on the individual needs of pupils . . . There is one more space to be filled in the classroom which may reduce the flexibility for reorganising teaching in different ways. (Bassey, 1995, p. 10)

Suggestions have been made that teachers could increase the time given to whole class teaching of different kinds to the benefit of their students, citing performance data in mathematics and science from Pacific Rim and other selected countries in particular (e.g. Reynolds and Farrell, 1996). These have been critiqued widely (e.g. Alexander, 1996) because they do not appear to account for cultural difference. For example, in the case of Pacific Rim countries it is necessary to take into account:

- the high status of teachers within society because of religious and cultural traditions which place a high value on learning and education;
- the cultural stress reflecting Confucian beliefs about the role of effort and the importance of individuals striving and working hard;
- the high aspirations of parents for their children;
- the high levels of commitment from children to doing well.

Experiences and Perceptions

There has been a tendency in the past to ignore or dismiss the reported experiences of teachers, pupils, parents and governors. Two quotes provide apt illustration of the research findings on teaching and learning conditions. The first is from a 9-year-old pupil in an English school:

> I am a nine year old in a class of 38, and obviously my teacher cannot give us each the time we need. If one of us brings a piece of homework that we have done

> on our own, he cannot look at it very closely. This happened to me recently when I brought in a piece of homework that I did about a canal walk. If there hadn't been so many people in the class my teacher could have talked about my work with me and then written something on it. Surely eight and nine year olds [referring to the Labour government's decision to reduce class sizes for 5–7 year olds only] need as much attention as five to seven year olds. Why should my sister . . . get all the luck? (reported in *The Independent*, 12 June 1997)

This experience of one student confirms studies in New York City secondary schools which provide evidence that overcrowding is having significantly negative effects on instruction and learning in the system, that it is 'sharply' linked to lower student achievement among children with low socioeconomic backgrounds, and that both students and teachers feel deeply disaffected (Rivera-Batiz and Marti, 1995). Graphic illustrations of the effects of overcrowding come from students and teachers. A parent of a pupil in an elementary school in Oregon reported her son as saying, 'Mom, it's so crowded in there, they're breathing on me' (Smith, 1995); and a teacher of 14–15 year old students commented that in her classroom there was 'very little room to manoeuvre in terms of desk formation, so you've got a very static kind of teaching style' (Boyle, 1996). According to Fernandez and Timpane (1995, p. 6), reporting on the effects of overcrowding, 'the more dense and overcrowded the classroom, the more teachers and students will revert to habitual teaching techniques and learning patterns' — just the opposite of the diagnosis of what is needed to advance teaching and learning provided earlier in this chapter by Linda Darling-Hammond.

Research indicates clearly, then, that increasing class sizes and the consequent overcrowding in classrooms have detrimental effects upon students and teachers. The quality of teaching and learning is ultimately adversely affected even for the best teachers because of the physical, psychological and emotional attrition exacted by the demands placed upon them, not only by the system managers, the increased student numbers or the distribution of teaching resources, but also by the demands placed upon them by their own moral purposes. If governments really are concerned to raise standards of achievement, then the debate on class size effects needs to be moved on from the clichéd rhetoric of, 'traditionalists' versus 'trendies', the ineffectiveness of 'modern' teaching methods, the 'poor stewardship' of the incumbent government or, 'under funding'.

School Cultures

Just as conditions in classrooms affect the ability of teachers to provide the best learning opportunities for students, so the school culture provides positive or negative support for its teachers' learning:

> When culture works against you, it's nearly impossible to get anything done. (Deal and Kennedy, 1984, p. 4)

Schein (1985) defined culture as 'the deeper level of basic assumptions and beliefs that are shared by members of an organisation, that operate unconsciously, and that define in a basic "taken for granted" fashion an organisation's view of itself and its environment' (p. 6). Nias, Southworth and Yeomans (1989) use 'culture' to describe the different realities that people construct for themselves; and Westoby (1988) refers to organizational culture as 'social habitat', including the informal, ephemeral and covert as well as the visible and official. Essentially, then, culture is about people in the organizational setting and is characterized by the ways in which values, beliefs, prejudices and behaviour are played out within the micropolitical processes of school life. It is the culture of the classroom, department or school which is often described as the ethos or climate; and it is the creation and management of the culture or cultures which, according to Schein (1985), is the only thing of real importance that leaders do.

In reporting research in America on what matters most to teachers in their workplace context, McLaughlin (1993) is critical of metaphors of the '*school as a formal organization*' as directing attention to, 'incentives, management structures, oversight and accountability, governance, technology and material aspects of the workplace' (p. 99). The research revealed the importance of the '*school as workplace community*':[3]

> The school workplace is a physical setting, a formal organisation, an employer. It is also a social and psychological setting in which teachers construct a sense of practice, of professional efficacy, and of professional community. This aspect of the workplace — the nature of the professional community that exists there — appears more critical than any other factor to the character of teaching and learning for teachers and their students. (McLaughlin, 1993, p. 99)

Whilst it is possible to identify such community cultures in many primary schools (Nias et al., 1989), this is not always appropriate for larger primary or secondary schools; for, despite the abundance of school mission statements and developmental plans, they may amount to nothing more than an agglomeration of, or even compromise between, different departmental sub-cultures, competing 'interest groups' and the influence of powerful individuals (Talbert and McLaughlin, 1994; Hargreaves, A., 1994).

In Canada, Andy Hargreaves (1992; 1994), and in England, Jennifer Nias and colleagues (1989), have written extensively about forms of school culture which have different implications for teachers' work and professional development opportunities. Hargreaves identifies 'broad' forms: individualism, balkanization, collaboration, and contrived collegiality (see Figure 4.1).

Individualism

Like others, Andy Hargreaves recognizes that habitual patterns of teaching alone behind the closed doors of the classroom cuts teachers off from the possibility of

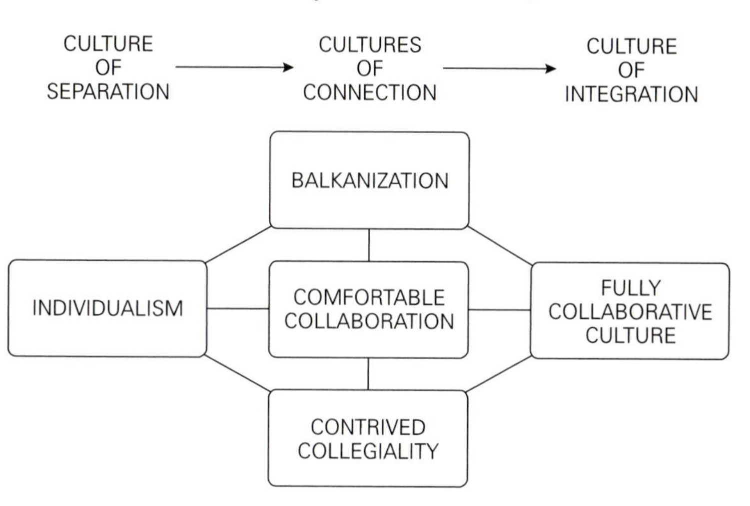

Figure 4.1 School management cultures (adapted from Hargreaves, 1992)

feedback, promotes unaccountable autonomy and insulates them from direct criticism (Rosenholtz, 1989; D. Hargreaves, 1982; Lortie, 1975; Ashton and Webb, 1986). However, citing Flinders (1988), he also notes that isolation is an adaptive strategy because it protects the time and energy required to meet the immediate learning demands of students, and so does not necessarily indicate that teachers will adopt safe, non-risk forms of teaching or will necessarily be resistant to change:

> It was not the walls of privatism that needed cracking in this school district, but the social milieu and conditions of work which so effectively undermined the confidence and devalued the knowledge, wisdom and credibility of its best teachers. (McTaggart, 1989, cited in Hargreaves, A., 1994, p. 171)

If the culture of individualism is not complemented by professional development opportunities in which knowledge, wisdom and expertise can be shared and through which collective espoused visions of good teaching can be tested against individual realities, then there is little hope of continuing professional development. Nor should we forget that some teachers' life histories, training, and organizational contexts teach them that privacy is a safe option. This is particularly so in reform contexts in which the only privacy left and the only area for discretionary judgment is the classroom.

Balkanization

As a form of culture, balkanization also separates. It remains prevalent in many secondary schools where teachers work in isolation or in isolated departmental groups. Teachers will identify with and be loyal to the group rather than the school as a whole. Groups will compete for resources, status and influence in the school.

Collaboration will occur only if it serves the interests of the group. This form of culture is likely to pose problems for teachers who wish to extend their knowledge of teaching and learning beyond the traditions and norms which inform their particular subject or phase reference group, and for headteachers who wish to promote a broader view of professionalism across the school.

Collaboration

Much research suggests that collaboration is an essential ingredient of teacher development and thus school improvement (Rosenholtz, 1989; Mortimore et al., 1994; Purkey and Smith, 1982; Reynolds, 1988; Hopkins, 1996). In England, a seminal study of five primary schools demonstrated the virtues of 'collaborative cultures' in terms of staff relationships, curriculum planning, and teaching and learning climate (Nias et al., 1989; Nias, Southworth and Campbell, 1992). In such cultures, however, collaboration may not extend to classrooms and so may not pose a threat to teachers' independence. It may be cooperation masquerading as collaboration and remain at the level of talking about teaching, advice giving, technique trading (Little, 1990, cited in Hargreaves, A., 1994, p. 210). It may not extend teachers' thinking about or practice of teaching. Such cultures of '*comfortable collaboration*' will be concerned primarily with the immediate, short-term, practical issues to the exclusion of systematic critical inquiry. The prime concern of teachers (and headteachers) will be to develop and sustain camaraderie on a personal level but resist challenge on a professional level. In *collaborative cultures*, working relationships are likely to be: spontaneous, voluntary, development oriented, in which teachers exercise discretion often initiating tasks or responding selectively to external demands. Whilst collaboration will take place within formally established structures, it will go beyond them:

> . . . in their most rigorous, robust (and somewhat rarer) forms, collaborative cultures can extend into joint work, mutual observation, and focussed reflective inquiry in ways that extend practice critically, searching for better alternatives in the continuous quest for improvement. In these cases, collaborative cultures are not cozy, complacent and politically quiescent. Rather, they can build collective strength and confidence in communities of teachers who are able to interact knowledgeably and assertively with the bearers of innovation and reform. (Hargreaves, A., 1994, p. 195)

Of course, for collaboration of this kind to work, all or most staff must 'give up' at least a measure of their independence.

Contrived Collegiality

A collaborative culture may not indicate democracy. Indeed, it may be an administrative device imposed by the principal. Andy Hargreaves describes the working relationships in this form of culture as being, 'not spontaneous, voluntary, development oriented, but fixed in time and space and predictable' (1994, p. 195). Working together is, therefore, a matter of compulsion, and the example of Norwegian reform earlier in this chapter indicates the likely negative consequences of mandated collaboration:

> . . . the sad thing about the safe simulation . . . of contrived collegiality is not that it deceives teachers, but that it delays, distracts and demeans them. (Hargreaves, 1994, p. 208)

Building a professional development culture in bureaucratic settings in which compliance is the norm, is not easy:

> Most of us spend our working lives in bureaucracies. We come to understand that working alone is normative, while sharing takes time, and cooperating is difficult — even, in some cases, suspect. New personnel quickly learn that meetings often don't lead to anything but more meetings; that stopping the usual flow of work in order to do something different requires enormous effort; that protecting one's turf, whether it be a classroom, a research project, or a program, is what one is supposed to do; that gatekeepers are hired specifically to keep the bureaucracy running; that paperwork takes a large part of everyone's daily life; and that the role of top leadership is to keep all the parts of the bureaucratic chain working, making sure that the obligatory myths and symbols are a consistent part of organizational life. (Lieberman, 1992, p. 152)

Lieberman recognizes that cultures change over time. The ways in which they change will relate to the introduction of new relationships, the development of existing relationships, the challenges of the external environment and the influence of the school principal. Contrived collegiality may, however, represent a stage in the journey from individual or balkanized cultures towards more culturally embedded forms of collegiality and collaboration.

These forms represent only one dimension of culture. However, they provide a useful lens through which the general ethos or milieu of the school may be viewed and reviewed. Like teacher confidence, cultures of professional development need to be created and nurtured within the broader development purposes of the school. It is important to note that if collaboration is an effective means for teacher development, it will impact upon the quality of students' learning opportunities and thus, indirectly or directly, upon their motivation and development.

In 'individualism', 'balkanized' and 'comfortably collaborative' cultures, it is likely that development will be evolutionary to the point that it becomes extinct without external intervention. Despite their limitations, cultures of contrived collegiality, may act as a 'bridging' process towards more collaborative cultures in providing added opportunities for development. However, in a collaborative culture, where critical reflection and experimentation are the norms, development will be continual. So at any given time there are likely to be differences both within and between schools in terms of their phase of development. Culture is dynamic and subject to change, and the kinds and pace of change will vary in response to the

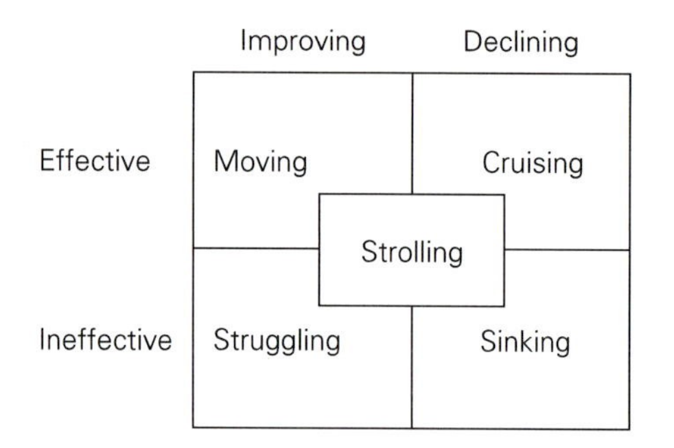

Figure 4.2 An effectiveness and improvement typology of schools (Stoll and Fink, 1996)

needs of and demands upon the individuals who make it up and the system itself. In America, Rosenholtz (1989), in a study of 78 elementary schools, found that those which were 'moving' (in which teachers learned from one another and from outside, and in which improvements in teaching were seen as a collective responsibility and enterprise), were more effective than schools which were 'stuck'.[4] In developing this work, Stoll and Fink (1996) looked at school cultures from two dimensions — i) effective–ineffective; ii) improving–declining — and proposed a typology of five cultures (see Figure 4.2).

Moving schools are those in which people work together, keep developing and provide 'value added'. *Cruising schools* are perceived by all to be effective but could be doing better in relation to their resources, staffing quality and student intake. *Strolling schools* are 'average' but are 'meandering' into the future. *Struggling schools* have the will to improve, but lack the expertise to do so, unaided. *Sinking schools* lack the will and the skill to succeed.

All of these schools need to focus upon professional development, but in different ways. It is interesting to speculate that the moving, cruising, strolling development cultures parallel those of individuals who may have 'plateaued' whether in the expert, proficiency or competent phase of their lives. Professional development in each of these cultures, as for each of these individuals, will require different kinds of plans and processes. For example, struggling, sinking and possibly strolling schools will require intervention which is transformative in its purposes and outcomes, whereas intervention in cruising or moving schools may be less radical.

Schools in many countries have experienced a 'breakdown period' because of imposed structural and curriculum reform efforts. By contrast, it is those schools that have shared goals, a sense of responsibility for making a difference, collegiality, a culture of continuous improvement, a belief that learning is for everyone and never stops, a willingness to take risks, a sense of interdependency in support and care, mutual respect, openness, and that celebrate personal and organizational achievement by building rather than undermining self-confidence, which have been able to rediscover values rather than be content with survival. However, even in those moving schools where continuous learning is an organic part of school culture, change is not always easy and must be led by principals who are clear in their vision and committed to promoting learning for teachers as well as students.

The Role of the Principal in Professional Development

Since culture will affect and be affected by its leaders, it will need to be actively managed. For example, whilst it is agreed that one characteristic of effective schools is goal consensus, the standard means of attempting to achieve this, it is claimed, tend to be rational — discussions, formally documented statements, evaluation and review procedures. However, this is not enough. Hallinger and Murphy (1985) distinguish between cognitive goals (specific statements about desired results) and affective goals which concern the mission of the school and describe the organization's core or primary values. These non-rational goals act as a source of identification and motivation for staff, giving meaning to their work, and binding them to the organization (Staessens and Vandenburghe, 1994, p. 188). Thus, a vital function of leaders is to manage both rational and non-rational goals in their daily interactions with colleagues.

Headteachers need to be both managers, designing and implementing plans, focusing upon task achievement, dealing with structure and systems, with the immediate future and the status quo, *and* leaders who articulate a vision, promote shared ownership, and engage in evolutionary planning (Louis and Miles, 1990), dealing with culture, the long-term and change. It is beyond the scope of this chapter to provide a wide-ranging critique of the range of leadership theories that have been developed over the last 50 years or more. Rather, it will discuss the kinds of leadership which are likely to promote teachers' professional learning and development.

Responsibility for the professional learning culture of the school is at the centre of the cultural and educative leadership roles of headteachers. It is pivotal to enabling teacher development and, through this, school improvement. Indeed:

> In a community of learners, the most important role of teacher **and principal** is that . . . of leading learner. One who engages in the central enterprise of the schoolhouse by displaying and modelling the behaviour we expect and hope students . . . (and teachers) . . . will acquire. As one bumper sticker puts so well: 'You can't lead where you won't go.' (Barth, 1996, p. 29)

The role that the principal takes in supporting professional development is, then, a critical variable in determining whether it is seen as an 'add on' to the policy implementation roles of teachers or whether it is an integral part of the conception of school as a dynamic community of learning for adults as well as for students. Thus major factors in judging the effectiveness of principals are their interpersonal skills and learning orientations. The relationships between the principal and teachers provide a model for all relationships in the school; and ongoing or continuing professional development inside and outside the classroom is directly related to the capacity of schools to achieve development.

Empirical research into the development of knowledge and skills in employment with workers at different levels in the engineering, business and health care sectors of 12 medium to large organizations in England is relevant, also, to leadership in schools. It confirms that:

> . . . a manager's indirect impact on learning through the allocation of work, as a role model and by creating/sustaining a microculture which supports learning from peers, subordinates and outsiders, is no less important than his or her direct impact through advice and encouragement, appraisal and feedback. (Eraut et al., 1997a, pp. 16–17)

This research is particularly important to thinking about *learner* support rather than support through *training*. It identifies four main approaches to the facilitation of learning:

- *Induction and integration* focusing primarily on people becoming effective members of their work unit and the organization as a whole.
- *Exposure and osmosis* described as the process of learning by peripheral participation (e.g. observations and listening) in which the learner has not only to be alert and receptive but also to work out what he or she needs to know.
- *Self-directed learning* which assumes that the learner takes a more active role, learning from doing the work and finding out on their own initiative what they need to know.
- *Structured personal support for learning* which involves the use of supervisors, mentors or coaches . . . [Here] the climate of the workplace is likely to significantly affect the quality of learning support. (Eraut et al., 1998, pp. 23–4)

In the educational world of the present and the foreseeable future, success will depend, 'not so much in trying to control people's behaviours as in helping them control their own by becoming more aware of what they are doing' (Elliott, 1977, p. 111). If teachers are not provided regularly and appropriately with opportunities for self-renewal of vision and purpose, helped to acquire new habits, or review existing habits of thought, disposition and practice, then their capacities to contribute to the task of enhancing the quality of students' learning opportunities and to the development of their colleagues' thinking and practices will be limited from the outset (Rudduck, 1991, p. 138). Growth will be stunted.

In their empirical work with teachers on the micropolitics of educational leadership, Blase and Anderson (1995) provide a number of insights which relate directly to the types and levels of opportunities which different kinds of school leaders are likely to promote. They identified three kinds of leadership.

Normative–instrumental Leadership

> Although this form of effective leadership is based on principal control and teacher compliance, it relies on the use of strategies and purposes consistent with teachers' professional norms and values. (Blase and Anderson, 1995, p. 113)

In this kind of leadership principals work 'through' teachers to articulate their (the principals') visions, goals and expectations in order to influence them to 'buy into' their agenda. While this has been shown to be effective (Hoy and Brown, 1988; Bennis and Nanus, 1985; Leithwood and Jantzi, 1990), teachers themselves rarely identify their fundamental needs, values and aspirations (Blase and Anderson, 1995, p. 106). School principals who exercise 'power through' strategies, are likely to see their roles as motivating teachers to implement their own or externally derived goals rather than involve them in consideration of their worth or relevance. Although normative–instrumental leadership has been shown to be effective, it does not fundamentally enhance teachers' professionalism and autonomy, though it may sometimes appear to do so. Indirectly, then, strategies of control serve to maintain the subordinate role of teachers as operatives.

Facilitative Leadership

Blase and Anderson generated seven major facilitative strategies which enhance teacher empowerment:

1. *Demonstration of trust in teachers* (associated with individual teacher's classroom actions, rather than school-wide concerns) . . .
2. *Developing shared governance structures* (moving a meeting time, involvement of all staff in decision making, attendance and involvement as equal members, support of decisions regardless of personal disposition etc) . . .
3. *Encouraging and listening to individual input* ('hearing' teachers' words and feelings, valuing opinion, creation of non-threatening environments) . . .
4. *Encouraging individual teacher autonomy* (teachers feel in control of classroom affairs) . . .
5. *Encouraging innovation* (creativity/risk taking) . . .
6. *Giving rewards* (through praise and recognition of day to day difficulties) . . .
7. *Providing support* (staff development opportunities, determined by teachers, availability of time, materials, finance, assistance in personal and professional problem solving). (Blase and Anderson, 1995, pp. 111–12)

Empowering Leadership

This kind of leadership draws upon traditions of participation, equity and social justice. Its aim is not to improve teacher morale, decisions, and pupil achievement, but to 'eradicate power differentials and reconstruct the workplace as a just, democratic community' (Keith, 1995 cited in Blase and Anderson, 1995, p. 129). It aims for a 'power with' approach which goes beyond the enacting of the seven features of facilitative leadership. What is 'just' or 'equitable' may vary from culture to culture, but in each case will be defined by critique by the community of ethical values such as equality, human rights, participation, 'the common good' (Starratt, 1991).

In each of the above kinds of leadership, it is possible to identify the kinds of teacher development and levels of reflection which are likely to be encouraged by structures and visions. For example, it is unlikely that reflection beyond the technical will be supported in the normative–instrumental model of leadership. In the facilitative model, critical reflection by teachers may be supported, but the values and contexts which underpin the teaching and learning cultures will not necessarily be examined. In the empowerment model, on the other hand, reflection of a critical emancipatory kind is likely to be compulsory! The kinds of school learning cultures which are likely to dominate in each of these leadership contexts are compliance, cooperation and collaboration respectively.

In England, recent research into the kinds of leadership behaviour which would best suit current and future generations of people in different kinds of organizations identified *liberating leadership*, characterized as that which can 'balance freedom and constraints achieved by tight goal-setting' but be 'loose on procedural progress' (Tampoe, 1998, p. 38). Liberating leaders are those who *release* the empowerment within individuals rather than empower them per se. The study found that they:

1. Have a strong belief in their own and other people's capabilities and set out to release this latent power in others and themselves.
2. Enthuse their followers and put enthusiasm into whatever they do.
3. Act as protectors of others, i.e. they support their followers against attack from outside interests.
4. Through a process of tutoring and mentoring develop the self-esteem of followers such that they have the potential to become effective achievers or contributors themselves.
5. Manage by using an effective combination of direction, delegation and listening.
6. Enhance the worth of their followers by ensuring they are in tune with their environment and are producing effective outcomes.
7. Respect others and believe that they, given the opportunity, will contribute to the success of the organisation through their own inner conviction and drive.
8. Personalise rather than generalise their leadership approach, in that they do not seek or use a single 'best' practice approach but set out to create an empathetic relationship in which leader behaviour matches the needs of those being led.
9. Release the latent self-leadership capability of their followers, i.e. they behave in ways that encourage their followers to take charge of their environment and take responsibility and accountability for their own actions.
10. Democratise hierarchical work environments by using the structures, processes and procedures to strengthen and enable followers rather than control them. (Tampoe, 1998, pp. 4–5)

The most authoritative series of empirical studies of headship with a clear theoretical orientation have been conducted in Canada by Leithwood, Begley and Cousins (1992) at OISE's Centre for Leadership Development. They provide insights into the three parts of the '*leadership problem*', defined as, 'how to influence people to strive willingly for group goals' (p. 6):

> The leadership problem . . . has three parts: developing a widely shared, defensible vision; in the short run, directly assisting members of the school community to overcome obstacles they encounter in striving for the vision; and, in the long run, increasing the capacity of members of the school community to overcome subsequent obstacles more successfully and with greater ease. (p. 8)

Without a focus upon and involvement in the continuing professional development of their teachers, other staff and themselves, it is difficult to conceive how the 'leadership problem' can be met.

Crowther and Postle (1991), reporting research in the Australian context, were in no doubt of the importance of the principals' role in establishing positive learning conditions for teachers:

> To the extent that principals insist that professional growth be viewed as an ongoing, long-term process, teachers will feel a sense of security and personal identity that will contribute to their sense of professional worth. On the other hand, where principals fail to demonstrate leadership in these areas, the perceptions of teachers regarding professional development tend to be marked by a degree of futility and cynicism. (p. 96)

Leadership Development

> It was easier to be a principal before. All this discussion has resulted in a feeling of frustration and discouragement. There are so many expectations, and I experience a lack of competency, which is not a good feeling. So much ought to be done, and time is a critical factor. (cited in Moller, 1997, p. 14)

This principal is Norwegian, struggling during a time of structural reform. Yet he could have been of almost any nationality. Over recent years, the role of the principal has increased in its complexity as reforms have spawned greater and more diverse demands on time, energy and expertise. Headteachers are now 'caught up in a quasi-market system which constitutes effective school leadership as entrepreneurial vision and energy . . . [and] . . . what has been called the chief executive "dimension" of the role in the past seems likely to become its defining characteristic in the 1990s and beyond' (Grace, 1995, pp. 42–4). As the culture of new managerialism in schools grows and headteachers become increasingly distanced from direct cultural experience in classrooms (Grace, 1995, p. 113), and as the importance of shaping the professional development ethos and attending to internal relationships increases, so the need for headteachers to attend to their own development as learners has become essential.

Leading in a school, like leading in a classroom, requires the use of both the head and the heart (Sergiovanni, 1992). It requires leaders who not only know and are known by their staff but also know themselves. Howard Gardner has proposed that there are eight intelligences which each of us has to a greater or lesser extent: logical mathematical, linguistic, musical, spatial, bodily-kinaesthetic, naturistic, intrapersonal, and interpersonal. Gardner's concept of 'multiple intelligences' is complex and controversial. However, it is interesting to consider these last two in relation to the successful creation and management of professional development cultures.

Intrapersonal intelligence

> The core capacity at work here is access to one's own feeling life — one's range of affects or emotions: the capacity instantly to effect discriminations among these feelings and eventually to label them, to enmesh them in symbolic codes to draw upon them as a means of understanding and finding one's behaviour. (Gardner, 1993, p. 240)

Interpersonal intelligence

> The core capacity here is the ability to notice and make distinctions among other individuals and, in particular, among their moods, temperaments, motivations, and intentions. (p. 240)

Gardner suggests that:

> The less a person understands his feelings, the more he will fall prey to them. The less a person understands the feelings, the responses, and the behaviour of others, the more likely he will interact inappropriately with them and therefore fail to secure his proper place within the larger community. (p. 255)

Much of the research literature on principals' behaviours and effects supports the need for these intelligences (Blase, Dedrick and Strathe, 1986; Sergiovanni, 1984; Sharman, 1987; Hoy and Brown, 1988). However, there are two variables which must be taken into account — the time available and their own phase of development.

Time

Although there is a general acceptance of the multi-dimensional role of principals, and the increasing and competing demands on their time, there are relatively few studies of their use of time. In America, Bredeson conducted a study of the practice of five high school principals. He analysed interview data, documents and records as well as their daily activities and found that, notwithstanding individual role definitions, adaptations and priorities, three '*metaphors of purpose*' characterized the ethos of the principalship — maintenance, survival, and vision. These revealed much about the shared cultural associations of principals.

> Regardless of personal leadership style, 89% of the principals' total number of daily activities were intended to 'keep the school doors open and the process going' . . . Daily routines . . . revealed the predominant maintenance role. (Bredeson, 1989, pp. 306–7)

His research demonstrated the difficulties in finding time to view the present holistically and speculate about the future (i.e. to vision). Significantly, it revealed, also that more than 60 per cent of time is spent in interpersonal activities, most involving face-to-face contact. The brevity, fragmentation and variety of principals' activities is confirmed by studies in England (Davies, 1987) and Israel (Gally, 1986).

Phase of Development

It is only recently that there has been a recognition that principals, like teachers, will be in different phases of their development. Not all will be 'expert', or feel comfortable with the 'turbulence', 'change' and 'uncertainty' which characterizes education. Not all will have well-developed people skills, nor be natural 'transformational' or 'liberating' leaders, either by disposition or ability. Studies of headteachers in their early years indicate that many experience frustration and anxiety (Daresh, 1987) and have unrealistic expectations of change (Parkay, Currie and Rhodes, 1992). Principals in one Canadian study, for example, reported difficulties in managing inherited hierarchical structures (Leithwood and Montgomery, 1984). Studies of secondary school headteachers in England and Denmark (Day and Bakioglu, 1996; Reeves, Mahony and Leif-Moos, 1997) provide further evidence that developments in the thinking and practice of headteachers, as in teachers, are complex. Different developmental phases have been identified:

- Initiation: a period of idealism, uncertainty and adjustment;
- Development: a period of consolidation and extension;
- Autonomy: a period of conservation and resistance to external change;
- Disenchantment. (Day and Bakioglu, 1996, p. 207)

These phases are affected by life history, health, previous role preparation, inherited school culture, external environments, personal belief factors, and the ability to manage stress. Reporting findings of a large-scale study of occupational stress among 2,638 headteachers of primary and secondary schools in the UK, Cooper and Kelly (1993) found that 'handling relationships with staff' was one of the principal categories of job stressors, and that, 'A continuous process of mid-career development for heads is absolutely fundamental if they are to avoid managerial burnout at a later date' (pp. 141–2).

Headteachers' commitment, efficacy and motivation cannot be taken for granted. However effective and efficient they are, they can no longer 'single-handedly pull and push organisational members forward by the force of their personality, bureaucratic clout, and political know-how' (Sergiovanni, 1992, p. 119). In research in English primary schools, effective headteachers relied upon three professional attributes:

- they saw their work as being concerned with developing their staff;
- they were patient, tenacious, assiduous, persistent in striving to see their beliefs put into practice across the school;
- they could synthesise and link ideas and information. (Southworth, 1993, p. 77)

Headteachers are first and foremost educational leaders of educational communities — and this core role is likely to become more, rather than less important over the next decade.

> The principal for the next decade must remember that he or she is a person whose work as an educational leader is first, foremost, and always with persons — persons who are physical, intellectual, spiritual, emotional, and sound beings . . . As a person in the community, the principal of the 1990s and beyond will be concerned with several things. Recognising that communities and their occupants flourish in caring, nurturing environments, these principals will seek to utilize a caring ethic to guide their decisions and actions . . . They will view teachers, students, parents, and others as colleagues, partners, co-learners and (where possible) friends. And they will relish the challenge of working with these groups to [build] a community of learners in which all persons can flourish. (Beck and Murphy, 1993, p. 195)

There are clues here which point to the key areas with which headteachers must be concerned. In setting the scene or creating the conditions for professional development they are in the business of shaping and working with school culture, creating structures in which teachers and children can learn effectively, and managing change. Moreover, they will be expected to call upon knowledge, skill, intuition and experience in order to achieve this. This is no small challenge for those who already may feel isolated and frayed around the edges as a result of persistent and increasing demands made upon them over the years at a time when, for some, energy levels may be declining and health, family and a sense of mortality are increasingly important factors in their consciousness.

Conclusion

This chapter has explored the potential that different policy contexts, classroom conditions, school cultures and leadership dispositions and behaviours have for promoting and inhibiting teachers' dispositions towards and capacities for development. Whilst principals cannot affect events initiated outside the school, they have a crucial role in creating professional learning cultures which encourage teachers to engage routinely in individual and collective, formal and informal learning, alone and with others. In such cultures they are more likely to continue to be challenged and supported, and committed to teaching to their highest potential.

The next chapter explores this theme further. It examines ways in which processes of appraisal and personal development planning may contribute to the development of individual and corporate learning cultures.

Notes

1 This section is based upon a critical synthesis of literature pertaining to class size and the quality of teaching and learning (Day, Tolley, Hadfield, Watling and Parkins, 1996).
2 For a critical review of research on self-efficacy, see Pajares (1996).
3 For a detailed discussion of these organizational settings, see Talbert and McLaughlin (1994).
4 Rosenholtz's claims for the benefits of teacher collaboration have been criticized because of seven items on her teacher interview instrument, six were concerned with giving and receiving help and advice, and none with reflection, shared decision-making and collaborative planning (Hargreaves, A., 1994, pp. 188, 210).

Chapter 5

Self Renewal: Appraisal, Change and Personal Development Planning

Much of the literature on 'effective schools' and 'school improvement', asserts that institutional and individual personal professional development needs should be synchronized or at least reconciled. Appraisal would appear, therefore, to offer an ideal mechanism through which both needs may be addressed. However, because appraisal takes place over a set period each year or two years it will be limited in its ability to effect change. Many (though not all) internal and external changes create challenges from which teachers may learn. Moreover, teachers' 'critical learning' phases will not match with appraisal systems nor with each other's. Indeed, if the research on teacher learning, development phases and working conditions discussed in earlier chapters is taken into account, the quest for synchronicity must be tempered by the realities of learning and development which are neither linear nor entirely rational or predictable. This chapter, therefore, focuses upon appraisal linked to career-long professional development planning and change as a means of development which is '*interactive with*' rather than '*reconciled to*' both individual and school needs.

The system of appraisal (sometimes called performance appraisal, sometimes review) in schools exists in different forms in different countries. Essentially, though, it is management inspired, providing a formal opportunity for the needs of teachers and their contributions to classroom, school and community to be evaluated through formal interviews. The interviews are based upon data collected about performance by the appraisee and the appraiser (usually a line manager). Such data includes classroom observation(s). The agenda for the appraisal interview is agreed between the appraiser and appraisee. In some countries (e.g. England) it must be linked explicitly to classroom achievement targets. The results of the appraisal are used for different purposes in different countries. For example, in Hong Kong they are directly linked to promotion prospects, whereas in England this is not yet the case. Access by others to the results also differs from country to country.

At its introduction in England in the late 1980s, it was predicted that appraisal would be too infrequent for monitoring purposes, unnecessary for identifying low performing teachers, and likely to lapse into an expensive piece of bureaucratic tokenism after the first couple of years (Eraut, 1989). Ten years later controversy continues to surround its effectiveness.

> Evidence shows . . . that the way appraisal is being used varies considerably and that, in some cases, schools have either stopped undertaking appraisal altogether or are using a model of appraisal unsuited to these purposes. In these schools, the outcomes of appraisal in terms of training needs do not lead to action and are not being linked either to school development planning or to teachers' own professional development planning. Unless these . . . central elements are more explicitly linked, the potential for teachers to develop and schools to improve will not be realized. (Millett, 1995, p. 15)

A government report on the appraisal of teachers from 1991–96 indicated its continuing lack of integration with teacher and school development:

> Overall the impact of appraisal on teaching and learning has not been substantial. In only 20% of schools visited by HMI had appraisal led to observable improvements in teaching, and then on a minor scale for the most part.
> . . . appraisal has remained too isolated from school development and INSET planning . . .
> . . . only a minority [of teachers] are able to identify improvements in their teaching as a result of appraisal . . .
> . . . Nearly half of the schools visited . . . reported delays in implementation. Reasons given included staff turnover, especially at senior level, and difficulties in finding time for appraisal interviews. (OFSTED, 1991–96, p. 10)

The most authoritative study of appraisal surveyed 109 LEAs over a two-year period (Wragg, Wikeley, Wragg and Haynes, 1996). Among its findings were that 49 per cent of teachers reported that they had changed their classroom practice as a result of appraisal, and 69 per cent that appraisal had offered personal benefits. However, the authors point out that these findings can be interpreted in different ways.

> A Department for Education official, when told of the findings, replied, 'That's good news. If appraisal had not taken place it would have been zero per cent who would have changed what they are doing, so 49 per cent is not bad.' It might equally be argued that appraisal should help everyone modify practice, so if 50 per cent say they did not, then this is a high failure rate. Optimists see a half full bottle, pessimists see a half empty one. (Wragg et al., 1996, p. 79)

Additionally,

> The difference between 49 per cent who say they altered their teaching and the 69 per cent who claim they derived personal benefits, is an intriguing one. How can people feel a process to be beneficial if it does not alter or improve what they do? . . . If they set themselves goals that related to school, rather than classroom practices, then their actual teaching may not have been directly affected.

> . . . Many [teachers] mentioned a 'boost' simply through being given attention . . . others enjoyed the therapy of an intimate conversation. (p. 80)

Twenty seven per cent stated that they had not gained any personal benefits from the exercise;

> Many of the sceptics had clearly not enjoyed good personal relationships, but some were simply cynical about the general value of the exercise, concerned about the introduction of performance related pay on the back of appraisal, or they felt they were too old to learn new tricks. (p. 81)

Significantly, the authors of this study commented on the ongoing tensions between school and individual needs, the limitations of time and funding, issues of confidentiality, and difficulties of personal change:

> Appraisal should be properly resourced . . . appraisal needs proper time and money . . . One of the reasons why so few teachers change what they did in the classroom may have been because there was not enough time, given the many demands on them, to be fully de-briefed, and appraisers were not freed to follow teachers up to see if agreed plans were actually being implemented. (p. 203)

Underpinning the use of appraisal in schools, are particular conceptions of the role of teachers and the work of teaching. Research into appraisal practices in 32 cities in America (Wise, Darling-Hammond, McLaughlin and Bernstein, 1984) identified the existence of four basic conceptions of teachers which provide a useful framework for judging appraisal schemes. Teaching was viewed as either *labour*, a *craft*, a *profession* or an *art*. As labour, the teachers' role is to implement schemes designed, directed and monitored by external authorities who supervise and inspect. It would not be difficult to associate external inspection systems, the grading of teachers, and league tables of test results with this. As a craft, it is assumed that there are specific, generalizable skills or competences defined by external authorities who monitor by periodic inspection. The introduction of national performance standards with prescribed lists of competences associated with 'the good teacher', such as those for beginning teachers, subject leaders, 'excellent' teachers, heads and would-be heads might be taken as one expression of this view. In contrast, in teaching as a profession it is assumed that teachers require a repertoire of qualities and skills that may be differentially applied according to the teacher's discretionary judgment as expressed through their 'pedagogical tact' (van Manen, 1995). These skills and judgments will be self and peer developed and monitored. In teaching as an art, evaluation by self or peers relies upon holistic judgments that recognize the unpredictable, personalized nature of teaching. It is clear, then, that national and local school cultures and contexts will affect both the design of appraisal systems, the ways in which they are implemented, and their effectiveness. This may

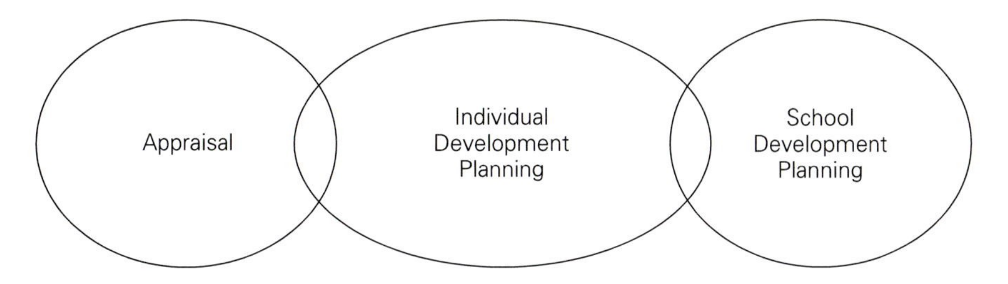

Figure 5.1 The relationship between individual development planning, appraisal and school development planning

account for the different, apparently contradictory findings of research studies cited above.[1]

It is not only the actions of individuals which need to be changed to bring about improvements in teaching but also those underlying structures which limit and restrict the options available (Elliott, 1982). Where the school culture does not promote sharing of thinking and practice as part of its everyday interaction — where it perpetuates cultural myths that everything depends upon the teacher, the teacher is an expert, and that teachers are self-made through experience (Britzman, 1986) — then the core appraisal processes of disclosure and feedback will continue to pose difficulties for teachers who interpret autonomy as the right of privacy. In these settings, teachers are likely to collude in the language of development while continuing to pursue previous practices.

Yet formal appraisal systems are important in order to promote development which continues to ensure that individuals and schools regularly review changing curricula, changing student needs and the changing demands of politicians and parents, and to provide support for self-renewal, and underpinning purpose of continuing professional development because, in changing times, existing mental maps or frames may, 'cease to fit the territory' (Pascale, 1990, p. 13). Appraisal, then, should not be seen as separate from school and individual teacher development planning if both individuals' work processes and the social architecture of the school are to be developed. Figure 5.1 illustrates the reciprocal relationship.

Planning for Process and Product

Because appraisal has a dual function in mapping onto individual and school development planning it will be both 'product' and 'process' oriented.

The *product* model has been described as one in which

> . . . the main value of the appraisal process lies in the value of the product it will generate. This product is, in the first instance, . . . a . . . comprehensive and up-to-date information base on teacher performance for the use of LEAs and governing

> bodies . . . This information base will then be used to achieve the purposes of appraisals, namely to improve professional standards through recommendations as promotion, remediation or training. (Winter, 1989, p. 49)

Winter contrasts this with a *process* model in which

> . . . the value resides in the process of carrying it out. It is the process itself which will result in professional development. Any outcomes are unique to the individual practitioner and the specific content. Whereas the product model seeks to generate authoritative ('accurate') assessment of teacher performance (so that learning experiences can be prescribed, subsequently, for the teacher) the process model seeks, in itself, to stimulate effective learning by the teacher. It would not generate 'information' about teachers' work, but insight for those teachers themselves to use in improving their work. (p. 50)

If appraisal does not result in a product, then it will have little meaning for those who are responsible for managing the system. Yet if it does not promote learning, if the teacher does not develop as a result, then it will quickly be viewed as a waste of valuable time and energy. Those systems which are concerned only with product represent oversimplistic models of CPD. To focus upon both process and product requires that appraisal is part of a larger ongoing scheme of professional development. In *other words, whilst product is necessary, getting the process right and, more importantly, adopting the right process, is essential.* There is, for example, a different kind of product which can arise from appraisal. If development is recognized as part of an ongoing development process for individual and school, then *because* it occurs at regular, set intervals, it can be used as a 'staging post' for all teachers to review their progress, both in relation to their own development and that of the school. The appraisal interview in this scenario becomes a professional development interview which enables an action plan for further development which logs into both institutional and individual needs. The action plan becomes a product, which is itself provisional. Because appraisal is acknowledged as a staging post only, the process of collecting information about classroom teaching and work outside the classroom can also be regarded as a 'special accelerated' period of supported inquiry conducted over a relatively short period of time, to supplement other information collected in the 'normal' course of development planning. If the period leading up to appraisal were to be designated as a time when teachers could take advantage of particular development opportunities associated with review which were supported by the school, then the appraisal system itself would be seen as contributing in a special way to ongoing teacher development. The school might, for example, set aside a part of its development budget or 'directed time' in order to support self and peer classroom observation and inquiry, or to provide time for reflecting upon and redrafting professional development journals or profiles, either alone or with a colleague.

Appraisal schemes which are part of ongoing development recognize and capitalize upon teachers' capacity to be self-critical. They assume that teachers have a store of practical knowledge about practice and have built in opportunities for this to be made explicit, where appropriate, and utilized. They recognize that teachers cannot be developed (passively) but develop through active participation. If we begin from the premise that the final decisions about practice will be taken by the person engaged in practice then it follows that teachers must develop the capacity to be self-critical. Many (hopefully most) teachers will be 'connoisseurs or potential connoisseurs' (Eisner, 1979, p. 197). Yet, as we have seen, the capacities to be self-critical and develop self-monitoring strategies are often either limited by socialization, psychological or practical factors (such as time, energy, and isolation in cultures of individualism or contrived collegiality) or discouraged by classroom and managerial climates in which individual growth is perceived as unconnected to organizational development.

Attempts to promote appraisal as part of continuing professional development are, therefore, unlikely to meet with success unless there is an active consideration of the psychological and social dynamic in its planning, process and evaluation. Ownership, commitment and motivation are essential:

> . . . effective change depends on the genuine commitment of those required to implement it, and that commitment can only be achieved if those involved feel that they have control of the process . . . Teachers will readily seek to improve their practice if they regard it as part of their professional accountability, whereas they are likely to resist change that is forced on them. (McCormick and James, 1983, p. 27)

Since the process of appraisal involves disclosure and feedback, is unlikely always to be comfortable — even where extensive negotiations have taken place, contracts have been made and forms of confidentiality ensured. Consciously interrogating one's own work will almost inevitably raise doubts about what under ordinary circumstances appears to be effective or wise practice (Sergiovanni, 1984). Yet the raising of doubts is only the first in what will be a number of potentially painful steps along the road to change — a road which can be littered with obstacles of time, energy, resources and, perhaps more important, self-doubt.

Change and Changing

> . . . if we accept that the practitioner's own sense of self is deeply embedded in their teaching, it should not be surprising to us that they find real change difficult to contemplate and accomplish. (Rudduck, 1991, p. 93)

There are three precepts about development and change which must be taken into account if appraisal is to contribute to the development of individual and corporate learning cultures:

- Professional development is not something that can be forced, because it is the teacher who develops (actively), and not the teacher who is developed (passively).

- Change which is not internalized is likely to be cosmetic, 'token' and temporary.
- Change at deeper sustained levels involves the modification or transformation of values, attitudes, emotions and perceptions which inform practice, and these are unlikely to occur unless there is participation in and a sense of ownership of the decision-making change processes.

Difficulties of imposed systemic structural reforms which fail to account for the individual and collective cultures into which they are planted have been widely documented (Fullan and Stieglebauer, 1991; Fullan and Hargreaves, 1992; Fullan, 1993b). The same applies to attempts to generate change internally. However 'friendly' a suggestion for change is, unwillingness or inability to change may have its source in the personal or professional life and values of the teacher, lack of self-confidence, or the cultural contexts of their work.

Change processes will inevitably contain elements of uncertainty and tension and a need for support in what will be at least temporarily a risk-taking burden of incompetence (Fullan, 1992, in Day, Hall Gammage and Coles, 1993). Understanding individual teacher histories and local school and classroom contexts and cultures is, then, crucial to successful change processes.

> The programmatic approach often falsely assumes that attempts to change how people think through mission statements or training programmes will lead to useful changes in how people actually behave at work. In contrast our findings suggest that people learn new patterns through their interactions with others on the job. (Beer, Eisenstat and Spector, 1990, p. 150)

Whilst appraisal systems have a part to play in professional and school development, they cannot guarantee successful outcomes. School and classroom cultures, collective and individual dispositions towards learning and the influence of those in whose interests new ways of thinking about and practising seem to be desirable will help or hinder. At one end of the continuum, creative and dynamic teachers will relish the possibilities raised by appraisal. At the other, appraisal systems may be 'prisons of constraint' to teachers who lack self-confidence in their own abilities or a sense of participation in shaping change initiatives (Fullan and Hargreaves, 1992). Invitations to 'be developed' may be seen to imply present inadequacies. Traditional cultures of teaching mean for many teachers that:

> - it is not always easy to receive help;
> - it is difficult to commit oneself to change;
> - it is difficult to submit oneself to the influence of a helper; help is a threat to self esteem, integrity and independence;
> - it is not easy to see one's problems clearly at first;
> - sometimes problems seem too large, too overwhelming, or too unique to share easily;
> - it is not easy to trust a stranger and be open with him or her. (Egan, 1982, pp. 296–7)

Homeostasis and habit will at the very least hold back change that the teacher does not recognize as being needed. First, learned techniques acquired over time, reinforced by years of 'single loop' learning in organizational cultures which do not encourage development, can be powerful negative forces and can make the process of appraisal more threatening. Teachers may obfuscate or delay change on the grounds that they do not have time; that it has been tried before and did not work then, so why should it work now; or that the students are not ready for it yet. Appraisal, however 'user friendly', involves confrontation and challenges to values, routines and established practices, and disclosure of these, whether by self or with the help of others, may threaten the comfortable stability of practice.

Most individuals and organizations are dynamically conservative (Schön, 1971) and unless they perceive that change is *relevant* (to the needs of the students), unless they themselves are *ready* to engage in change, and unless they are assured of *support* not only for the change implementation but also for the time and energy which will be needed for its refinement and redefinition in local classrooms and school contexts, they will be unlikely to give it more than the minimum attention required by those who insist upon it. The principles of 'sustained interactivity' among local communities of practice (Huberman, 1993b) which underpin much of the partnership and network learning described in Chapters 8 and 9 of this volume, provide one means of countering this and achieving what Fullan (1991) describes as the 'institutionalisation' and 'continuation' phases which follow 'initiation' and 'implementation'. More importantly, they promote cultural change from within by means of:

- mobilisation of broad support;
- principal commitment;
- embedding into classroom practice through structural changes and incorporation into policy;
- skill and commitment of a critical mass of staff;
- procedures for ongoing assistance, especially for newcomers;
- removal of competing priorities;
- inbuilt evaluation;
- assistance, networking and peer support. (Fullan, 1991, in Stoll and Fink, 1996, p. 45)

Change need not be always radical. It may be evolutionary (implicit, unconscious, natural); additive (sudden modifications of values, practices); or transformative (conscious, planned with particular improvement end in view) (Rossman, Corbett and Firestone, 1988). Teachers, like schools, will be in particular states of readiness to engage in additive or transformative change. Inquiring teachers in inquiring schools, however, will be in 'a continual learning mode' (Senge, 1990, p. 142). In their classic study of five primary schools in England, Jennifer Nias and her colleagues found that:

> Both teachers and heads saw professional learning as the key to the development of the curriculum and as the main way to improve the quality of children's education. Although they responded during the year to internal and external pressures

> for change, the main impetus for their learning came from the shared belief that existed in all the schools that practice could always be improved and hence that professional development was a never-ending process, a way of life . . . Teachers who wanted to improve their practice were characterised by four attitudes: they accepted that it was possible to improve, were ready to be self critical, and to recognise better practice than their own within the school or elsewhere, and they were willing to learn what had to be learned in order to be able to do what needed or had to be done. (Nias et al., 1992, pp. 72–3)

Teachers are willing to engage in change according to whether they perceive a need, diagnose a problem, and conceive of a response to the problem that is both within their intellectual and emotional capacity, and appropriate to their personal, educative and ideological perspectives and the context in which they work, and have access to support. Inquiry into practice by self and others and the confrontation of this, which is inherent in the appraisal interview and concurrent target setting, can entail destabilization risks to both personal and professional self-image and self-esteem (Argyris and Schön, 1974; Nias, 1989; Winter, 1989). Adverse internal and external circumstances can complicate efforts to change. Teachers' personal and professional selves are inextricably bound up in their teaching and thus inquiry into their teaching; and the emotional non-rational factors central to processes of investigation and change which are personally as well as ideologically and educatively significant can cause ripples of change throughout all facets of life which are not always positive (Dadds, 1993; Day and Hadfield, 1996; Day, 1997b). For classrooms and schools to become and be maintained as settings for adult learning, priority must be given before, during and following appraisal to providing time, with others, for articulating and examining purposes, processes and outcomes of teaching and learning.

In work with teachers in America designed to improve student achievement in reading, Stallings and her colleagues found that teachers are more likely to change and sustain change when they:

- become aware of a need for improvement through their analysis of their own observation profile;
- make a written statement to try out new ideas in their classroom the next day;
- modify ideas to work in their classroom and school;
- try the ideas and evaluate the effect;
- observe in each others' classrooms and analyse their own data;
- report their success or failure to their group;
- discuss problems and solutions regarding individual students and/or teaching subject matter;
- use a wide variety of approaches: modelling, simulations, observations, entry of video tapes, presenting at professional meetings;
- learn in their own way continuity to set goals for professional growth. (Stallings, 1989, pp. 3–4)

Critical Friendships

Moving into 'double loop' learning and decreasing isolation may be achieved through the active encouragement of *critical friendships*. These can be a means of establishing links with one or more colleagues to assist in processes of learning and change so that ideas, perceptions, values and understandings may be shared through the mutual disclosures of thinking and practice, feelings, hopes and fears. The results of this kind of interaction, if successful, will be deeper levels of reflection, experimentation, and greater potential for change and higher teaching standards. The process will also generate documented information which may be used by teachers as part of an appraisal interview. Below is a summary of some of the advantages and disadvantages of the use of a critical friend.

Advantages of critical friends (from inside or outside the school)

Providing they are skilled and trusted, they can:

1. lighten the energy and time loads for observation (enable teacher to carry on with teaching, maintain his or her duties), often relieving the teacher of the burden of collecting and analysing his or her own data;
2. be used to check against bias in self-reporting;
3. offer, where appropriate, comparisons with classroom practice elsewhere;
4. provide post-lesson critical dialogues;
5. act as an informal resource which teachers may use at times appropriate to the needs which they perceive;
6. stimulate reflection in, on and about teaching and learning contexts, conditions and purposes.

Disadvantages of critical friends (from inside or outside the school)

If they are unskilled and not trusted:

1. Unless they become a regular part of the classroom over time, then children and teacher may react to their presence in such a way as to cause untypical behaviour.
2. The exercise may be time consuming and counter-productive — critical friends must spend time together before and after the work observed.
3. Critical friends need themselves to be or become skilled, committed inquirers with sensitive and high level communication skills.

Whether teachers invite colleagues from in school or someone from outside (e.g. from a local higher education institution) will be a matter for their discretion. However, it may be worth noting that some research suggests that, 'It is preferable from the user's point of view to learn from a peer far enough from home so that: i) asking for help can't be interpreted as a self-indictment; ii) invidious competition and comparison is reduced; iii) the ideas can be challenged with impunity;

iv) they can be credited to their new user (Hopkins, 1986). Whatever the choice, elements in successful critical friendships will be:

1 a willingness to share;
2 a recognition that sharing involves:
   a. disclosure,
   b. opening oneself to the possibility of feedback;
3 a recognition that disclosure and feedback imply being prepared to consider changing;
4 a recognition that changing may be:
   a. threatening (to self-esteem and current practice),
   b. difficult (it requires time, energy, and new skills),
   c. satisfying, and
   d. emotionally demanding;
5 a recognition that the degree to which people are willing to share may, therefore, be restricted.

Adults learn when they are provided with regular opportunities for reflection, based on 'lived experience'. They learn by doing, and benefit most from those situations which combine action and reflection. Elliott's (1984) comments upon the lack of a rich stock of self-generated professional knowledge, seeing the cause of this as being the traditional isolation of teachers' practice remain true today. Clearly then, the message would seem to be that appraisal and professional development should present opportunities for less teacher isolation, more time for reflection upon and about action, outside as well as inside the classroom, and more active engagement in planning for development. Collegial cultures and critical friendships are central to the successful promotion of continuing professional development and appraisal schemes which support rather than erode teacher autonomy, and which encourage teachers to respond positively to change. They reinforce a sense of responsibility by affirming confidence in teachers' professionalism. Such confidence will only be built, however, if teachers are supported in career-long learning, and this means that appraisal must take account of their needs as persons and as professionals. School development is unlikely to be effective, then, unless leaders actively promote processes of interaction between individual and whole school appraisal and development planning in which teachers' personal professional development needs are recognized, supported and based upon self-managed personal development planning.

A Framework for Career-long Development Planning

No amount of rational planning either by individuals or organizations can predict or cater for all development needs. However, school cultures in which there are ongoing reflective conversations with self and others optimize the ability to recognize and respond to significant events in individuals' lives around which pivotal decisions might revolve (Sikes et al., 1985) alongside the development of school development planning. The problem with much present planning, where it exists, is that it tends to be short term, reactive and problem based. Figure 5.2 provides a planning framework which 1) takes account of the long-term needs of teachers over a career for coherence, progression, continuity and balance 2) by relating these to the different facets of teachers and teaching which contribute to the maintenance and their learning lives and the needs of the school to ensure the provision of high quality teaching. The teacher is described as person, member of a community of professionals, classroom practitioner and organizational player. The framework suggests a range of direct and indirect benefits that are likely to result if the needs of teachers in each of these roles are addressed. It assumes that professional development by definition must extend beyond classroom practice and that 'learning from experience' alone is not enough; and it provides support for the personal and professional thinking, emotional and practice needs of the teacher.

The framework suggests that long-term development is the responsibility of the school and the teacher; and that both leaders — whether principals, middle managers or subject coordinators — and the culture of the school or department will affect the extent to which the direct and indirect benefits are realized.

The framework was developed during an 18 month research and development project funded by the DfEE involving more than 200 teachers from 20 schools representing all phases of school education across 8 local education authorities (Day, 1994b, 1996). Its aims were to design and trial support materials to assist teachers in preparing their own personal development plans within whole school management and review procedures. It was based on teacher profiling and is presented here as an example of how schools might introduce the use of personal development planning for their staff in ways which encourage personal ownership and increased effectiveness. The project itself was an example of university–LEA–school collaboration, and reflecting this, the research and development team consisted of eight headteachers and teachers (one from each of the participating LEAs), two higher education representatives and one independent consultant. During the project schools:

- used the materials to evaluate their organizational cultures;
- modified the materials and, where appropriate, developed further their management support;
- designed strategies to support and monitor the introduction of personal development planning in cooperation with teachers.

Teachers:

- planned their own personal development;
- considered the use of personal development plans in relation to whole school development and appraisal/review procedures;
- where appropriate, participated with higher education establishments in establishing criteria for accreditation of their learning, experience and achievement.

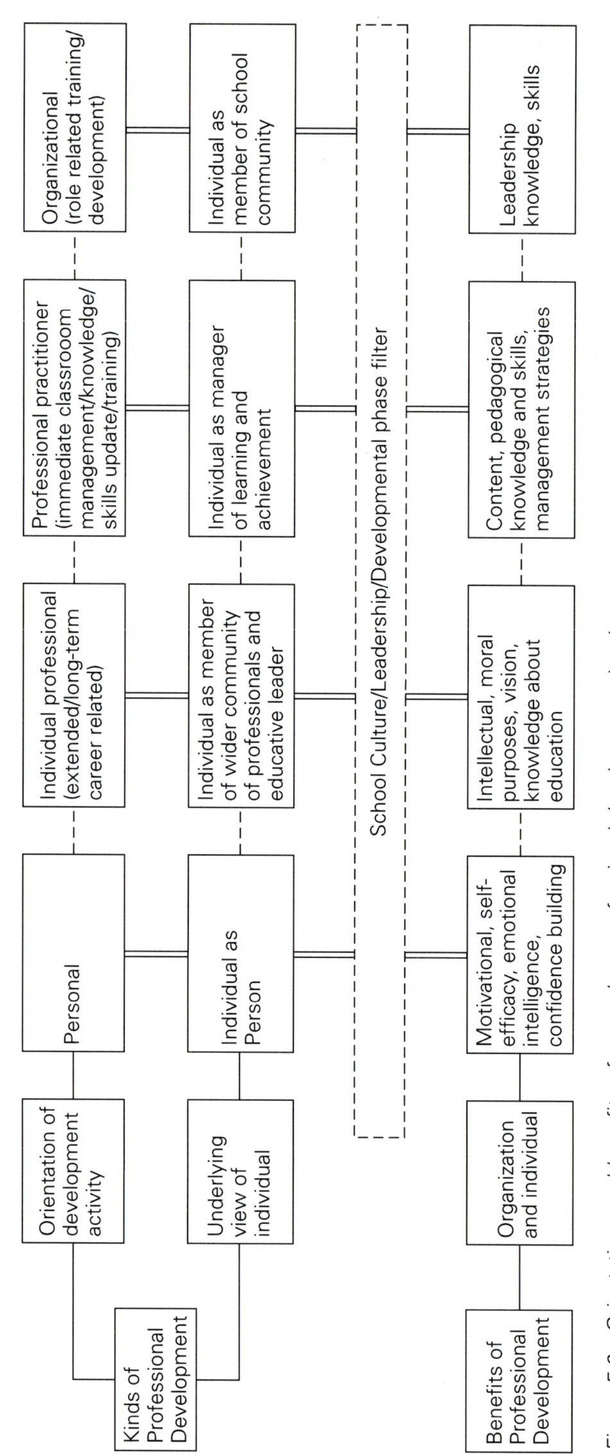

Figure 5.2 Orientations and benefits of career-long professional development planning

Ten assumptions about professional learning and development underpinned the project.[2] Professional development should:

1. acknowledge teachers' limited access to the intellectual knowledge of a phase or subject field;
2. ensure regular opportunities for systematic reflection of different kinds (as being essential to growth);
3. take explicit account of contexts of teaching, cultures and sub-cultures of schools and experiences of teachers;
4. promote teachers' routine interrogation of individual beliefs, institutional patterns of practice and the relationship between these;
5. acknowledge the limitations of private learning and ensure the provision of learning partnerships (by critical friendships);
6. place classroom practice in the larger contexts of school practice, the needs of society and the educational lives of children;
7. ensure review and support the renewal of moral purposes, professional expertise and the emotional intelligence of teachers;
8. stimulate accelerated development, change and, where appropriate, transformation of beliefs and practices through opportunities for teachers to participate in professional development activities which are designed to lead to a range of outcomes which are of direct or indirect benefits to themselves, their students and schools;
9. ensure in terms of resource allocation over time a balance between the interests of individuals and schools;
10. ensure coherence, differentiation, progression and continuity and balance of learning opportunities over a career.

The personal development planning project materials which were designed represented a structured attempt to utilize existing research knowledge about teacher learning, professional development, leadership and organizational cultures, in order to assist participants to examine their thinking and practice with critical friends or key colleagues. Through examining personal histories and the organizational contexts in which they worked, teachers were able to construct a 'lifelong learning' profile which related to the four kinds of development needs identified in Figure 5.2:

- Personal (non vocational)
- Professional (career, long-term learning needs)
- Classroom practitioner (immediate knowledge, skill needs)
- Organizational (role preparation, enrichment)

Two models of dissemination and support were used. In the initial (six months) phase, the project team designed a set of personal development planning materials. In the second phase, over the following 18 months, these materials were trialled in schools across 9 local educational authorities (districts) by volunteers. The materials were then revised in the light of the evaluation conducted through questionnaire and interview. Each school in which the materials were trialled had a coordinator with both managerial and interpersonal qualities and skills whose roles were: i) to make sure that all colleagues knew of the project and its aims; ii) to establish the best support structures for critical friendships within their own school contexts; and iii) to ensure that all participants received systemic support in processes of review and planning. Coordinators met through regular network meetings. The project thus provided an example of 'sustained interactivity' (Huberman, 1993b). The focus was not directly upon curriculum development but upon *personal* development. Thus for each individual, the use of the materials had personal significance.

The values which informed the work of the project team were made explicit in the materials themselves:

> We believe that any model of personal development planning needs to recognize that:
>
> - management must be concerned with supporting the development of the whole teacher;
> - a climate must be created in which all learning activities, formal and informal, planned and unplanned are recognized and valued;
> - all staff must have opportunities to be involved in processes which enable them to identify their own learning needs and to clarify these in relation to their development as a person, member of a profession and classroom manager;
> - achievements and successes must be emphasized and built upon.

The use of the term 'Personal Development Planning', was important as it represented a recognition of the necessity to focus upon teachers' needs in a national reform context which continues to emphasize the primacy of organizational needs. The materials, review and planning processes did not exclude the latter, but placed them within a broader holistic developmental framework. The review and planning materials themselves, therefore, focused upon both personal and management review in the knowledge that much teacher development takes place in and is influenced by the contexts in which they work. The materials were intended to stimulate thought and discussion, and to lead to the production of teacher development records based upon a framework for career-long development planning. Such ongoing teacher development records would bring together review, analysis and planning. Information collected for the purposes of appraisal could thus be informed by and contribute to the record.

The values which underpinned the design of the record were that it should:

- be owned by the teacher not the school;
- focus upon enhancing teachers' self-esteem and confidence by recognizing achievement;
- provide a means of feedback on learning to teachers through reflection and analysis of key learning moments;
- encourage the planning of short-, medium- and long-term development;
- enable teachers to evaluate their learning;

Section 1: What Have I Done? (a summary record)
This is a curriculum vitae of the kind many teachers compile prior to job application: a summary list of achievements set out in a quantifiable way, a 'professional record'. It is descriptive, in note form and date order. It records *what* has been achieved, e.g. it might include keeping a running record of the activities you are involved in. This includes experiences and activities in school (relevant whole school events, team meetings, development time with other staff, meetings with colleagues who visit the school).
Section 2: Self-evaluation/Review of Critical Incidents and Key Learning Moments (including role competences where appropriate)
This involves the process of *selecting* and listing key examples of particular on- or off-site 'landmark' incidents, situations, events, roles, activities, competences which are of particular relevance to learning, achievement, growth, contributions to the school. Many of these may relate to items listed in Section 1. It is a form of qualitative and quantitative, interpretative, self-reflection and evaluation, also recorded in note form. It *may* require the informal assistance of a 'critical friend' or 'key colleague', and may involve theorizing about the practice.
Section 3: Application to Thinking and Practice
The section illustrates the application of gains made and recorded in Sections 1 and/or 2. This involves written reflection on *how* thinking and/or practice has changed as a result of the 'critical incidents' selected in Section 2; the recording of new understandings, knowledge, skills or concepts; and **examples of these changes in practice**. The situations themselves are described briefly, placed in their social and institutional contexts, and comments from self (and others if appropriate) on **the learning/achievement gained** are recorded. Wherever possible, **third party verification** is sought as a check on self-perception. This implies the active and formal use of a critical friend/'key colleague'. Additionally, it implies **confrontation** by self or others, as well as reflection, and the ability to evaluate.
Section 4: Decision-Making (goal setting)
This involves action planning based upon the synthesis of experiences recorded in Sections 1–3. It is a form of development planning for personal, individual professional, teacher-practitioner and organization growth.

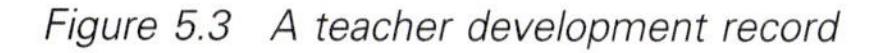

Figure 5.3 A teacher development record

- not be too time consuming;
- not be too long;
- be portable;
- provide opportunities for development discussions with others;
- be more than a simple accumulation of data;
- be of use to teachers in individual development and school accountability processes.

It was not, therefore, another way of constructing a curriculum vitae (though it might contribute to that). It is presented in Figure 5.3 as one example of a teacher development record which might be introduced at departmental or school level as part of a discussion on planning to support individual and school development.

Responses of the Teachers

Teachers and head teachers across the participating schools spoke of the ways in which participation in the project had affected their personal development, understandings of whole school development and leadership, and learning support. In terms of *personal development*, the project had offered a structure for identifying and focusing upon their own needs, valuing their own achievements, *'reawakening' the link between their personal and professional lives*. Many also stated that the project had given them 'clearer ideas' of their development. They were 'more aware of the need to sit and plan', to 'think through the development experiences', to 'focus on their use of time'. Others claimed that involvement in the project had made them, 'more aware of strengths and weaknesses', 'present and future aims', 'my own role in relation to the school', and they were, now, 'more aware of the experiences I needed'. Many also wrote of their *increased confidence and self-esteem* — 'I have more to offer than I thought' — and a *greater awareness of the need for planning career development*: 'It gave me the opportunity to analyse, target needs, plan', '. . . more confidence in seeing a career move . . .', '. . . time to reflect on my own strengths, classroom practice, weaknesses, areas in need of development . . .', and '. . . provided much needed structure to our personal and professional development planning'. A novice teacher found 'the energy to discipline herself' to complete the tasks, although there were problems with time. She learnt to, 'value the school environment', become aware of 'gaps in myself' and development needs. It had made her think. 'We so often accept things without question. I think about health and happiness. I am looking for the priorities and learning sometimes to say "no".'

The project had helped teachers in thinking of their career development. Many had become, 'more involved with management with a view to a career move'; 'been made more aware' of the experiences they needed, and their role in relation to the school. Others wrote of their increased confidence in the context of their resolve to gain promotion. The project, for one, had also 'helped me to see what I am doing now is a stage in my development, and that I needn't feel guilty about not being where other people are!' Many teachers were '. . . beginning to think about professional development in a more structured way . . .', becoming 'clearer about the precise nature of long- and short-term targets'.

In the context of whole school development, teachers claimed that the project had also provided 'a greater awareness' of their individual contributions to the department and school, a greater understanding of management structures and school cultures, and a greater sense of the importance of collaborative work. An experienced teacher talked of her growing awareness of the idea of 'management', and realized that she had already begun to put these skills to good use. In her school there was the opportunity to take a meaningful role in the management of the school as a member of a team. This message appeared to have taken a higher profile in the minds of Head, Deputy and members of staff in the school: 'The level of trust, already healthy, increased as did the respect for each other.' One teacher talked about considering one's development in 'a wider context — individual development first and aims of the school, second — how to fit the needs and aspirations of both together'.

Participation in the project tasks had clearly demonstrated the need for more detailed planning of processes of whole school planning in order to realize and support the development needs of staff so that both individuals and schools could benefit. There was evidence that some schools had grown to recognize the need to use the potential of staff to contribute to whole school development planning more fully. By the time one design team member visited a school six months into the project, a Personal Professional Development Policy, based upon the materials and built from the common experience and contribution of colleagues, had been put into place and was being implemented. In another school, staff were: '. . . considering a more democratic approach to whole school management as a result of the project. Individuals were beginning to see management as part of the whole.'

The project had been particularly useful in the understanding and introduction of appraisal for professional and school development purposes. In several schools, elements were being used, 'as a framework for personal development (target setting), and whole school planning and appraisal'. Many teachers referred to the project as 'having great value when it comes to being appraised', 'supporting staff development programmes', and 'allowing the review process to become part of the planning strategy . . . running parallel to and independent of the appraisal system'. Participation in the project had helped to identify a complementarity of individual and school needs. In particular, for many, it had served to highlight and promote interaction between personal and institutional development issues, often being used as a basis for school management planning.

Participation in the project and use of the materials had also provided a heightened awareness of the importance of learning support in the process of personal planning in the school context. The project's tasks called for concerns to be shared, and support by the school for development needs identified by individual teachers. The evaluation identified an existing supportive culture in one school: 'the level of success, in terms of depth of understanding and interpretation, firstly, depends upon the amount of personal concern and respect for others, which already exists there.' In another, however, the leadership culture was less supportive. The headteacher was remote from staff and the senior management team unbalanced in terms of gender — one woman and four men. Differences between head and coordinator about the philosophy of the project caused a delay in its launch. These problems undermined people's confidence, and concurrent 'union problems' over time commitments within the school, made the initiation even more difficult. 'Morale was precarious,' many staff were in a position of 'retreat', and not ready to talk about 'feelings' or 'development'. The coordinator allowed time to lapse and then arranged for the group of participants to leave the premises for some hours together. This was designed to enable them to take ownership of the development of the pilot. There remained the danger, however, that 'lack of awareness and interest from "the top" would stifle any real whole school movement and progress, and destroy the energy and confidence of key staff.'

School coordinators had clearly played a key catalytic and supportive role, 'making people feel at ease at the beginning of the scheme', 'keeping the momentum going', and providing time 'to meet with individual staff and as a team'. In each of the schools, the importance of the coordinator's role, in relation to personal and whole school aspirations, was highlighted and the qualities needed by a coordinator, working in circumstances in which differences of philosophy with the head existed, identified.

In a nursery school, qualities of 'commitment' and 'dedication' minimized the 'inadequacies' of resource provision; and in an upper secondary school, the co-ordinator was: 'full of enthusiasm and extremely sensitive to the needs of the staff and the pressures upon them. He appeared to have the complete support and confidence of his head and immediate colleagues.'

Coordinators themselves referred to a wide range of skills used and developed during the period of coordination:

- Management skills — planning, leadership, reviewing, organizing and advising.
- Interpersonal skills — counselling, negotiating, persuading, supporting and delegating.
- Listening — the single most frequently highlighted skill.
- The importance of tact and patience.

A central strand in the strategy for the piloting of the materials had been to encourage participants to consider the benefits of learning not only through independent self-review and the development of reflection but also through sharing this experience and its outcomes with key colleagues through 'critical friendships'.

In summary, the effects of school participation in the Personal Development Planning Project had been a supported, structured framework which had created conditions for a powerful form of teacher and school development. Almost all teachers and schools had:

- grown in self-confidence and self esteem;
- raised their awareness of the complexities of management;
- recognized the importance of their contributions to whole school development;
- identified and targeted more clearly professional and career development needs;
- participated actively in the growth and development of collaborative management cultures, thereby increasing their involvement in and commitment to the visions and goals of the school;
- developed critical professional friendships with particular colleagues in school in extending forms of self-review and reflective practice;
- contributed to a greater interaction between whole school and individual review and development planning;

- affirmed that effective self-review and planning is central to the effective development of appraisal schemes;
- joined with colleagues in other schools to establish personal development planning networks.

Variables which affected the achievement of these benefits were:

i) the provision of time to reflect and interact;
ii) the involvement of a 'significant other';
iii) the quality of leadership in the school;
iv) the balance of professional development opportunities available;
v) the provision of a practical planning framework based upon an explicit value stance, rooted in research and practice knowledge.

Conclusion

If they are to be successful, appraisal and individual development planning must be underpinned by the notion of encouraging rather than restricting teacher autonomy. They must demonstrate a recognition of the need for teachers to retain a high degree of control over the direction of their work and the confidentiality surrounding their contributions, whilst at the same time providing access to appropriate critical support. Without this, the growing tendency over the last decade to regard 'development' as 'training' which may be achieved in short, sharp bursts and which must be directly related to policy implementation, and the perception of appraisal as a bureaucratic means of contractual accountability, will be reinforced. The consequences of adopting and developing wholly competence-based profiling systems — for example, for use within models of appraisal designed to benefit only organizationally defined needs — will ultimately lead to the downgrading of teachers as autonomous, responsible and accountable professionals to teachers as operatives who implement, rather than mediate, the curriculum. Confidence, commitment and morale in these circumstances are likely to decline. In the Personal Development Planning Project, emphasis was placed upon self and collaborative generation of knowledge by means of in-school and inter-school professional learning networks and partnerships with colleagues from school and higher education.

Personal development planning recognizes teachers' active, shaping roles in the change process, and provides support appropriate to their individual needs as well as those of the organization and communities in which they work. Effective professional development must be based upon planning models which themselves are founded upon educational principles which recognize the need to encourage lifelong learning which is both private and public, individual and collective, and in the interests of the teacher and the school (sometimes more of one than the other).

There are six principles which underpin the notion of personal development planning. First, teacher development which supports teacher learning is lifelong, continuing if not continuous. Second, it must be self-managed but the joint responsibility of teacher and school. Third, it must be supported and resourced. At certain times it will involve others — teachers cannot be self-sufficient. Fourth, it will be in the interests of the teacher and the school, though not always simultaneously. Fifth, there must be an accounting process; and sixth, whilst every teacher has a right and responsibility to engage in development over a career, it must be differentiated according to individual need. Personal development planning which is underpinned by these principles will enable the career-long development of teachers as whole persons, recognizing that (i) 'There is a natural connection between a person's work life and all other aspects of life . . .' (Senge, 1990, p. 307) and, therefore, that personal mastery in all aspects of life must be supported; (ii) that teaching is, 'bound up with teachers' lives, their personal and professional histories the kind of people they have become' (Hargreaves, 1994). Records should enable a balance of learning and development opportunities which at any given time might be focused predominantly upon *personal* need (of the teacher as human being), and long-term *professional* need (of the teacher as a member of a learner community of professionals), as well as practitioner need and the needs of a particular school.

The creation of personal development planning support mechanisms over a career, which involve opportunities for both the enhancement of job skills and the development of personal and organizational vision, are not simply desirable for teachers in the twenty-first century, they are essential. Appraisal and school development planning must be supported by cultures of individual and collegial development which encourage openness and trust, notions of human fallibility rather than infallibility, collaboration rather than competition, participation and ownership rather than passivity and compliance. They will be practical but will define practicality in ways which broaden rather than narrow teachers' visions of teaching. They will embrace teachers' subject knowledge, pedagogical skills and their intellectual, spiritual and emotional health needs. Above all, they will be part of a school culture which is clearly and explicitly committed to the education of the whole child through the service of educators who are themselves whole people.

Notes

1 For a detailed discussion of appraisal for professional development see Day, Hall and Whitaker (1998).

2 Day, C. (1996) 'Professional learning and school development in action: A personal development planning project', in McBride, R. (ed.) *Teacher Education Policy: Some Issues Arising from Research and Practice*, London, Falmer Press; Day, C. (1994) 'Personal Development Planning: A different kind of competency', *British Journal of In-Service Education*, **20**, 3, pp. 287–301.

Chapter 6

School-led Professional Development: A Case Study

> Teachers themselves can be active in promoting changes of style or content which will lead to significant developments across the curriculum. (School Principal)

Successful schools are those which recognize that building effective teacher–teacher and teacher–student connections and practising good stewardship can only be enacted if teachers themselves are routinely engaged in continuous learning (Fullan, 1995). This chapter provides an illustration of how school-led professional development in one school over the period of a year enabled a variety of individual and organizational needs to be taken into account in developing practices aimed at building the school as a dynamic, professional development community. The study raises issues of leadership, learning and change in the management of 'insider led' school-based development. The summary of the case study is divided into four sections. The first provides the social setting for the scheme, its historical context and purpose within school development planning. The second section provides a summary of the planning, processes and outcomes of the three school-based development projects, principally from the participants' viewpoints. The third section provides a formative evaluation of the scheme itself. The fourth raises issues of the costs of teacher inquiry, collaboration, leadership, ownership and control.

The Context

Branston School and Community College is situated in the village of Branston some four miles from the centre of Lincoln, England. The school catchment area is wide and includes several villages, many of which have experienced considerable growth in recent years as its dormitory function has grown. The 1200 strong student intake is, therefore, of a broad social mix, but predominantly rural. Most students are 'bused' in and out of the 11–18-year-old mixed comprehensive school. The school was largely purpose built and includes a sports complex with sports hall, swimming pool and youth wing. Its aims were:

> to provide for every student an equal opportunity to attain his or her fullest personal development; to provide students with the confidence and maturity to handle whatever life may have in store; to provide, through the resources of our College, a welcoming setting for a varied programme of community activities; to encourage good home–school relationships; and to foster the fullest professional development of staff.

In the spring term of the previous year, the Principal of the school had called a full staff meeting in school time. At this meeting support was sought and given for development which indicated both 'the Principal's perception of major areas for future development and his belief in Branston teachers as their own experts'. The Principal had written the detailed submission which was approved both by the Academic Board, Heads of House and the Governing Body of the school. The areas for investigation were selected by the Principal and agreed by the Academic Board prior to being 'offered' to the staff of the school; and the following criteria were established:

1. Projects should centre on an important school issue (of curriculum or learning styles, and related organizational/structural implications).
2. Projects should be collaborative — participation in them, the process, should be regarded as an important outcome in itself, as a way of supporting the view that school self-analyses and self-renewal are key aspects of a teacher's professionality.
3. Projects should lead to, or clearly prepare for, an actual change.
4. Project teams should be deliberately and clearly linked to the normal, on-going processes and bodies which in theory 'manage' curriculum maintenance and review (e.g. Academic Board or Heads of House or staff conferences) so that the danger of isolation is avoided, and so that the proposal has maximum status and impact. Every effort should be made to relate projects to other aspects of school development, including other school INSET, secondments, departmental curriculum development etc.
5. Projects should always clearly relate to classroom interactions. The stimulation of direct consideration of, or research into, what happens at the point of learning should be an aim. Teachers should be encouraged to become their own researchers into classroom phenomena.

The Principal's view of teachers as experts and their involvement in 'generative' roles was both a valuing of their capacities to evaluate actively and design as well as to deliver the curriculum, and a recognition of their resistance to implementing passively other people's ideas. Traditionally, most of the resources and effort to promote curriculum and teacher development concentrate on the initiation and developmental stages themselves, and little, if any, are devoted to monitoring (i.e. the systematic collection of information) and evaluation (i.e. making judgments, whether formative or summative, based upon information collected). The scheme avoided this temptation in two ways:

Internal Monitoring

First, the Principal continued an involvement in the work through the overall scheme coordinator who had the explicit responsibility of reporting back to him, and through 'Adcom' (the Academic Development Committee) some members of which were participants in the projects.

External Evaluation

In addition to internal monitoring, one condition of LEA (School District) support was that 'full documentation and evaluation' would be ensured. The Principal had already expressed his wish for, 'a major evaluation by a significant credible outsider . . . It is extremely important that when we succeed we have "proof" . . . We also need sympathetic outsiders to tell us what is happening as we go along . . . People who will really listen to us as we try to manage our own school development, and later be able to report our feelings as people, our perceptions as professionals, our achievements as educators . . .' The Staff Bulletin reported further that an external evaluation would provide the Branston scheme with the necessary status and support for the 'teachers-as-experts' approach to curriculum development. Thus evaluation involved the presence of the evaluator as non-participant observer at team meetings, and the conduct of interviews with those involved in the scheme at regular intervals during the year.

Immediately following the scheme's approval, the Principal issued a 'Launch Pack', outlining the rationale and methodology of the scheme, and asking teachers to indicate their desired involvement in one or more of the project areas at one of six levels:

LEVEL OF INVOLVEMENT (tick the box nearest to your present wishes)	
1.	*No* involvement — on reflection the scheme is unsound.
2.	*No* involvement in 1986/87. Too many priorities this year, but count me a sympathetic non-participant.
3.	*Some* involvement — am interested in hearing speakers, whether colleagues or outsiders, and in reading reports etc., but not in group membership, discussing, writing or visiting other institutions.
4.	*Significant* involvement — am interested in hearing speakers, considering reports and issues, exploring issues as a member of a group, possibly helping write brief reports, possibly suggesting INSET activities, possibly visiting other institutions. Prepared to set work for supply (substitute) teacher on one or more occasions next year if the group requests me to undertake a task for them, so I can take time out.
5.	*Major* involvement — am interested in coordinating the work or findings of a group, and playing a leading role in the tasks listed in 4 above, possibly organizing outside visits, speakers in, ensuring colleagues' work is coordinated, written up and disseminated to group bodies such as Adcom, Academic Board, Heads of House, staff meetings, etc. Willing to accept one–two periods reduction in class contact (if timetabler can manage) in order to undertake research or team leadership role.
6.	*Ultimate* involvement — am willing to eat, drink and sleep research and development, freely to give up the hours between 4–10 pm each night, if necessary, marking books before breakfast in order to keep up. Able to vow, as the Good Lord is my witness, that I will earn the professional staff at Branston a national reputation for pioneering work in school-based INSET.

The projects focused upon (1) curriculum description; (2) learning about learning in classrooms; and (3) pastoral support systems.

The numbers of teachers involved constituted almost half of the total school teaching staff of 73. Each group had a leader who was allocated two periods each week off timetable, and the groups themselves were allocated between 10 and 20 days of teaching supply cover to enable members to conduct their investigations.

Those who had expressed interest in team membership/coordinator roles were approached and the staff common room bulletin indicated which individuals had been selected. This was a significant moment in the history of the development of the scheme, since it not only marked its practical launch — only six months after its inception — but also emphasized management support for principles of ownership and collaborative participation through the ways in which the process was organized. There was a deliberate move by the Principal to distance himself from his initial 'ownership' of the scheme by placing control of its development in the hands of the individual project leaders (almost all of whom held 'middle management' roles in the school) and by appointing an overall coordinator whose role was to liaise, facilitate and promote dissemination. The projects, it seemed, were to be pursued by communities of equals and success would therefore be the result of collaboration.

> The climate in the school is good for this kind of action research. It's right for this school at this stage in its development . . . it's got a tradition for progressiveness and forward thinking. Here is a project which is central in that it is going to look at curriculum and curriculum delivery, and this is what many staff think their schools should be addressing themselves to now.

Teachers as Experts, Teachers as Researchers

Curriculum Descriptions Group

> All teachers are concerned with the curriculum. It's fundamental to what we do . . . What we all do is to close our classroom door and shut the school out.

The group of six teachers from across the curriculum disciplines led by the Head of the English Department, aimed to produce a summary of the curriculum offered to Branston pupils, such that all staff could gain some insight into the experiences children were receiving in areas other than personal specialisms. This project was divided into two areas:

- discovering what the curriculum is, and how it is delivered;
- investigating a means of presenting a description of the whole curriculum in a comparatively immediate and accessible form.

During Term 1 of the project, members devised a questionnaire, to discover and describe the framework of the curriculum, the overlap of subject areas and interests, and what complementary material and approaches were present. This was approved by Heads of Department and then administered to all staff who taught 11-year-old students. The questionnaire format was adopted as being 'the most expedient means of soliciting information from a comparatively large number of subject areas'. Despite doubts as to its adequacy the questionnaire results did provide the desired base for analysis and description. Term 2 was spent in 'pupil pursuits' in order to 'gather a flavour of the curriculum on offer'. In this exercise, five members of the group observed the same class of 11-year-old students on each day of the same week in order to gain an overview of curriculum in action. Teaching purposes were taken into account, activities in lessons were recorded sequentially and timings were taken. In addition, pupils were interviewed. The results were analysed and discussed, and provided the information for a display which was to form the centrepiece of a presentation designed to disseminate the group's findings to all colleagues. The group worked on the displays during Term 3 and presented the results in Terms 1 and 2 of the following year at two separate meetings.

The group reported on issues concerning the curriculum (balance of age and experience of staff; possibilities of gender stereotyping) and the relationships between the ways in which different subject departments 'delivered' the curriculum. Some of the findings are illustrated in this excerpt from the final report:

> Far more listening by students takes place than might normally be supposed — in many subjects far less was anticipated. Less discussion takes place than might be expected. Similarly, far less exercising and developing of reading and writing skills takes place than might have been supposed . . . The project raised many pertinent questions, the answers to which cannot but help shape future curriculum planning, and indeed it suggested further areas where INSET research would be rewarding to both researchers and researched. For example, such an area could be an attempt to effect a comparison between (1) how children learn (best) with (2) how children are expected to learn. The percentage of time children (should) spend working individually, in pairs, in groups, in classes etc. needs to be researched. This work would need to be in careful conjunction with an analysis of what is taught (or learned) (1) by example, (2) by telling, (3) by investigation etc. A weighing of physical skills, what children learn to do, with mental skills, how children learn to think, needs to be made and a measure taken on the amount of curriculum time devoted to each. Finally, the more staff can observe other staff teaching, and students learning, the more will be the general awareness of what the curriculum really is.

Learning about Learning Group

Support for this kind of project was fundamental to the Principal's belief in teacher-as-expert; and the purposes were described as being:

1. to stimulate the teacher-as-researcher/analyst model;
2. to emphasize classroom experience as worthy of primary, personal analysis by teachers themselves, as the obvious and, in fact, only possible 'experts' in promoting learning.

None of the group had any previous experience of classroom research. The most important intended outcome was described as 'an increase in confidence among teachers that they can discuss, theorize about and be active in the management of learning (or the environment in which it happens) and that they are the natural experts at analysis of its features'. This coincided with the group's aspirations for a heightened awareness of what they were doing which would 'rub off in conversation with other people'. Members agreed to focus upon classroom interaction initially and they began by observing their own classrooms, focusing upon areas of particular personal interest. The main aim of this was, 'to enable us to clarify our ideas about possible fruitful areas of research'. These observations were then shared in the group. Impressions recorded at the end of the first term were described as 'striking, particularly the "blinkeredness" and isolation of much student experience in the classroom'. As a result of discussion, the main areas of interest which emerged were: teacher questioning as an aspect of teacher/student exchanges; and how best to motivate students and encourage them to take greater initiative in their learning. A decision was made to focus first upon the volume and types of teacher questioning through the observation of colleagues' classrooms from within and outside the immediate project group. This was to fulfil the group's agreed secondary aim, 'to acquire experience of methods of research, especially of observing each other teaching'. An aim which was of equal importance, however, was, 'to achieve a greater sense of team identity, greater ease of coordinating the group's work and . . . being able to meet to discuss common ground'.

To help in the systematic observation of teacher questioning, the group used its own schedule. They wanted to discover how many times in a school day students were invited by teachers to reflect upon their own experience. The major difficulty in using the system was in achieving a consistency of interpretation of different categories. Members were aware of this and other difficulties but decided to, 'trust our instincts'. This pragmatic and apparently naive approach to research processes was mirrored by the group's decision to look at classrooms on the basis of 'whether the observer got on with the teacher' rather than any other. The result was that no two people looked at the same subject:

> Observers were left with the impression that rather too often questions were just a method teachers had of controlling or dominating a discussion, rather than provoking thought. They could in fact dull the student's receptiveness to the occasional really valuable question.

Six members of the group each observed at least 70 minutes worth of lessons, recording the types of questions used by teachers on an analysis sheet. The strongest impression formed by the group was of the sheer number of questions generated by teachers. This surprised both the observers and the observed. The most startling case involved a teacher who had been happy to have a lesson of hers observed though rather apologetic that the lesson would not involve many questions. In fact, 110 questions were recorded in 35 minutes. Whilst seasoned researchers from outside schools will find little to surprise them in this information, it is worthwhile emphasizing that many of the teachers were learning this for themselves for the first time and were deeply affected by their discoveries.

As a result of this, the team decided to try to view the experienced curriculum from the pupils' viewpoints, and five members engaged in student pursuits, each following a different student from the same mixed ability class of 11–12-year-olds through a day's lessons on different days of the week. The final report reflects the learning which occurred from the student pursuits:

> One of the strongest impressions to emerge from this section of our research was of how isolated many of the students seemed to be — from their teachers and from their peers. A well motivated and academically able girl whom we observed even managed to remain unaware of the excitement caused in a science lesson by a minor fire in another part of the laboratory. Perhaps more interesting, however, was that her periods of deep concentration would be broken regularly — typically about every twelve minutes — by a pause for taking stock or simply relaxing. During the science lesson already mentioned, for example, she left her table ostensibly to fetch some apparatus but in fact simply to be able to wander round and look out of the window. In a remarkedly sophisticated way her learning was already largely self-directed. This girl was in many ways exceptional but for different reasons the activities of their peers and their teachers seemed to have very little impact on at least two of the other students to be observed, boys of average and weak academic ability. One member of staff commented on the latter that school was a phenomenon in his universe that wouldn't hurt him if he didn't hurt it. In this context it seemed significant that observers commented on the very small amounts of time when students were expected to produce or discuss work in groups. This was corroborated by the findings of the Curriculum Descriptions Group which suggested that the first year spent more time engaged in listening than in any other activity and very little time learning through structured discussion.

This part of the work naturally led on to investigating group work as a means of countering the sense of isolation noted in the student pursuits. Six members of the team volunteered to act as observers in different departments. They found that, 'While there was some debate about whether group work could provide an appropriate teaching technique in all subjects and for all abilities most members of the group had their belief in its potential confirmed.' It was the team leader's belief that of all the questions raised by his team's observations, 'the ones about how group work can be implemented, structured and evaluated are probably the ones most worth pursuing. Certainly, they seemed to get as close as any others to the central, underlying question: What happens when students learn?'

The Role of the Tutor Group

> We've got a different job in that we've got to have done something by next September.

This statement illustrates the urgency of this group's task. Initially, the project had been described as having 'the potential for initiating major, whole-school review' of the pastoral curriculum, with the aim of providing 'examples of practice and some real lines of development for future teams of tutors'. By the time it was launched, there had been a 'statement of intent . . . on an eventual move to horizontal (year) groups'; and by the end of the first term an 'imminent change from a vertical to a horizontal pastoral system' was reported. Ten staff were involved actively in the project, five of whom were Heads of House under the current pastoral system, and not all were committed to changing this. The first term was spent by the whole group meeting together at two-weekly intervals at lunchtimes to discuss the advantages and disadvantages of change, to assimilate literature about horizontal pastoral systems and to define the role of the tutor. Additionally, the whole team attended a part-time, externally directed, in-service course on pastoral care. At the end of the first term, however, there was still a certain amount of ambiguity and uncertainty perceived concerning the role of the project group. It had become clear during the first term that its role was not to conduct research in order to describe or make recommendations for change but rather to plan for the implementation of a policy decision taken by the Principal which did not have the unanimous support of staff: 'We felt that there was a need . . . to justify this change. There was no staff consultation on a major scale at all.' Although the Principal responded to this feedback by producing a paper and holding a staff meeting, as far as the progress of this group's work was concerned, 'a term had been lost'.

During the second term, members of the team, now aware of the necessity to plan for the implementation of a new system, visited schools already operating a horizontal pastoral system, and the spring and summer terms were spent working in five pairs to design tutor materials for use with each of the five school years. Commitment to the original project had been damaged and meetings of the whole project group, 'petered out like a car running out of petrol'. However, despite, 'conflicting views, attitudes, opinions within the team . . . I think we are working towards a common approach . . .'; and in terms of implementing as distinct from recommending or initiating change it was clear that some success was achieved.

Emerging Patterns and Issues

In the interviews conducted during and after the projects by the external evaluator, participants and non-participants talked about their reasons for involvement or non-involvement in the projects, their hopes and fears, their achievements and the constraints. Although interviews to elicit experience and opinion were conducted individually, there was a remarkable degree of consensus within each project group both in the early interviews (those conducted during the projects) and after the formal ending of the projects. Seven issues in particular were raised which are pertinent for further consideration by all those involved in the management of school-led curriculum and professional development:

1. The climate — contextual constraints
2. Ownership and control

3 Self-reflection and collaboration
4 The fatigue factor
5 Group leadership
6 Dissemination
7 Enhanced professionalism

The Climate

School-based work of all kinds occurs within at least three major contexts — national, local (school) and individual (social psychological) — and these will affect attitudes of participants and non-participants to learning and change. One group leader had referred at the beginning of the project to previous 'years of discontent', during which teachers' associations had been in dispute with central government over pay and conditions of service; and a member of another group had seen the projects as coming 'at the end of a bad year as far as morale goes', and that 'nowadays morale is so low that people would be reluctant to give up their time to do something like that again'. Previous development activities had been initiated under a previous Principal in which individuals had placed considerable time and energy without seeing their recommendations translated into action. Thus it was perceived as vital that this Principal '. . . persuade the staff that what's going on is actually going to be acted upon, that any initiative which he takes . . . has got to be clearly focused'.

This view was reinforced in interviews which were conducted with staff who were not project group members. Referring to the 'Learning to Learn' project, one had 'doubts about what's going to happen to it . . . I can see the result being a lot of files and reports'. Another was not against changes in the pastoral system, but, 'There's too many changes . . . and we're going to have to do most of it in our own time'. The following statement is typical of those expressed by many non-participant staff about the speed and nature of the changes:

> Sometimes you feel as a member of staff that he [the Principal] is going along too fast . . . we teachers are a bit jealous of things that we've already established, and are very wary of change . . . he's going uphill in a way because unfortunately the previous head did not always have the backing of the staff . . . People need the human touch . . . Someone to . . . be prepared to listen to people's criticisms . . . fears . . . you can sometimes forget that you need to talk to people.

Attitudes to involvement in changes (the conscious act) and changing (the ensuing processes) will inevitably be affected by these and other more personal factors. While most were positive about the ideas themselves, one had been 'seriously put off because it would have been tinkering with my time'; another had 'too much on my plate'; and a third had 'lost my missionary zeal'. However, it was reported that 'without doubt the biggest single factor in people deciding that they would not get involved was time.' In evaluating any project which does not involve all staff but is expected to influence them, it is important to actively seek their views. Other voices, though potentially dissonant, are important to building ongoing dialogue in learning communities.

Ownership and Control

The Principal's underlying intention had been to engage colleagues in collaborative activities for the 'common good' of the school so that there was a moral imperative implicit in his selection of the projects. The assumption (untested until the projects got underway, though implicit in the principle of voluntarism) was that this would be shared by the project members. This raises an important issue for those who seek or are offered school support for professional and curriculum development: the 'institutional needs' dimension may conflict with the personal or group needs dimension. In any needs identification procedures and development programmes, the match between felt individual and institutional need is bound to be potentially problematic. The Branston Scheme implicitly recognized this, but did not fully account for it, although the Principal did see the scheme as being the first of three one-year phases which would take into account differently perceived needs. Nevertheless, as this chapter has indicated, some problems arose in the course of particular projects in which changes in school policy, perceived as necessary by the Principal and senior management colleagues, conflicted with the views of some of the staff members involved.

The work of one of the project groups was circumscribed by the knowledge that the Principal had already taken a controversial policy decision to change the pastoral system. It was not, perhaps, surprising, that even the project group itself was characterized by occasional dissension and conflict. One of the group commented: 'It's like building your house on poor foundations.' Many staff were not committed to the planned change, 'even in our own team', and there was initial and continuing resentment that 'there had been no staff consultation on a major scale'. It was 'very difficult early on to get a nice climate at meetings', because 'there's a lot of ill feeling and a lot of dissension'. A member of the group summarized the difficulties that, ultimately, caused the project group to split into year group pairs in order to set the scene for the new system:

> Every meeting we have, somebody puts a spanner in the works about something. If we'd all been committed we'd probably have got our ideas together by now . . . I think there's a feeling at the back of people's minds that, 'I'm keen, but am I wasting my time? Will the things that we have suggested be taken up'.

Clearly, these project members felt that they were being denied the opportunity to conduct a 'reconnaissance' of pastoral systems and to consider relative merits before reporting on these to colleagues: 'We were overtaken by events . . . so that the work of the group, in the summer term, seemed to stop, because we were so busy trying to get everything ready for the tutors to operate in September.' Commitment to a process of investigation designed to implement an imposed innovation in the most efficient way was not universal and was far from the ideal of teachers-as-researchers with which the group had begun.

In the other two groups, however, it was clear that members had similar interests, motivations and prejudices, and that school and individual needs coincided. For one member of the 'Curriculum Descriptions' group, involvement in the project was a 'natural extension' of work in a particular subject area in which a curriculum had been designed and developed. He anticipated that this would help him to look at 'broader issues'. Another had 'always been interested in cross-curricular links' and had tried to build these up in his previous school. His 'prime motivation' was to 'try and find out what is being done elsewhere'. A third member was keen to 'learn more that will help me develop, help me be a better teacher' and he too wanted 'a lot more cross-curriculum activity to take place'. A fourth project member expressed similar sentiments, feeling that 'there should be a tie up between what we're doing and other departments'. 'I always do reflect a lot on what I do. I always have done. I'm that sort of person really' seemed to characterize the backgrounds of those involved in 'Learning about Learning'. The key activities of observing classroom action, whether from the viewpoint of the teacher or the pupil (as in the pupil pursuit tasks) suggested that this was a 'doing' group: 'It's all very well to sit and philosophize about education, but unless it's going to do something then . . . I've got 101 things I can be doing . . . The reason that a lot of people are doing this is that they're at the heart of it . . . We're deciding what we're doing as we go along.' Yet, despite this, much of the group's time was spent in designing observation schedules, analysing results and hypothesizing on the processes and outcomes of teaching and learning. Perhaps the key feature of the work of these groups is that it did not threaten the existing order in the school.

It seems, then, that school-based development which meets institutionally perceived needs is likely to be more successful when these coincide with those of the individuals involved. Expressed differently, school leaders need to take account of principles of ownership and change when taking an initiating role in school-based curriculum development. Work undertaken which attempts to support curriculum and staff development through teacher research, runs the risk of being seen ultimately as an instrument of control in which the research is prescribed by needs or policies defined by an individual or group of staff who hold senior positions within the management structure of an institution.

Self-reflection and Collaboration

> It was well worth doing . . . the chance to see what's actually going on in school . . . just to see what activities were going on has helped me . . . It's been an eye opener . . . We've enjoyed the tasks we've set ourselves . . . the minutiae of educational research looking at the data and drawing conclusions. The very process we've enjoyed, as well as the final benefits.

The model of teacher professionality promoted by the projects explicitly recognized the importance to teachers' learning of the use of their personal, practical knowledge and, as a means of utilizing this, a dialectical process of reflection both 'on' and 'in', if not 'about', the action. Participants across all groups spoke of personal gains that had been made as a result of the activities of visiting other schools, discussing values and ideas with colleagues, reading, looking at life in classrooms. The projects had provided '. . . an opportunity to look at other people's ways of looking at things' and although in one group, 'a majority think that we didn't achieve as much as we ought . . . all in all I'm glad I had the experience'. 'If nothing else comes of this . . . approach, it will have brought me into contact with more pieces of material, and I've been made aware of other methods . . . topic areas . . . which cannot but help.'

Three gains in particular are worth highlighting in the context of professional development and change. The first concerns the recognition — perhaps the re-recognition — of *the gap between intentions and practice*:

> There's the inevitable problem that you have a vision of what you want to do, and what you actually accomplish is only going to be a fraction of that vision.

The second concerns the changing of individuals' perspectives of their own work from a narrow departmental to a broader school context:

> I think it's helped us all to see the school as an organism, that whatever you contribute can inevitably only be a part of the whole. And it's been interesting to see how other parts of the organism work, what they contribute.

A third gain identified related to the *collaborative nature of the work which brought teachers from different disciplines together*. Two comments, in particular, illustrate the perceived value of this:

> The biggest value is just opening communications between groups of teachers who would otherwise not necessarily talk about teaching . . . I've never done that before . . . It's valuable not just to confirm hunches that you may have had yourself, but to share those with other people and see that they too share them.

> I think it was important that we did spend time together as a group in school time. I think that adds a greater kudos to what we do . . . that the school thought it important enough to give it time.

It is sometimes assumed that schools are social and sociable places. Writing after the project had ended, one member made this comment:

> I think that in a big place like this the biggest weakness is that staff don't know each other. They pass like ships in the night . . . We began to appreciate people far more, and . . . working together like that you get a greater appreciation of people.

> You get to know them better. And I think the better you know somebody, the better the opportunity of achieving things working together.

The Fatigue Factor

Time, energy and emotional and intellectual commitment were identified by the project participants as being the biggest single factors affecting both motivation and energy levels. It was generally observed that, 'a lot of people have given up considerable amounts of time' to the work. This theme was repeated through all the groups:

> I think I put in far more time than I was actually given . . . so having an afternoon or morning session a week working on it [the project] wasn't a bonus, but it did make us feel that we were doing something which other people were going to look at.

> If you're given time to observe a lesson, then you're going to have to spend many times that to do anything meaningful with it afterwards.

> The spin off was to be given the opportunity to study in working time . . . That was one of the very positive things where you've got that time and it's a facility, and I think that in itself is a very motivating factor . . . The question is, would we have done it without the scheme?

> You might get a couple of periods, and this is classed as time off, but in reality it isn't necessarily time off because you've taken a substantial part of that time in setting work for classes that you'd normally be teaching, and then you've got to go back and mark all the work that they've done . . . It's a relocation of resources . . . not a free gift.

It would appear that in terms of economics as well as professional growth the scheme provided 'value for money'. However, there are two further issues which relate to provision of time support. The first is that not every member of every group will necessarily provide the same level of commitment, and this may have adverse effects upon the dynamic and learning processes of groups. One leader spoke of the need to 'reconcile' himself to people's individual commitments — which ranged from one who 'just stopped coming to meetings with five seconds notice each time', to others who 'after Friday night's meeting which finished at five o'clock . . . spoke for a further twenty minutes about it'. The second is the issue of fatigue.

It was observed in two of the groups that, 'People started getting fairly tired through the year', and one group's work began to 'peter out'. Additionally, when asked whether they would wish to continue to participate in school-based development work in the following year, a significant number of participants stated that they 'wanted a break from it'. This was not, it seemed, because they were no longer interested, nor, for the vast majority, because they had had negative experiences.

One, for example, had been studying on his own for a number of years, and so wanted to 'tick over on my responsibility and enjoy my teaching'. Another said that he would probably continue what his group had been doing after a year's break. A third stated that he 'felt it was detracting from my lessons quite a lot.'

It is worth reflecting on the issue of involvement in projects which require extra time and energy in relation to the notion of 'bounded' or 'containable' time. The problems of research fatigue and increasing lack of confidence by individuals in their ability to focus upon the central task of teaching need to be taken into account at the planning stage. It is incumbent upon those who manage school-based development to ensure also that 'commitment' does not become associated with 'overload'.

Group Leadership

The roles played by group leaders are crucial to the degree of success of the various enterprises and, in view of this, it is surprising that no leadership training and team building programmes were provided prior to the beginning of the projects. Team leaders' commitment and credibility were not questioned by colleagues, and while some were viewed as 'middle management' figures and others as 'very much grass roots' this did not seem to be an issue in the functioning of the groups. One member of the senior management team was 'impressed by the methods employed for getting the teams together, and the quality of the debate'. Nevertheless, it is clear from the reports of the projects that leadership knowledge and skills are essential prerequisites.

Dissemination

Both the 'Curriculum Descriptions' and 'Learning about Learning' groups had entered the projects with expectations that they would share their findings with their colleagues in the school. Both hoped that their work 'will affect the work of the school', and that the information would 'enable people to understand what they are doing . . . what's happening in the school . . . then decide is this the right thing, is this the right way to do it? What changes do we need?' One member stated that 'it is very important in a large school with so many different subjects that the left hand should know what the right hand's doing and when and how'; another envisaged it as 'an exercise in information sharing which then could be used department to department . . . as a means of breaking down subject barriers'. However, whilst these groups planned for dissemination by producing, and in one case presenting, their findings, no detailed consideration was given to the very principles of participation, collaboration and ownership which had characterized their own learning throughout the projects. In effect the hope for adoption or use of the findings was in part based on an act of faith, a belief that if they had intrinsic merit and were perceived as being 'valid', then acceptance by others could be achieved through traditional modes of dissemination (for example, a report and presentation).

Enhanced Professionalism

In an interview after the project had ended, the Principal stated that:

> At the moment what's important to me is that kind of [open] attitude and awareness and openness, especially in view of the fact that teachers do feel kicked about and treated as menials. It's more important to me that their sense of professionalism has been increased . . . than that any specific change has been achieved.

Overall, he said, the scheme had been valued. It had 'made people feel that there is life after their classroom lessons.' It had been welcomed as being important in 'making people aware of issues in education . . . because it means that we are looking at ourselves to see what we are doing with children . . . which will either confirm or help people to look again at some of the ideas.' The scheme itself recognized that 'as teachers we want to do something about our own profession, about what's going on here. We want to examine it . . . to look objectively at what we are doing.' He recognized, however, that those directly involved had been 'people that one would expect to come through', who had 'seized the opportunity . . . It was a vehicle for them to express themselves'.

Conclusion

The school-based development work described in this chapter was the idea of the recently appointed school Principal, variously described by his colleagues as 'an ambitious professional', who 'sees himself as a fairly cerebral and dynamic head who would like to get his staff and, probably, to encourage some of his colleagues to think about the curriculum perhaps on a slightly more advanced level'. He was 'a quiet operator, thinking and planning, calculating . . . in logical and sensible ways.' In a very real sense, then, the scheme was an embodiment of the Principal's ideals, values, and vision. It had begun, in his own words, 'with the thought that effective change is people changing and is grass roots'. He had been convinced that a 'top–down hierarchical' approach to curriculum and professional development would not work, and that the approach he had taken had 'as good a chance as anything else of success in achieving change, which in a school is so linked to people internalizing'. He had been aware of the need to establish a 'right timescale for change', and had consciously determined to take advantage of his 'honeymoon period' in school: 'One of the glories of being new is that you're already at the threshold before you start. People expect you to have your own agenda, expect changes.' Nevertheless, he recognized the 'tension between wanting to use your power as headteacher to empower the staff and then wanting to retain the controlling voice — which in certain respects I do.'

A senior management colleague described the management model:

> It was top–down only to provide the initial impetus. Once the impetus was there then if we nurtured it then it should develop — as indeed it has developed. So to the extent that we opened doors to enable staff to progress, we opened those doors where we saw there was a need. So although the staff could claim ownership, in fact the options which were available to them to bid for had been diagnosed and offered by the management team.

This 'mandated ownership', while attractive, clearly results in problems of commitment for those who do not share the leader's value system; and empirical evidence in the Branston scheme provides support for this. One of the interesting factors in this scheme was, however, the long-range vision and alternative future strategies of the Principal. He described this as only the first stage of school-based work — 'the start of an ongoing INSET strand' — which, it was hoped, would eventually provide every member of staff with opportunities to participate. Even before the formal end of the scheme, an invitation had been issued for colleagues to participate in a new scheme. This 'invited bids for development time from individuals, groups, or departments on any area', though 'whole school research/development, or at least whole departmental ones, remain likely to get preference over individual, self-contained ones'. The scheme attracted bids from two departments (the 13 staff in these were allocated a total of 21 'supply' cover days) and 19 individuals who were allocated between two and six periods each week in order to pursue investigations into a range of curriculum issues.

Essentially, leaders of school-based professional development must adopt principles of collaboration based upon teachers' ability as learners and active participants. In doing so, they must adopt strategies which take account of a number of learning and change principles.

Figure 6.1 is an attempt to operationalize these. It represents a planning–action–review–planning cycle which accounts for the need of all those engaged in school-based teacher development to engage in a process which minimizes potential problems caused by disjunction between, for example, individual and institutional need. It recognizes that 'need' may be identified by any individual or group or by collaborative need identification procedures but that the key to progress is in contract-building and contract-making. It is at this stage that the kinds of responsibilities and answerabilities (by management to teachers and vice versa) for the duration of the work may be clarified, established and negotiated. The model avoids making judgments about the effectiveness of particular management stances, so that the opportunity exists for 'pro-tem' power and authority relationships to be negotiated. However, it is implicit that where the culture or ethos of the institution is expressed through antagonistic management–staff relationships, then success will be difficult to achieve.

The final words in this chapter are those of the Principal who had initiated the idea, who had been passionately convinced of the necessity for professional research and development to be seen as an 'utterly natural part of every schoolteacher's role within his own institution'; and who had undertaken considerable searching and lobbying for resources from outside the school to support the project:

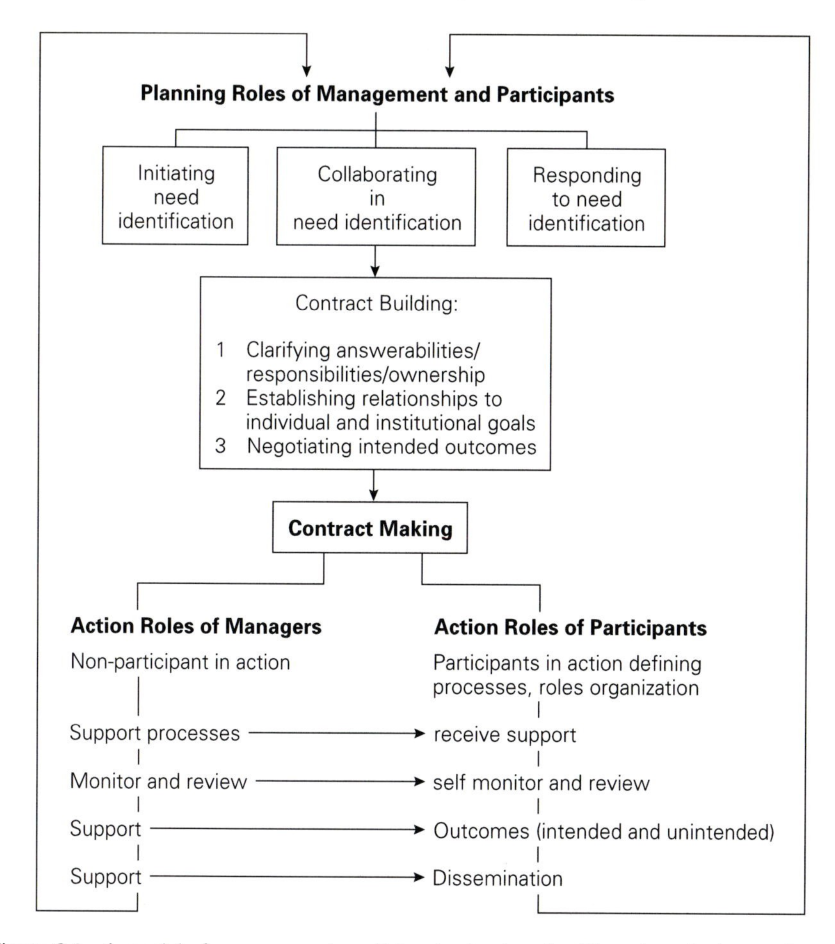

Figure 6.1 A model of management–participant roles in school-based curriculum and professional development

Of course, the projects were perhaps not equally successful, and certainly not in the same ways, but my own subjective view is that the process at least began to diffuse into the bloodstream, and although neither the projects nor their reports may have broken new ground, that they happened here was enormously significant for our future development. Some tied in directly to whole school curriculum and structural changes (though the question of the relationship between teacher groups and whole school policy, as determined by senior management, is itself worthy of a separate report) while others were far more akin to basic research, with no immediate outcome. This was a deliberate mix. I myself believe that the year paved the way for a better understanding of several major school changes, as well as acting as a spur to professional in-house activity. For example, when in the following year at stage 2 of the campaign 'Teachers as Experts' I invited bids for research development time, over 20 staff responded individually and 10 more as members of departments. Two of the resulting individual projects are forming the major part of a Diploma in Professional Studies, and this is one more necessary step forward.

Professional activity of the school-based sort just should be validated, by certification as well as in other ways. School-based work certainly proves to be very cost-effective in terms of 'activity generated per pound of resource', but of course it needs some funding. Overall, despite our imperfections, we have, I believe, shown that there truly is an appetite for school-based, teacher-centred collaborative research. I also believe that this school is healthier and stronger because of the activity its members have participated in than it would otherwise have been. I intend to continue to pursue the 'teachers as experts' approach.

Chapter 7

In-service Education and Training (INSET): Limits and Possibilities

The more elaborate, richer concept of professional development outlined in earlier chapters does not eschew INSET in the form of courses, but locates it in a wider learning context, as contributing to the repertoire of learning modes now used to promote growth of individuals and institutions, and taking place both on- and off-site. Because it is a part of an array of strategies for development, its intrinsic limitations, like those of other learning modes, are recognized alongside its potentialities. This chapter, then, will focus upon the ways in which INSET can contribute significantly to the development of teachers and their schools. Conditions of teaching and limited resources mean that formal learning opportunities inside and outside school are minimal and, often, in teachers' own time. All the more important, then, that they are purposeful and relevant to the learning needs of the teacher. INSET is defined here as a planned event, series of events or extended programme of accredited or non-accredited learning, in order to distinguish it from less formal in-school development work and extended partnerships and inter school networks which are discussed in Chapters 8 and 9. The chapter discusses the management, purposes, processes and outcomes of in-service education and training. It examines policy and institutional contexts and their increasing influence upon INSET agendas; and focuses upon issues of impact and effectiveness.

One important message which emerges from research into INSET effectiveness is that it contains two complementary elements:

> **Education** which helps you decide what to do.
> **Training** which helps you to do what is necessary more consistently, effectively and efficiently. (Steadman, Eraut, Fielding and Horton, 1995, p. 67)

This is a useful bifurcation for it implies that there are different purposes and orientations which will result in different kinds of professional development.

INSET is intended to provide intensive learning over a limited period and, although it may be jointly planned, it usually has a designated leader(s) whose role is not only to facilitate but also actively to stimulate learning. Where it is timed to 'fit' the needs of teachers in relation to their phase of experience, career development, demands of the system, lifelong learning cycle or systems needs, it is likely to succeed in *accelerating growth*, whether that growth is additive (taking knowledge, skills, understanding forward a step) or transformative (resulting in major changes in beliefs, knowledge, skills or understandings). Whilst the traditional concept of INSET as an activity or series of activities isolated from the learning life of the school or as the principal provider of teacher development is dying, it remains true that in some schools staff receive little advice on their development. This is due to an inadequate understanding of the concept and an inability or unwillingness to engage in planning which relates to establishing an appropriate balance between individual and system needs. Even now, in many countries:

> New teachers are welcomed but left alone; INSET is left to individual choice and so goes to the most ambitious and those with the least need for it; most INSET is in the form of courses, takes place off the school premises, and is for the benefit of the individual: It does not grow from institutional needs nor is there any mechanism for disseminating the outcomes within the school. (Hargreaves, D., 1994, p. 430)

INSET Contexts

In the distant past, education and training provided mainly by those outside the school was the formally recognized arena for teacher development. This was known as in-service education and training (INSET). With the growth of site-based management, and national initiatives in curriculum and assessment reform aimed at raising standards of teaching and learning in classrooms, INSET has become only one of a range of professional development opportunities available to teachers. The INSET agenda has moved from being largely determined by individuals who chose from a 'smorgasbord' of activities on offer from external providers to being largely determined by the managers who 'sponsor' INSET.

Whilst all countries agree on the importance of INSET, historically there has been little attempt in any European country to establish systemic career-long differentiated support for the continuing professional development (CPD) of teachers. An examination of the contents of the 1994 *European Yearbook of Comparative Studies in Teacher Education* (Sander, 1994) indicates that in all 21 countries represented, the emphasis in resource terms was on initial teacher training. In-service was voluntary (Austria); was not coordinated (Denmark, Italy, Spain); was not conceptualized (Belgium, France, Netherlands); or was top–down, short-course dominated (Portugal, United Kingdom). In America, in-service relies upon individual's self-motivation and commitment to career advancement (Hawley and Hawley, 1997), whereas in Japan the priority is on collegial, collaborative development where the role of peers is influential in INSET which is based upon networking (Shimahara, 1997). Whilst many countries have moved towards school-based INSET (cheaper and apparently more cost effective), there is no evidence of any systematic evaluation of the benefits of the use of particular models, nor any acknowledgment that learning involves change (of thinking and/or practice) and that this often needs long-term support. Attempts both at local and national levels to provide INSET support for the CPD needs of teachers and schools are rarely conceptualized beyond the rhetoric of statements such as, 'They should result in improvement'.

In all of these countries, however, the context in which in-service now takes place has been or is being irrevocably altered in parallel with government-initiated reforms. In England, a national Teacher Training Agency has been given responsibility for establishing a 'cradle to grave' set of nationally accredited training courses. These are targeted at 'key stages' of an institutionally related career development, but with no explicit consideration of effective learning models or the long-term intellectual and professional development needs of individual teachers (Day, 1997c, pp. 39–40). Nor, as in other countries, do INSET activities 'capitalise fully on what we have learned about the importance and variability of local contexts . . . in-service activities tend to be linked to special projects or to discrete components of reform and to embody a relatively traditional conception of classroom experience' (Little, 1993, p. 144). Whereas in the past participation in in-service was usually a matter of individual choice, in many countries there is now a minimum requirement. Since the late 1980s, purposes related directly to the implementation of mandated policies in the classroom and school management have dominated the INSET agenda. Much INSET has become driven by national, local and, even in some cases, school initiated managerial policy agendas. Teachers are seen as 'delivery agents', acting in accordance with statutory demands of the employer. There is a tendency now to regard development as training which may be achieved in short, sharp bursts and which must be directly related to policy implementation. Studies in Australia, England and Sweden indicate that both teachers and administrators may favour an emphasis on technical rationality in professional development programmes (Sachs and Logan, 1990; Gilroy and Day, 1993; O'Donohue, Brooker and Aspland, 1993). If this trend remains unchecked, the consequences may be the downgrading of teachers as autonomous, responsible and accountable professionals (with a responsibility for the moral purposes of education) to mere functionaries (with a responsibility for uncritical delivery of knowledge and skills).

So, whilst teachers now have more opportunities for INSET, they have:

- less opportunity for extended learning;
- less choice over what they learn;
- less support for study unless they belong to a targeted group.

If local patterns of resource allocation which tend to favour the training model persist or become the only route to professional development for most teachers, then:

> Rather than developing reflective practitioners who are able to understand, challenge and transform their practice, in-service education in its current form encourages the development of teachers who see their world in terms of instrumental ends achievable through the recipes of 'tried and true' practices legitimated by unexamined experience or uncritically accepted research findings. (Sachs and Logan, 1990, p. 479)

Professional development in this conception has been described as a 'deficit model' in which INSET is seen as a straightforward activity making good deficits in a teacher's repertoire (Gilroy and Day, 1993).

Long ago, Jackson contrasted the 'defect' approach with the 'growth' approach to INSET. The former is based upon an external view that teachers do not have the level of knowledge and skills necessary to motivate students to fulfil their achievement potential. The goal is, therefore, to equip them with these. The proponents of the latter approach affirm that teacher growth is necessary, but that 'In teaching, as in life, the roads to wisdom are many' (Jackson, 1971, p. 27); that teaching is a complex, multi-faceted activity; that good teaching demands more than the sum of knowledge and skills; and that schools and classrooms are not always environments in which professional learning is encouraged or supported.[1] If it is accepted that teachers, schools and policy-makers outside schools have legitimate interests in improvement and redirection in contractual, moral and professional accountability contexts, then notions of 'defect' and 'growth' approaches present a false dichotomy. Rather, INSET should not focus predominantly on one at the expense of the other. It should present a range of learning opportunities related to all those interests and should seek not only to meet short-term, but also legitimate longer-term development needs since the contexts in which it operates are those of personal, professional and organizational change.

Over recent years, governments have realized that successful change requires the active cooperation of teachers. Thus, they have reasoned that restructuring schools, providing nationally directed curriculum reform and targets for student achievement will not in themselves improve teaching practices or student learning and achievement (Elmore, 1992). These will be more likely to be implemented successfully if teachers' knowledge and skills are upgraded. In Australia, Logan and Sachs (1988) suggest that where INSET is supported by governments and their agencies it is for three reasons: i) to stimulate professional practice; ii) to improve professional practice; and iii) to implement social policy, and that the latter subsumes the two former reasons:

> The purpose of improving schools and stimulating professional development is, on this view, to increase the capacity of institutions and individuals to contribute to the process of societal restructuring. That is, the purpose of professional development is to assist with social policy implementation through school improvement. (Logan and Sachs, 1988, p. 9)

They argue that in-service activities which have no immediate bearing on specific social policies and issues need to be supported because schools and individual teachers need to develop and maintain their capacity for renewal in order both to improve the quality of current services and to meet new demands. However, the development of centrally promoted INSET has tended to be at the expense of, rather than complementary to, INSET opportunities chosen by the teachers themselves.

The Management of INSET

Needs and Purposes

Because externally provided INSET represents a temporary intervention into teachers' learning lives and because schools operate within limited budgets it is important that budget-holders establish principles for its support which are clear to all parties involved. For example, is the focus of the INSET programme on: 1) policies set by national or regional priorities; 2) school-wide improvement linked to an organizational development plan; 3) individual teacher's growth linked to personal development planning and appraisal? Logan and Sachs (1988), using learning rather than location as an organizing concept, identified three orders of learning served by in-service:

- *re-orienting* in which teachers develop their capacities to make 'significant revisions' to current practices as a result of the introduction of new teaching methods, different working conditions, changed management procedures or expectations, or as a result of a change of role;
- *initiating* in which teachers are inducted into new roles (social initiation) or incorporate new ideas and practices learnt through reorienting programmes into classrooms and school life (technical initiation);
- *refining* in which teachers' current practices are strengthened and extended.

They designed a useful checklist for designing or evaluating in-service education proposals which are seeking the support of schools:

Name of project:

1.	Is this an in-service education project?	Yes	No	
2.	What type of program is it?	Reorienting (Current Duties) . . . . Reorienting (New Duties) . . . . Initiating (New Positions) . . . . Initiating (New Practices) . . . . Refining (Current Practice)		
3.	Does the program address policy implementation, school improvement or individual development?	Social Policy . . . . School Improvement . . . . Individual Development		
4.	Is it school or classroom focused?	School	Classroom	
5.	Is the outcomes configuration realistic in respect to goals, and to the collection of evidence and use?	Goals Evidence	Yes . . . . Yes	No . . . . No . . . .
6.	To what degree do the expected outcomes match the priorities of the sponsor?	High	Medium	Low . . . .

In England, Bolam (1986) linked INSET needs and purposes through a matrix which enables the management of INSET in terms of system and individual needs (see Figure 7.1). The typology of the kinds and benefits of personal development planning provided in Chapter 5 provides a comprehensive means of planning which enables principles of differentiation, coherence, relevance, progression and continuity and balance to be applied to INSET as part of CPD over a career. The model is a useful reminder also of the need to consider short- and longer-term purposes.

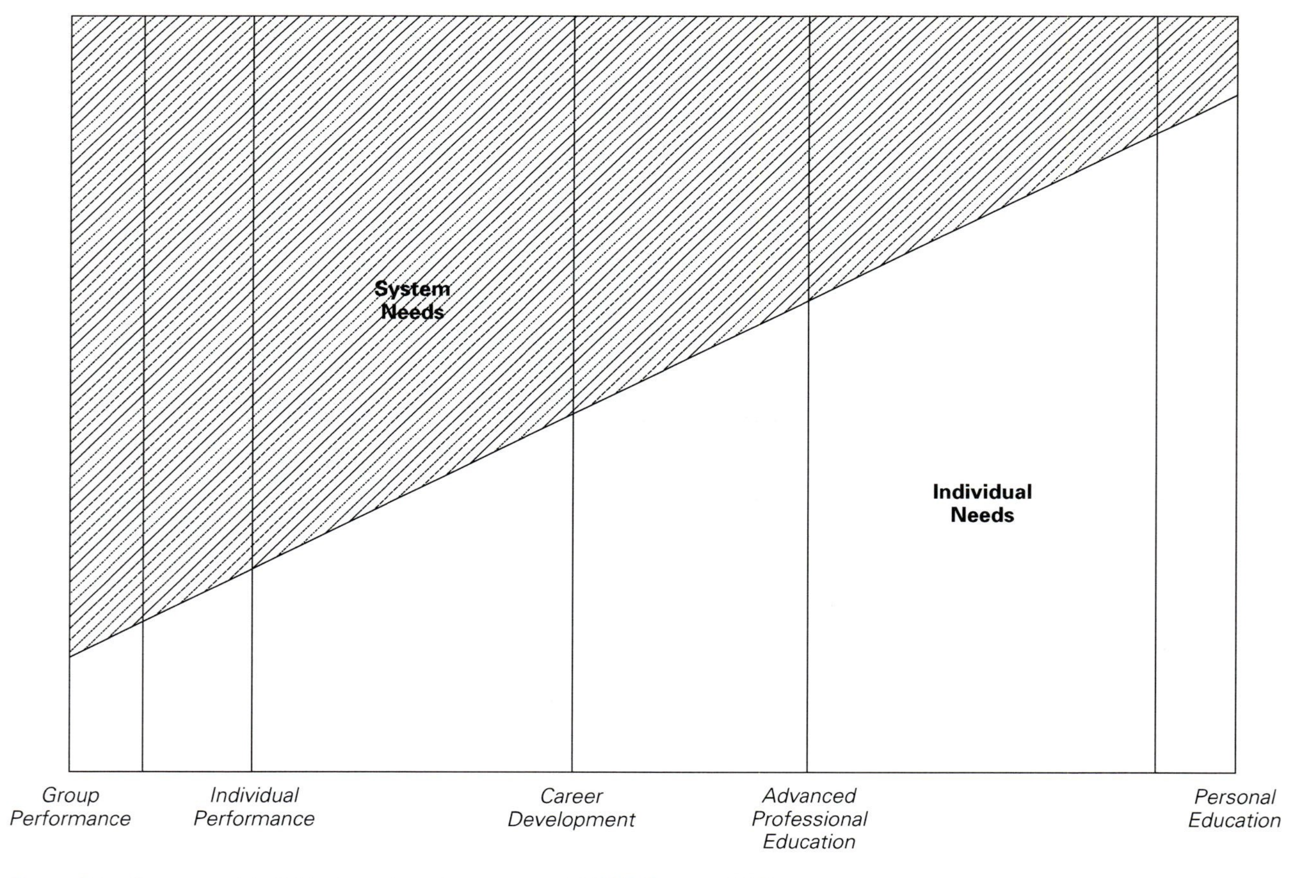

Figure 7.1 *System and individual needs and purposes of INSET* (Bolam, 1986)

If INSET activity is about the promotion of reflection for the purpose of individual and/or systemic change, it is important that purposes are clearly formulated and that processes are informed by adult learning and change theory. Because the intervention is temporary, if the activity is to have a lasting impact its planners must take account of the need, where appropriate, for preparatory and follow-up work so that the learning experience may 'map on' to the histories and futures of the natural learning lives and working environments of the participants, to their personal development plans and those of the school. INSET effects are most likely to be sustained when they can be adapted to and supported by local classroom and school contexts (McLaughlin, 1993). However, since it is only one of a number of learning strategies used by teachers and schools, direct cause and effect relationships between INSET, change and effectiveness must be regarded as problematic — macro-, meso- and micro-level contexts will inevitably complicate matters, as will the quality of the INSET activities themselves. For example, although the general purposes of all INSET will be to contribute to efforts to enhance classroom teaching, and through this to provide the best possible opportunities for learning and achievement by all students, not all INSET will focus directly upon classrooms themselves. To do so would be to oversimplify teachers' work. It follows that all INSET will not necessarily directly or appropriately result in observable change in the classroom. Indeed, there are inherent difficulties in separating out the influence of INSET from other pressures for change in the classroom.

> Those who fund INSET can appreciate that the path from new idea to classroom goes via a sequence of awareness, learning, ownership and application, and that a premature desire to evaluate classroom outcomes inevitably means that essential intermediate stages of INSET will be judged to have failed when that may not necessarily be true. (Steadman et al., 1995, p. 75)

Teachers present at INSET events must: i) acquire the intended knowledge, skills and attitudes; ii) incorporate them into practice; iii) in ways which influence students' learning and achievement; and iv) possibly influence other teachers in their school (Eraut, Pennycuick and Radnor, 1987). Yet teachers' and students' own dispositions and learning agendas may not match those of policy-makers and INSET leaders. Nevertheless, there is evidence that INSET can and does exercise powerful effects on the thinking and practices of teachers and thus, indirectly, upon the quality of students' classroom learning experiences.

This is the case especially where INSET is able to focus upon their particular development needs, and those of the school. The interaction between these is, however, more complex than is often recognized by INSET providers. National, district and school development needs must be routinely addressed in order to meet necessary change imperatives and learning and achievement expectations and standards. However, where INSET does not take account of the development phases of teachers, their core moral purposes and intellectual and emotional development needs, it is unlikely to enhance their capacity for skilled commitment over the longer period. Classroom and school improvement efforts are thus likely to be diminished.

Two further descriptions of purposes provide different but complementary perspectives. The first focuses upon the 'fundamental' purposes of staff development — emphasizing the teacher as a person. According to this view, INSET should:

- make people feel valued in the job they do;
- enable them to do this job well so that they receive the positive feedback essential for job satisfaction and for motivation;
- encourage them to derive excitement and satisfaction from their involvement in change;
- make them feel willing and competent to contribute constructively to the development of the school. (Bradley, 1991, p. 2)

From this perspective, maintaining and building self-efficacy, motivation, commitment, enthusiasm and cultures of professional care are central to the conceptualization and planning of INSET. In the second description, 10 purposes of professional development which may be applied to INSET are identified. These purposes account for the moral, social and instrumental responsibilities of teachers. They recognize the need for lifelong learning in a world which will continue to change, and they imply that schools themselves have a significant part to play in providing formal as well as informal opportunities for continuing teacher development.

1. Continuing development and adaptation of the teachers' subject matter and pedagogical repertoires:
   matched to novice-expert phase of teaching development.
2. Ongoing learning from experience, reflection, and theorizing about how best to meet individual and collective needs of the students:
   matched to level of reflection.
3. Ongoing learning through mutual observation and discussion with colleagues:
   matched to change needs of disclosure, feedback and collaboration with peers.
4. Continuing development of the capacity to contribute to the professional life-cycle of the school, e.g. through policy-making, internal reviews, management roles:
   matched to contribution to the wider professional community of learners.
5. Continuing development of the capacity to interact with clients and stakeholders, both as a class teacher or form tutor and on behalf of the school as a whole:
   matched to building partnerships with other stakeholders.
6. Continuing proficiency in relevant, up-to-date subject matter and continuing development of ways to make it accessible to students:
   matched to subject knowledge change needs.
7. Ongoing collection of evidence about policies and practices in other schools:
   matched to networking needs.

8 Ongoing access to new educational thinking relevant to improving the quality of the school:
matched to intellectual development needs.
9 Continuing acquisition of relevant knowledge about one's changing society, both to support good communication with students and other stakeholders and as a basis for reviewing curriculum priorities:
matched to lifelong learning needs.
10 The need to gather intelligence about and later implement the decisions of external policy makers who have jurisdiction over the school:
matched to contractual accountability needs.

(based on Eraut, 1995, in Guskey and Huberman, 1995, pp. 245–6)

School-provided INSET

In recent years there has been a move towards school-based, school-focused, school-initiated school-provided INSET, largely for two reasons. First, it appears to cost less and be a more efficient way of addressing practical school matters of immediate relevance; and second, it appears to devolve responsibility for decision-making closer to the focus for decision implementation — the school and the classroom. It does, therefore, seem to avoid problems of match, relevance, knowledge transfer and utilization encountered in more traditional off-site models of in-service work with teachers. The school-provided models which tend also to be school-based, have their critics. They can lead to insularity and 'parochialism' (Henderson and Perry, 1981; Helsby and Knight, 1997) and inhibit possibilities for critical reflection (Bullough and Gitlin, 1994). In the early 1990s, a government commissioned report in England pointed to the dangers in exclusively school-based models of 'recycling mediocrity' (Alexander, Rose and Woodhead, 1992).

School-provided models of professional development may come to be seen as compensatory if they focus predominantly upon teachers' responsibility for improving instruction but give little or no attention to organizational or social factors influencing their instruction and the curriculum. This is likely to promote a more limited conception of teaching and being a teacher than has hitherto been the case. If school-provided professional development (led by the imperatives of implementing policy) remains the only route to professional development for most teachers, opportunities for teachers to extend their professionality will be constrained. Thus, the seductive discourse of practicality — where this is interpreted as meaning that only that which is able to be translated into practice is valuable or legitimate — is ultimately a limit on the creative development of teacher education practice. Writing about in-service education in schools in Queensland, Australia, Sachs and Logan (1990) claimed that in-service education 'which is predominantly concerned with practicality tends to result in the unintended outcomes of controlling and deskilling teachers' (p. 474). Indeed, concepts of practicality and relevance, they suggested, 'contribute to the development of instrumentalist ideologies which emphasize a technical approach by both providers and consumers of inservice education'

(p. 477). The emphasis upon teachers' experiential knowledge and immediate needs reinforces the view that teachers need only to know how to manage teaching and that, by implication, understanding its broader purposes and contexts is less important.

> Rather than developing reflective practitioners who are able to understand, challenge and transform their practice, in-service education in its current form encourages the development of teachers who see their world in terms of instrumental ends achievable through the recipes of 'tried and true' practices legitimated by unexamined experience or uncritically accepted research findings. (Sachs and Logan, 1990, p. 479)

Quality and level are also key issues in relationship to the costly school-based training 'professional development' days which are compulsory in England and common in many other countries. In England, Cowan and Wright (1990) surveyed the use of 110 of these and found a lack of coherence and continuity, lack of follow through, and an expressed feeling of cynicism, frustration and dissatisfaction among teachers. More recently Newton and Newton (1994) conducted a similar survey in 99 primary and 94 secondary schools from five local education authorities. They found that most primary school events were concerned with an awareness-raising information-giving, related to preparation for classroom teaching. They were characterized by immediacy and largely determined by current events.

In a survey of 2000 secondary school teachers in local education authorities (School Districts) in the UK between 1991 and 1993, 'fewer than one in three believed that the system of professional development had improved or that the organisation of INSET within the institution was working well' (Helsby and Knight, 1997, p. 151). Though closer analysis revealed that senior managers were more positive than teachers on the main professional grade, this was accompanied by evidence that these same senior managers had greater access to local education authority support for their own INSET. The survey confirmed that: 'access to INSET courses appeared to be governed by the availability of funding, school priorities and therefore teachers' relative position in the hierarchy' (Helsby and Knight, 1997, p. 153).

Research published by the NFER in England, based upon a national survey and follow-up work in primary and secondary schools in five local education authorities, provided empirical evidence of the lack of appropriate infrastructures for the effective continuing professional development of teachers. Its authors reported that the lack of a national policy or framework was an impediment to the necessary long-term planning of teacher education, and referred to 'un-met training needs which are increasingly emerging in this era of school-managed INSET' (Harland, Kinder and Keys, 1993, p. iv). This is reflected in most other countries in the world. Even where national policy frameworks are being developed they represent a narrow managerial perspective and so are likely to be adequate for the broader career-long learning needs of most teachers only to the extent that they complement other components. They may: i) cultivate emotional commitment to externally mandated changes at the expense of rational deliberation and critique about their worth and applicability (Hartley 1986); and ii) provide a metaphor of teaching as essentially an exercise needing only subject mastery and technical competence which can be updated and upgraded through regular bursts of short training events. Furthermore, the assimilation of subject-matter knowledge by means of awareness-raising, information-giving INSET fails to address problems of *transfer* into practice. New knowledge often requires considerable internalization and reprocessing, and may imply changes in teaching approaches for which there has been no planned preparation.

Effectiveness

> Change in the classroom which involves more than extending the repertoire by acquiring new skills will mean changing attitudes, beliefs and personal theories; and reconstructing a personal approach to teaching. INSET therefore needs to provide new experiences, support the anxieties which accompany not just the threat but the genuine difficulties of change, and give people time to reflect, work things out and think things through. (Steadman et al., 1995, p. 49)

All teachers have development needs which relate to the relationships between age, experience, expertise and commitment on the one hand, and to their continuing ability to exercise emotional intelligence in teaching situations and school cultures which demand the use of discretionary judgment and pedagogical tact on the other. A major issue, then, when planning INSET is how it contributes to the development of these abilities. Most INSET is of limited duration because centralized control of funding and content agendas for INSET, both locally and nationally, have restricted opportunities for attention to broader, equally significant agendas of personal and professional development (Gilroy and Day, 1993; Evans and Penney, 1994). This has resulted, for some, in a hierarchical needs analysis model of INSET (Hartley, 1989), which draws simple and inaccurate 'cause and effect' relationships between INSET, improved workplace performance and enhanced student achievement.

Teachers' professional development will be restricted rather than extended and fragmentary rather than coherent whilst the breadth of their learning needs continues to be ignored; and professional learning will come to be associated not with capacity building for the use of insightful judgment exercised in complex situations, but with one-shot events specifically targeted at immediate technically defined implementation needs as determined by others. In America, a two-year study of professional development investigated what constitutes 'high quality' professional development through interviews with 1000 teachers and teacher leaders, members of the public and educational researchers (NFIE, 1996). The analysis concluded that, if it is to be effective, professional development cannot be viewed as a programme of activities separate from the job of teaching. In England, Kinder, Harland and Wootten (1991) conducted a longitudinal study which examined the impact of various INSET activities, many of which were school-based, on the practice of teachers in primary schools over a 3–4 year period. *Impact on practice* refers to an explicit intention in the INSET activity to bring about classroom change through new teaching behaviour, e.g. supporting the transfer of new skills into the teachers' repertoires (Harland and Kinder, 1997). From their observations they derived a 'typology' of outcomes[2]:

1. *Material and provisionary.* This refers to new or revised physical resources which result from participation in INSET, e.g. worksheets, handbooks, which can but not necessarily will influence classroom practice. In order for practice to be influenced it may be that other processes are necessary in order for appropriate skills of application to be acquired — hence the use of 'provisionary'.
2. *Informational outcomes.* This refers to the acquisition of 'background' or 'extended' knowledge of developments rather than new knowledge or skills.
3. *New awareness.* This refers to 'a perceptual or conceptual shift from previous assumptions' and, as with 1 and 2 above will not necessarily lead to changes in practice.
4. *Value congruence.* This refers to the extent to which individual practitioners' versions of good practice coincide with those of the INSET providers.
5. *Affective outcomes.* This refers to increases in self-efficacy and confidence so necessary where there is a need to apply new knowledge or skills into practice.
6. *Motivational and attitudinal outcomes.* Similar to 5 above, this refers to enhanced enthusiasm and motivation which results from INSET activities, a necessary precondition to developments in thinking and practice.
7. *Knowledge and skill* refers to a deeper understanding of and critical reflexivity to curriculum content and pedagogy. However, the authors recognize a need to distinguish between the various forms of knowledge in assessing outcomes (Eraut, 1993)[3].
8. *Institutional outcomes* refers to the collective impact on groups of teachers and their practice.

Harland and Kinder found that 'value congruence' which was consistently perceived as coinciding with strength of impact upon practice played a significant role in determining outcomes. This refers to the 'fit' between the underlying educational values being promoted through the INSET activity and those of the participating teachers. Where there is 'fit' or where existing beliefs are altered, then, Harland and Kinder hypothesized, there is an increased likelihood of impact on thinking and practice. It should be noted, however, that just as value dissonance can lead to confrontation and no change, so value congruence can lead to comfortable collaboration. Learning in both situations may thus be limited.

Harland and Kinder's (1997) work provides a useful embryonic elaboration of a range of outcomes and underlines the case for identifying needs and designing CPD experiences from an individual's learning perspective rather than global prescriptions of systemic needs and forms of provision. It relates to and elaborates upon the classic craft-oriented approach of Joyce and Showers in America. Like Harland and Kinder, they were particularly concerned with the impact of INSET upon classroom practice. In developing a training-outcomes model they effectively extended the definition of INSET from that which is achieved only by attending courses provided by others (usually from outside the school and classroom) to that which is achieved by working alongside colleagues in programmes designed to meet specific needs over an extended period of time. Their model claims to focus, then, upon the most effective means of achieving classroom change (see Figure 7.2). Hopkins (1989, p. 88) represented their ideas in the form of a matrix which has been adapted further:

Level of Impact	**General awareness of new skills**	**Organized knowledge of underlying concepts and theory**	**Learning of new skills**	**Application on the job**
Training method Presentation/ description (e.g. lecture) of new skills	✔	✔		
Modelling the new skills (e.g. live or video demonstrations)	-------→	✔		
Practice in simulated settings	-------→	-------→	✔	
Feedback on performance in simulated or real settings	-------→	-------→	✔	✔
Coaching/ assistance on the job	-------→	-------→	-------→	✔

(adapted from Joyce and Showers, 1980, in Steadman et al., 1995, p. 44)

Figure 7.2 Learning new teaching skills (Joyce and Showers, 1980)

Potential outcomes are:

1. Knowledge or awareness of educational theories and practices, new curriculum, or academic content;
2. Changes in attitudes towards self (role perception changes), children (minorities, handicapped, gifted) and academic content;
3. Development of staff (the ability to perform discrete behaviours such as designing and delivering questions of various cognitive levels or the ability to perform clusters of skills in specific patterns as in a synectics exercise);

4 Transfer of training and 'executive control' (the consistent and appropriate use of new skills and strategies for classroom instruction). (Joyce and Showers, 1988, p. 68)

Their argument that the most effective training is that which provides for a combination of presentation, modelling, practice, feedback and coaching is compelling. In particular, the matrix suggests that the problem of transfer of knowledge and skills to the classroom context can be solved by practice, feedback and coaching components. They conclude from their examination of the research on training that:

- First, regardless of who initiates a training programme, participants must have sufficient opportunity to develop skills that they can eventually practice in classroom settings.
- Second, if the content of training is new to trainees, training will have to be more extensive than for substance that is relatively familiar.
- Third, if transfer of training is the training objective, follow-up such as coaching in the workplace will probably be necessary. (Joyce and Showers, 1988, p. 72)

There are five valuable lessons here for those whose responsibility it is to promote teacher development: i) any comprehensive programme must attend to the classroom application of understandings, knowledge and skills — a simplistic 'learn-apply' model does not work; ii) feedback and ongoing coaching are essential components in the process of transfer; iii) the disposition towards and commitment to learning must be present in the teacher as lifelong learner; iv) the organizational culture must be supportive of collegial relationships (opportunities to learn through peer coaching and feedback require a school culture which facilitates ongoing collegial relationships and strong leadership, 'manifested in priority setting, resource allocation, and the logistics of scheduling on the one hand and substantive and social leadership on the other', (Joyce and Showers, 1988)), p. 91; and v) resources must be targeted at long-term development, taking into account a balanced portfolio of learning needs.

It is easy to trace the influence of this model on the strategies for growth employed in school improvement networks which utilize external and internal learning modes provided through a mix of extended temporary external interventions and self-generated internal collaborative activity. However, Joyce and Showers' hypothesis that fully elaborated training systems develop metacognitions (learning to learn) attitudes (1988, p. 72) is not easy to sustain in the face of knowledge about the limitations of practice settings and of single loop learning. The matrix has been criticized on the grounds that: i) the components themselves provide a limited range of inputs; ii) the outcomes are limited (Robertson, 1992); iii) it does not appear to require teachers to engage in reflection (Logan and Sachs, 1991); and iv) it is expensive (Steadman et al., 1995). Furthermore, undue emphasis upon skills training at the expense of other developmental needs is further likely to fuel anxieties that teaching is becoming regarded primarily as a technical activity.

> The training-and-coaching strategy that dominates local professional development has much to recommend it when considered as a balanced part of a larger configuration, and when linked to those aspects of teaching that are properly rendered as transferable skills. But the training model is problematic. The content of much training communicates a view of teaching and learning that is at odds with present reform initiatives . . . Nor is the content of training set against the content of local belief, practice, and policy in any meaningful and detailed way. In addition, principles of good training are frequently compromised in practice. In particular, schools and districts demonstrate far less capacity for classroom consultation and support than is required by the training and coaching model. Those persons typically designated as coaches or mentors are far outnumbered by their clientele of regular classroom teachers. They are further constrained by school workplace cultures that perpetuate a norm of privacy and constrain advice-giving. Finally, to attain results from the training/coaching model requires a consistency of purpose and a co-ordination of effort that is not the norm in many districts. Rather, districts parade a litany of short-term goals in their response to various state mandates and incentives, local constituencies, or the individual enthusiasm of superintendents, school board members, or others. (Little, 1993, p. 144)

The Contribution of Higher Education

One of the few longitudinal empirical studies into the professional culture of teachers and the secondary school curriculum in England, found that most teachers interviewed accepted the new constraints upon their autonomy but described their work as requiring,

> . . . 'higher education-based entry qualifications . . . specialist knowledge . . . exercise of non-routine judgement . . . a service ethic and a commitment to doing the job properly as opposed to fixed working hours . . . [suggesting] an occupation that, in its complexity and emphasis on individual, informed, non-routine decision-making, requires professional learning and not simply technical training. (Helsby and Knight, 1997, p. 147)

At first sight, it would appear that higher education institutions are better able to offer those professional development opportunities which are oriented towards education than are schools — enmeshed as they are in school-provided efforts — despite the obvious limitations of psychological, social and geographic distance. However, higher education in-service courses have been criticized in the past for their apparent lack of relevance to school needs, their elitism (relatively few can take advantage) and the inaccessibility of the research knowledge base (seen to be held by expert guardians far removed from the reality of schools and children). Even now, little is known about their long-term effects upon the students or their institutions; and schools themselves do not always use their returning teachers well, preferring instead to relocate them in their previous roles.

Three assessments of the long-term effectiveness of award-bearing courses in England provide some comfort for higher education providers. The first found that

28 per cent of the comments from headteachers noted an improved motivation of staff who had attended, and 80 per cent of heads, LEAs and students valued long award-bearing courses for the increased professional confidence and competence gained by participants. However, in terms of relevance to school needs, school-focused INSET was the most highly ranked (Triggs and Francis, 1990). A project commissioned by the Department for Education provided evidence that this form of development had been valuable in terms of impact upon career development (including promotion), leadership skills, and classroom practice, although it was also found that employers rarely systematically used the new knowledge, understandings and skills gained (Bradley and Howard, 1992). A third study confirmed the findings of the first two, and concluded that although effects of these kinds of courses may not be immediately quantifiable, 'their long term consequences for the confidence and professionalism of teachers make them a worthwhile investment for the education service . . . INSET designed to promote reflection, insight, and confidence is of value to the system because of its effects on the quality of the teaching force' (Cope et al., 1992, p. 307).

Teachers' Preferences

An American study conducted in 1996 by the National Foundation for the Improvement of Education found that of the teachers surveyed, the main motivations for growing as professionals were to improve student achievement (73 per cent); to improve teaching skills (55 per cent); to increase knowledge (34 per cent); to meet people who share professional interests (9 per cent); career advancement (7 per cent); to maintain professional certification (5 per cent); and to earn more (5 per cent). One of the key recommendations was: 'finding time to build professional development into the life of the school through flexible scheduling and extended blocks of time when students are on vacation' (Rényi, 1998, p. 71).

When teachers in England were asked about their professional learning preferences, including INSET (Harland and Kinder, 1997) their responses, too, pointed to i) the need for *time* to meet with colleagues from their own and other schools to discuss current issues and concerns; ii) to engage in curriculum development workshops which embodied the 'practicality ethic' (Doyle and Ponder, 1977); and iii) to learn from outside speakers and 'provider led' higher education programmes. By far the greatest influences on their professional development, however, were their own experience, beliefs and convictions and those of their colleagues.

Helsby and Knight's (1997) research in England confirms that, 'focusing on INSET as if it were the heart of professional development flies in the face of these teachers' reflections on their own learning' (p. 159) and that, therefore, professional development should be conceptualized as a much more wide-ranging, complicated process. However, it does not follow that all INSET is necessarily ineffective. For example, a small-scale qualitative research project which evaluated the effectiveness of short and more extensive INSET activities found that many were judged to be successful, that teachers used common core criteria for judging their quality, but that extended INSET met more long-term growth needs (Day, 1993c). Successful activities met teachers' expectations for:

- *Targeting needs* They were focused upon needs specific to the particular age range taught, i.e. relevant.
- *Content needs* They increased knowledge/awareness, reinforcing and reassuring current thinking but encouraging participants to see issues from different perspectives.
- *Utilization needs* They provided direct curriculum development benefits and application to classroom practice.

Three expectations in particular are worth elaborating further:

- *Process needs* Successful courses presented a balance of activities which were well-structured, involved working with colleagues and sharing experience.

In short, the teaching and learning processes should model good classroom practice. Even those INSET events which are targeted on a particular subject, year or phase group of teachers or on specific content or pedagogical skill acquisition will not necessarily engage them. As in classrooms, the teaching and learning processes will almost inevitably at any given moment actively engage only a proportion of the class. There are differences between class teaching and 'one shot' in-service events, however. Whereas in the former continuity, progression, differentiation and balance may be achieved over time, in the latter there is only one chance of success. If they are well planned and well led, short-term INSET activities can map on to individual professional and system learning needs where they are congruent, whether by accident or design, with the values of the participants, match the career, life-cycle and intellectual, knowledge or skill development needs of teachers at critical stages of their lives.

- *Leadership/Modelling needs* Successful courses were led by tutors who were well-prepared, enthusiastic, caring and aware of group dynamics.

Effective leadership is vital. In Australia, Logan and Sachs (1991) identified '*credible leadership*' as being a significant characteristic of successful in-service leaders. They found that:

> . . . credibility appeared to depend not on a person's assigned position but on his or her ability to make a worthwhile contribution in the eyes of the participants to achieving the task in hand . . . such people have . . . a sensitivity of the implications for each member in his or her school; a repertoire of instructional, interpersonal and group process skills; and management expertise. (p. 307)

These findings echo those of teachers in England reported in this chapter and those of successful in-service leaders in North America (Fullan, 1982; Joyce and Showers, 1988).

- *Time and energy needs*

A large part of the INSET budgets in the schools studied (Day, 1993a) was spent on providing supply cover for teachers to be released from their classrooms. Not all teachers released attended courses. Indeed, they engaged in a variety of activities: e.g. sharing a day's course with other schools; visiting other 'good practice' classrooms and schools; taking time out with a colleague to write policy documents; planning curriculum implementation. The most widely appreciated benefit, however, was the time to get away from the business of classroom life, to reflect 'on' as well as 'in' the action when energy levels were high:

> It's given us a breathing space . . . to stand back, reflect, think things out.
>
> It's very good that you can actually work in school without the children . . . However long you stay after school, an hour isn't long enough.
>
> The use of our own funding has given us the opportunity to spend time on certain elements of the curriculum in a shorter period of time than otherwise we'd be able to.

Hargreaves, writes of time as, 'the enemy of freedom . . . Time presses down the fulfilment of their wishes. It pushes against the realisation of their wants. Time compounds the problem of innovation and confounds the implementation of change. It is central to the formation of teachers' work' (Hargreaves, A. 1994, p. 95). He regards the use of the terms 'directed time', 'release time' and 'non-contact time' to describe time allocated contractually or by local managers for the purpose of planning or collaborative work (as embedded, for example, in reforms in Norway, England and Australia) as symbolic indicators of the 'expansion of bureaucratic control and standardisation in the development and delivery of their services' (p. 113). Clearly, where there is no consultation or choice, there is unlikely to be unbridled enthusiasm on the part of teachers to engage in mandated learning of which INSET is one part in contrived circumstances. So whilst the provision of time is necessary for INSET learning opportunities, it is not in itself sufficient to ensure that teachers will be motivated to learn.

These findings were reinforced by later research into INSET effectiveness in which common ingredients of successful INSET were found to be:

- inspiration — the sharing of visions of what is possible;
- exposition — the presentation of new content and ideas;
- discussion and other activities to advance conceptual understanding;
- opportunities for cross-reference of standards — judging one's own position in relation to others;
- training in new skills;
- opportunities to experiment, try out new approaches and generate teaching materials; and
- coaching from advisory teachers and/or colleagues. (Steadman et al., 1995, p. 28)

Teachers reported more complex learning needs which short staff development opportunities do not meet, but which are essential to long-term growth. They spoke through their learning biographies and interviews of the planned learning experiences which had been most significant for their development. One teacher wrote of the learning which resulted from attendance at a two-year part-time university postgraduate course:

> It challenged my attitudes and ideas subtly over two years . . . my practice used to be very product based . . . but now I can understand the child's work more and value it for what it is . . . you get to a stage when you need to have your attitudes educated . . . have opportunities to clarify your thinking . . . not carry on doing the same old thing every day.

A second teacher attending a part-time university course had been 'transformed as a teacher', and was 'more able to support the needs of the children'. Another spoke of a part-time non-accredited extended course which had been:

> . . . the start of my professional development . . . that opened my eyes. I learned to look outside the classroom, how things were affecting the work inside the classroom . . . management . . . how schools are run . . . and how the staff develop as a staff . . . timing was quite critical.

Yet another had found that attendance at an intensive three-day residential course had 'transformed me as a teacher, opened up new ideas, ways forward, working with staff.'

In addition to the needs met by short burst activities, these longer, more reflective and analytical in-depth learning opportunities had provided:

- *Critical friendship* in-depth opportunities for sharing and building knowledge and skills over time in a supportive but challenging environment.
- *'Vision' needs.* Participants had been enabled to relate their experience of practice to theory, to reconsider critically their assumption, predispositions, and values (the 'why' as well as the 'how' and 'what' of teaching), and the contexts in which they taught.
- *Skill development needs.* They were able to develop new skills over time.
- *Intellectual needs.* They were able to engage in systematic reading which, 'otherwise I wouldn't do'.
- *Personal needs* to build self-esteem, 'so important in these days when we're continuously being battered from all sides as regards our skills as professionals.

Concentration of finance and effort on short professional learning opportunities which predominantly focus upon institutionally defined needs may well, in the long term, result in cultural *isolation* and *parochialism.*

> It's giving you a narrow view . . . so I feel that it's going to be detrimental to your own development and that of the children.

Whilst teachers understood and were sympathetic to the need to respond to national initiatives in the short-term, many were concerned that their longer-term needs were being 'squeezed out'.

Conclusion

In-service education is a necessary and potentially powerful part of the continuing professional development of teachers. Most classroom learning involves reflection-in-action, an unconscious, routinized, intense, solution-oriented form of learning which, as we have seen, is ultimately limiting to teacher development. Opportunities to reflect on curriculum implementation and teaching skills tend to be available as part of the cycle of planning and evaluating teaching or in the introduction and implementation of new initiatives which are supported as part of school development. However, opportunities to reflect more widely and more deeply on purposes and practices are rare. Alongside the process of making theories that are embedded in practice explicit, the experiences of other practitioners and theoretical knowledge are important contributors to the development of the teacher. Both longer, extended accredited programmes and the short in-service courses have important contributions to make to teachers' intellectual and emotional capacities to provide high quality teaching. However, INSET's limitations and strengths need to be recognized, and related to purposes, processes and intended impact on practice.

The perception among teachers of a theory–practice divide, with experience of the former being of less relevance or use than the latter, is not always easy to dislodge. It is part of the history of becoming a teacher that 'theory' taught in universities and colleges is of limited value and cannot easily be applied to the practicalities of classroom organization and management, particularly in the 'busyness' cultures of classrooms and schools which demand 'learning to handle cases quickly and efficiently . . . by reducing (rather than extending) the range of possible ways of thinking about them to manageable proportions' (Eraut, 1994, p. 43).

There is unequivocal evidence, however, that teachers who have emerged from the 'novice' phase, do seek and benefit from broader perspectives on their work. Over a career, then, teachers should have opportunities for the creation and development of professional knowledge that includes 'unsystematized' personal experience, knowledge derived from practice settings, and propositional knowledge. Whilst exposure to propositional knowledge is not exclusive to INSET, it may be seen as a legitimate complement and contributor to the growth of practical knowledge with the proviso that 'to make practical use of concepts and ideas other than those embedded in well-established professional traditions requires intellectual effort and an encouraging work-context' (Eraut, 1994, p. 49).

Evidence from teachers themselves does not suggest a desire to return to the 'old days' when, for the most part, professional development was an individual's affair. Devolved finance does not in itself prevent management support for teachers' attendance at extended courses outside school. However, the pressure is likely to remain on many schools to encourage staff to engage in on-site activities which are self-generated and self-serviced and which thus implicitly discourage teachers from moving to deeper levels of development. Thus those who are looking for something more extensive or more intensive, may become increasingly frustrated and disenchanted. In the long term, this potential lack of investment in INSET as a key means of supporting professional development needs of staff at critical phases in their career, and their development as learners, may prove to have a negative effect upon the maintenance and enhancement of their motivation, experience, knowledge, and classroom practice. It is thus likely to hinder rather than help improvement efforts. This and previous chapters have, however, identified many ways in which INSET might be used as part of a range of opportunities in support of teacher and school development. The next two chapters provide further examples in the form of partnerships and networks for learning and improvement.

Notes

1 For a detailed consideration and critique of the 'defect' and 'growth' approaches, see Eraut (1987).
2 This typology has been used subsequently as a planning and evaluation tool (Kinder et al., 1991; Dormer and Foster, 1995; Lubben et al., 1995).
3 For a detailed analysis see Eraut, 1994, Chapter 3.

Chapter 8

Learning through Partnerships

This chapter focuses upon partnerships in which teachers and tutors from higher education institutions work together. (The term 'universities' will be used to encompass the range of higher education.) They are particularly suited to collaboration since both are in the business of knowledge creation. Though the historically generated divide and alienation between 'scholars' and 'practitioners' who work in very different cultures and respond to different demands has been well documented (Day, 1991; Cuban, 1992; Lieberman; 1992) there are increasing numbers of successful partnerships at pre-service and in-service levels, particularly those aimed at enhancing the knowledge creation capacities of individuals and professional communities.

In simple terms, a partnership is 'the relation which subsists between persons carrying on a business in common with a view to profit' (Partnership Act, 1890). In other words, partnerships are usually formed because each of the partners has something to offer to the joint enterprise which is different from but complements that which is offered by the other partners. There are, of course, different kinds or forms of partnership. In law, for example, there are 'senior' and 'junior' partners. In some businesses there are 'silent' partners; and in all fields there are partnerships based upon equality or principles of equity. Partnerships may be 'developmental' (responsive and evolutionary) or 'implementational' (imposed, formal, mechanistic and with a specific brief and limited timespan for action) (Biott, 1991). Developmental partnerships will often begin with the cultures of 'contrived collegiality' typical of implementational partnerships, but they have a greater learning potential because the ownership of the theme and process is controlled by the participants themselves. These extended partnerships, often called 'Networks' or 'Consortia' which recognize the advantages of involving schools, universities, LEAs and other stakeholders in collaborative work over time will be discussed in Chapter 9.

Partnerships between individual university tutors and schoolteachers are not new. Many teacher educators have their roots in schools and most teachers have been trained in universities. There is, therefore, an affinity of moral purpose and complementarity of practice (Day, 1997a). Paradoxically, this is sometimes accompanied by schoolteachers' scepticism about the perceived theory-bound esoteric world of the academic which contrasts with the practice-bound action worlds in which they work. However, the nature of 'partnership' has been changing over the last 30 years, partly as a direct result of educational reforms which have altered the balance of knowledge power: the usefulness, rigour and relevance of university research has been called into question and universities have been forced to compete for custom as their own standards of research and teaching have come under close finance-led, ideologically determined public scrutiny.

There are many examples of individual collaborations in response to research- and practice-led initiatives. The worldwide action research movement, which essentially embodies teacher–school–university partnerships for improvement, was born formally in England in 1978 through the foundation of the Classroom (now Collaborative) Action Research Network. In 1993, it launched the *International Journal of Educational Action Research.* A look through its pages demonstrates the considerable partnership activities between universities, schoolteachers and other professions. Examples of school–university partnerships may also be found in Australia (Sachs, 1997), America (Hollingsworth, 1997), Canada (Fullan, 1992), England (Day, 1985) and The Netherlands (Jansen, Reehorst and Delhaas, 1995), with individual teachers, departments, schools and consortia of schools. Partnerships of the past have usually been located in:

1. supervisory/monitoring relationships between tutors and teachers in pre-service programmes;
2. 'provider led' relationships between teachers and universities in which the latter offer a range of modularized award- and non-award-bearing in-service teacher development programmes — although negotiated school-focused, and school- and classroom-based projects have often formed a key component;
3. research and development relationships between university tutors and the education community. These may be sub-divided as: (a) pure research in which university scholars alone are deemed to have the technical expertise necessary to generate knowledge about teachers, teaching, learning and schools; (b) applied research in which university scholars lead others in curriculum and staff development projects; and (c) collaborative research in which university researchers work alongside teachers on needs identified by the teacher participants themselves in order to generate 'grounded' knowledge.

Whilst these partnerships represent accurately the functions academics are expected to fulfil by their employers, there has been criticism that much educational research seems to have little direct benefit to the schoolteacher and that many researchers themselves do little to enhance the capacities of teachers to generate knowledge. Michael Eraut presents a compelling case for reconceptualizing the relationship between higher education and the profession:

> The barriers to practice-centred knowledge creation and development . . . are most likely to be overcome if higher education is prepared to extend its role from that of creator and transmitter of generalisable knowledge to that of **enhancing the knowledge creation capacities** of individuals and professional communities. This would involve recognising that much knowledge creation takes place outside the higher education system, but is nevertheless limited by the absence of appropriate support

> structures and the prevailing action-orientation of practical contexts. (Eraut, 1994, p. 57)

He goes on to suggest the need for closer relations and joint responsibilities for knowledge creation, development and dissemination, suggesting collaborative research projects, problem-oriented seminars for groups of researchers and mid-career professionals and jointly planned programmes focusing up reflection on experience and, through this, 'escape' from some of its taken-for-granted features.

Involving others from outside the school is vital to the development of the learning lives of its teachers. One of the options that headteachers and teachers have is to build into their personal and institutional development plans the use of higher education personnel. The advantages of this are that:

- they are not connected to the authority structures or inspection mechanisms of the school;
- they are able to provide knowledge and skills which are complementary to those held by colleagues in schools and LEAs: e.g. knowledge of particular research techniques; access to a variety of research and knowledge perspectives upon, for example, methods of teaching; and knowledge of other schools. Reading, maintaining a broad 'critical' vision of classrooms, schools and schooling are essential parts of their job.

School leaders who care about providing a balanced learning diet for themselves and their staff have worked with higher education tutors and their departments to great effect. In addition to traditional taught post-experience courses, which provide support for the intellectual and vision growth so vital for mid-career teachers, there are many examples of:

- *Limited term development consultancies*, for example, related to preparation for external inspection, areas of school curriculum, teaching and assessment, or team building or appraisal.
- *External audit support*, for example, where the school has identified the need for a 'critical friend' to audit an aspect of school policy, provide an evaluation of the effectiveness of a programme of study, or even the strategies for supporting teachers' professional development.
- *Producing and disseminating research knowledge about education*, for example, about what is known nationally or internationally about whole class teaching strategies and their effects.
- *Generating educational knowledge* in which, for example, a colleague or colleagues from higher education work alongside a teacher or headteacher in order to assist in problem solving or the further development of reflective teaching practices. There are many examples of such collaborative action research work.
- *Building communities of intelligent practice* in which, for example, teachers from different schools or groups work together with education personnel over a period of years on a project which they (perhaps with

their LEA) have chosen as being essential to school development. Higher education personnel often play a number of roles, for example, those of consultants, critical friends, data collectors and analysers with teachers and coordinators (the glue in the system). These can be the richest of partnerships, since they represent *sustained interactivity* (Huberman, 1993b), combining the best of many worlds: the need of teachers and schools to work on agendas relevant to them; the benefits of sharing experience and practice across school environments and cultures; and the advantage of using wider research and knowledge perspectives over time. It is important to note, however, that where they are used predominantly as a means of uncritically implementing externally imposed innovations they limit growth and contribute to the 'technicization' of teaching.

There are costs to partnerships of these kinds, but in general the benefits far outweigh them. When used wisely, with clearly negotiated agendas and agreed ethical frameworks, and when set within long-term personal and institutional planning, they are good investments. Yet those leading change in learning communities, whether in the kind of school-led professional development described in Chapter 6 or in other settings, must ensure that the 'players': a) are convinced of their merits; b) feel a sense of ownership through participation in processes of decision-making; and c) have the intellectual, practical and affective support necessary to change.

The second part of this chapter focuses upon four different kinds of learning partnerships with teachers: (1) client-centred degree programmes; (2) non-accredited in-service programmes; (3) collaborative action research; and (4) partnership consultancy.

Client-centred Degree Programmes

In America, Hugh Sockett (1993) describes 'four primary principles for the governance of Masters level degree programmes designed to build a professional community of reflective practitioners', which he proposes as the core of professional development for mid-career teachers:

1 Practitioners must frame and set the problems.
2 The focus must be on the predicament of the unique case and its susceptibility to change.
3 Tacit knowledge and understanding must be acknowledged and described if possible.
4 Academic–practitioner relationships . . . should be defined as coach–practitioner relationships. (p. 44)

The 'coach' analogy is an interesting one, which Sockett explores a little further:

> For the academic to be a coach does not imply that he or she could do the practical job of teaching children better than the practitioner, for this is not a master–apprenticeship relationship. The coach usually brings experiences, ideas, and insights into a cooperating relationship. (p. 48)

The 'coach' role should not be confused with clinical supervision or monitoring, however, since it is founded, like critical friendship, upon the principle of equity, and is a negotiated relationship between equals.

Examples of good practice with regard to the formation of teaching partnerships for accreditation between higher education and schools for the promotion of lifelong learning and continuing professional education already exist. These provide a number of models on which collaboration for the further development of schemes for the academic assessment and accreditation of school-based learning might be based. They include:

- Direct sponsorship by a school (or group of schools) of a course or course module to address a particular need, e.g. to meet a skill shortage or provide knowledge updating. In this case the higher education institution 'bespokes' the services it provides to meet its clients' expressed needs.
- Leasing arrangements whereby an employer (or a consortium) pays a 'hire charge' to a higher education institution to provide a service from its existing 'product range', e.g. the delivery of a course or course module to company employees at one of its training centres at a time which fits in with business needs.
- Franchising agreements by which a higher education institution allows courses or course modules delivered by further education or tertiary colleges or 'in-house' by a school to be given credit towards one of its qualifications. Under such arrangements the higher education institution monitors the design and delivery of the course and the assessment of the learning outcomes in order to give quality assurance and safeguard the standard of its awards.
- Arrangements for the accreditation of prior experiential learning which may be used as equivalents against parts of award bearing programmes.
- The formation of consortia by higher education institutions and schools in order to make maximum use of the available resources and to ensure the highest quality provision of services at the lowest cost to any individual member.

The learning contracts which are central to the success of such partnerships will be tailored to individual needs, and will differ in their formality. They may be simple or complex, long term or short term, verbal or written. They are, however, essential, for they provide a recognition and reminder that teacher development is not only the responsibility of the teacher.

Non-accredited In-service Programmes

It is possible to plan and teach extended in-service events which focus upon particular needs associated with specific school roles in collaboration with LEAs, and which use a mixture of on- and off-site peer-assisted inquiry-based learning with appropriate conceptual and didactic inputs. An example of one such programme is detailed below.[1] It involved 40 primary school subject leaders from four different local education authorities (school districts) in England. The course was based upon principles of contracting, ownership and a recognition that the most important teaching and learning resource is the teacher him/herself. It extended over a period of ten working days between June and March, and was divided in six related phases:

June	*Phase 1*	Contracting (half-day attended by heads and curriculum leaders)
June–September	*Phase 2*	School based peer-supported classroom observations task (half-day)
September	*Phase 3*	First residential phase (three days)
September–February	*Phase 4*	School-based peer-supported negotiated curriculum development (two-and-a-half days)
March	*Phase 5*	Second residential phase (three days)
June	*Phase 6*	Networking continued (locally negotiated meetings)

The central theme of the course was the role of the subject leader and from this arose three related topics:

- leadership: helping qualities and skills;
- working alongside colleagues in professional and curriculum development in the classroom and in the staffroom;
- observing teachers and children in the classroom.

In addition to the course content work, members were required to undertake pre-course and interphase tasks which would be of practical relevance to their roles and their work in their own schools.

The residential phases and their contents were built around the school-based work and the initial contracting that had taken place. The dominant mode of organization was cross-authority small group work in which participants shared experiences and opinions critically; and 'pairings' of participants in order to provide 'close' support for school-based work. These were complemented by 'expert' inputs on issues related to the management of curriculum and professional development, which the planning group regarded as inseparable, and local authority group networking. This reflected the planners' desire to minimize or avoid problems of knowledge transfer and ownership which are often associated with the more traditional patterns of in-service, while at the same time avoiding the problem of parochialism which is associated with school-based work. The course was, in effect, an extended exercise in consultant-supported, school-focused development. It was designed specifically to enable teachers to reflect systematically on their thinking and practices and to confront these; and to provide active support for them both in their learning processes and in the planning, implementation and evaluation of changes which arose through the school-based developments which, with the learning networks, formed the cental core of the course.

Contract Building, Contract Making

An initial meeting was held which was attended by headteachers and their subject leaders. It provided opportunities for heads to meet and discuss expectations, needs and practices with their peers, and for the curriculum leaders to do the same. It also provided preparation for the first school-based task which involved classroom observations. More important, however, was that it introduced and actively encouraged the notion of contract-making:

1. **with self**, to give the commitment, time and resources in order to fulfil obligations as a profession;
2. **with schools**, to ensure that colleagues in school benefited from the participant's attendance on the course through regular feedback;
3. **with course members**, to agree with colleagues on the course to build trust through willingness to share and receive feedback; and to provide moral, intellectual and practical support as appropriate;
4. **with course organizers**, to attend all sessions; to fulfil written work requirements and to share these within negotiated frameworks of confidentiality; to contribute expertise and experience in small and whole group work;
5. **with LEA**, to ensure that the LEA benefited from the participant's attendance on the course through affirmation/enhancement of my current management practices in school; and to contribute to LEA in-service work where appropriate and through negotiation.

Below is an example of one such agreement reached between Headteacher and subject leader:

Needs of Subject Leader
- to look at the work throughout the school, i.e. aims, objectives, methods and evaluation;
- to involve staff in discussion;
- to develop professionally in order to fulfil the role.

Needs of Headteacher
- to provide on-going stimulus throughout the school as a back-up to basic fundamentals;
- to give staff opportunities to engender enthusiasm and interest in different curricular areas;
- to enable subject leaders to act as leaders and resource persons in these areas;
- to ensure use of all school resources.

Expectations of Subject Leader
- to implement course skills within the framework of the school;
- to be responsible for a specific area;
- to have specific times each week for subject development to take place;

- to provide feedback regularly to both head and staff;
- to liaise with relevant staff.

Expectations of Headteacher

- to provide opportunities for subject leaders to recognize the particular strengths of individual members of staff and to use them for the benefit of both children and staff;
- to emphasize the value of the stimulus created by topic work and a variety of approaches;
- to help the staff as a team to evaluate their work and the effectiveness of their teaching.

Support of Subject Leader

- to gain support and confidence of head and staff;
- to maintain a degree of confidentiality with head;
- to offer ongoing support after the course.

Support of Headteacher

- to ensure that opportunity to use the course experience for the benefit of children and other staff is provided;
- to ensure that a positive attitude to the benefits of the course was engendered at staff meetings;
- to provide opportunities for the subject leader to work in other areas in the school.

Responsibility of Subject Leader

- to the head, staff and children;
- according to the needs of the school, and the task set on the course.

Responsibility of Headteacher

- to the governors so that they would understand the purpose of the course;
- to the Authority that financed it;
- to the children and staff who would reap the benefits.

Constraints on Subject Leader

- lack of clarity about precisely what authority had been delegated;
- a lack of time in which to carry out responsibilities;
- a need for firsthand experience and knowledge of work being done in other areas of the school;
- an awareness of high expectations of other members of staff.

Constraints on Headteacher

- a need for an awareness of the effects on other members of staff who had not had the same opportunity;
- a need to avoid possible conflict by falling in with other people's ideas, if relevant;
- a need to recognize that an invitation to another teacher's classroom is necessary in order to work with any degree of ease;
- a need to show sensitivity in staff relationships.

Staff

- to adopt a positive attitude to members of the course;
- to show courtesy and a helpful attitude which will produce lasting benefits.

Headteacher

- to organize for unexpected emergencies, e.g. if time allotted to subject leader unable to be given;
- to view any criticism as constructive criticism from which benefit will be derived;
- to strive to be just and fair to all parties.

The Residential Phases

The residential phases of the course were intended to build on the contracting phase by providing opportunities for teachers to distance themselves from the classroom in order to reflect on and plan for action in a variety of ways. The curriculum of these phases was in part prescribed (in relation to the advertised content of the course), in part self-generated (through school-based issues) and in part negotiated (through the peer group challenge and support groups which acted as reference points and met throughout the year). Reflection on the learning process was legitimized through the provision of timetabled time for this purpose; and the phases made active use of participants' knowledge and experience and provided inputs which helped in planning and implementing the school-based tasks.

Peer-supported, School-based Research and Development

One course member described a school-based task as follows:

> I feel much relieved after spending half a day with Linda hammering out practicalities of the task. I am very thankful that course organizers have built this kind of 'moral support' in. We now approach the task with a greater degree of confidence . . . We found the time we spent pooling our thoughts really helpful and, we thought, satisfying.
>
> One of the most useful aspects of the course has been the opportunity of working with each other and having another person to bounce ideas off and to give moral support.

The task had been to 'plan and implement or evaluate/monitor a small-scale piece of curriculum development with one or more colleagues in school, including classroom observation'. The task had to take account of the developmental context of the school, but not be dictated by it. It was documented and shared with colleagues during the second residential phase. The emphasis upon school-based work was important, since it underlined the planners' acknowledgment of the 'practicality ethic' of teachers. They believed that course members would value the work if they perceived it as having direct and tangible practical benefits for themselves and their schools whilst also recognizing the added value of reflection and dialogue about the context of the curriculum development. It was recognized, also, that moral and practical support would be necessary, and so this was built into the work through pairing with peers and through network support groups which met regularly.

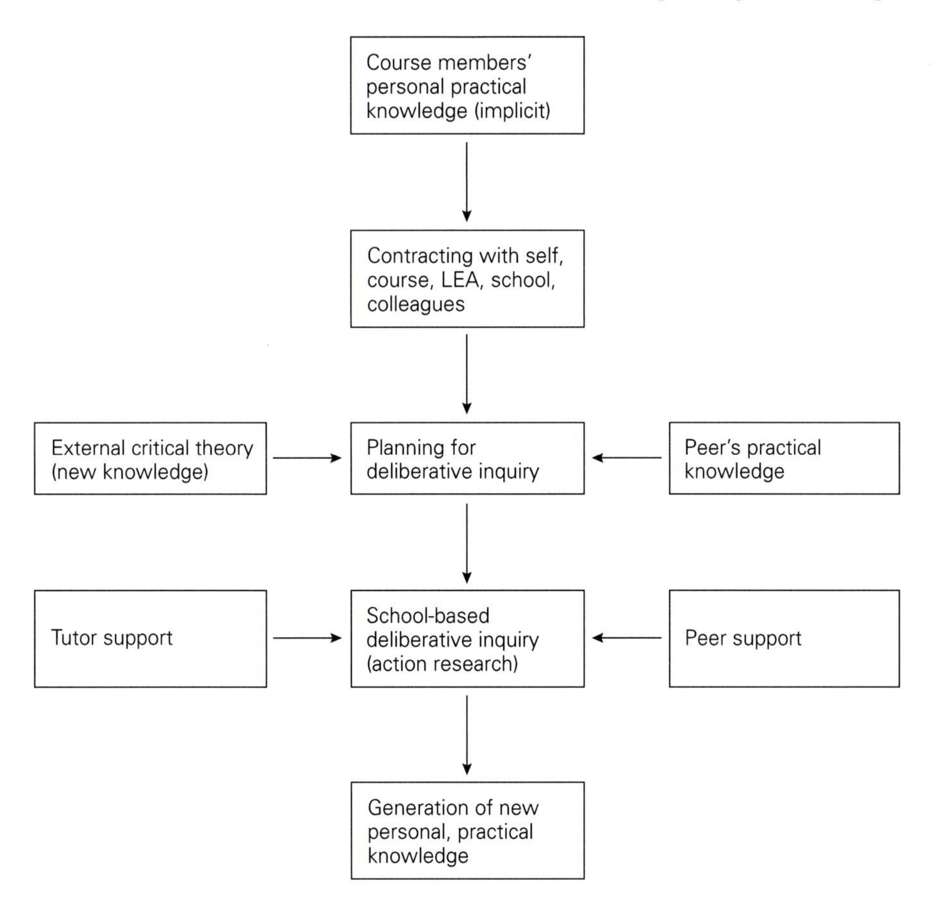

Figure 8.1 An in-service professional development process

Summary

It will be clear, then, that the course was designed specifically to enable teachers to reflect systematically on and confront their thinking and practices; and to provide active support for them both in their learning processes and in the planning, implementation and evaluation of curriculum development in school. This arose through the school-based action research which, with the learning networks, formed the central core of the course. The processes by which this was achieved are represented in Figure 8.1. Deliberative reflection and inquiry, contracting (with self and others), self and peer-confrontation, and the sharing of insights gained from this are essential ingredients in professional learning. Change means the private assumptions and practices must be shared and opened up for questioning by self and scrutiny by others. Therefore, the process of development is unlikely always to be comfortable — even where extensive negotiations have taken place, contracts made and forms of confidentiality ensured. Consciously suspending judgment about one's own work will almost inevitably raise doubts about what under ordinary circumstances appears to be effective or wise practice; and the raising of doubts is only the first in what will be a number of potentially painful steps along the road to change — a road which can littered with obstacles of time, energy, resources and, perhaps most important, self-doubt. Individual programmes of professional and curriculum development were, therefore, strengthened by peer support which was built into the course structure and processes. Teachers were thus enabled to confront their beliefs in the light of new personal and practical knowledge; and reflection and confrontation were seen as a necessary prelude to transformation.

This model of professional development recognizes that learning needs are complex. The course did not, therefore, belong to any one individual or one interest group. It was a partnership between 'those who know how' and 'those who know what', in which no one individual or group claimed a monopoly of wisdom. In this model, since teachers are seen as active causal agents in their own learning, the in-service design cannot be either masterminded or unilaterally controlled by the interventionist consultant/teacher educators. The work must, therefore, be collaborative, with a maximum flow of information between the stakeholders (in the case of this course the participants, schools, LEAs and university). To achieve this it is necessary to set up channels of communication which enable teachers and consultants to engage in a continuing dialogue about the nature of teaching and learning within agreed contexts.

Collaborative Action Research

> Despite the so-called revolution in teacher research around the world today where there is a lot of talk about teachers as producers of knowledge . . . a view of educational research is still dominant among classroom teachers that sees research as an activity conducted by those outside the classroom. For the benefit of those outside the classroom . . . and educational theory as what others with more status and prestige in the academic hierarchy have to say about them and their work. (Zeichner, 1995, p. 154)

A third kind of partnership is that of collaborative action research. Collaboration of this kind is not easy. It demands the establishment and maintenance of long-term relationships which are at the very least co-equal, in which teacher educators, student teachers and teachers are 'active agents in the production of a new pedagogic discourse, rather then merely the consumers of the professional knowledge produced by academics and education researchers' (Edwards and Brunton, 1993, p. 156). Problems of this form of practitioner research being 'colonized' by higher education academics have been identified (Elliott, 1991). However, it does potentially offer teachers the opportunity to engage in professional development through systematic investigation of practice with the help of a 'mentor' or critical friend from inside or outside the school which otherwise might not be available. What action research does in the context of teacher education is develop joint responsibilities for knowledge creation to enable teacher educators to address directly their concerns with the praxis of schoolteaching and the theory–practice dialectic, as part of their essential core task of contributing to teacher improvement. Clearly, however, issues of dependence and autonomy and roles and relationships need to be addressed within such work.

These complex learning partnerships are difficult to foster and sustain, since to some academics partnerships of this kind may represent new restrictions upon their choice and conduct of research. Collaborative work also can be labour intensive and requires of the actors technical and human relationship skills far beyond those necessary in more traditional research. Furthermore, the establishment of any working relationships must take account of existing cultures both within schools, within universities and between schools and universities. For example, a world which emphasizes the systematic gathering of knowledge, formal examination of experience, professional criticism and seemingly endless discussion of possibilities rather than solutions, is likely to contrast sharply with a world dominated by action, concrete knowledge and busyness (Day, 1991, p. 537; Cuban, 1992, p. 8). The disabling effect of the two task cultures upon long-term relationships should not be underestimated.

In the following example the researcher acts as a consultant providing the necessary moral, intellectual and resource support for teachers engaged in a process of self-examination. The work is not traditional, for role distance between the actor and his environment is not maintained. Because of this the 'researcher-consultants' achieve greater access to more valid information concerning how teachers learn and why they change (or do not change) — and thus to teachers' thinking — than were they to adopt more neutral or naturalistic stances.

Members of a secondary school English department invited the researcher to work with them in investigating their effectiveness: how far what they did in the classroom related to their intentions. Two sequences of six lessons each with classes of 14–15-year-old students were selected by the teachers and videotaped. By reviewing these video films and discussing them with the teachers at length, by interviewing pupils and examining the interactions within the lessons, the researcher was able to offer each of the teachers information which made it possible to re-examine and reflect upon espoused theory and to generate new personal theory. Each teacher's aim was to increase his/her professional effectiveness in the classroom, and five sequential stages were found to be necessary in order to achieve this:

1 Identification of inconsistencies within the prevailing theory of action through self-confrontation and reflection;
2 Evaluation of this confrontation as a means of informing future decision-taking;
3 Planning of new theories-in-use;
4 Implementation of those new theories;
5 Internalization of new theories of action and further confrontation, or return to confrontation of initial theory of action.

The research was client centred, in that the researcher intervened in the teachers' lives in order to seek questions perceived by them as relevant to their needs, to investigate answers to these questions collaboratively and to place the onus for action on the teachers themselves. The notion was that their personal investment in the learning enterprise would be maximized. All four teachers involved achieved change at classroom level in different ways according to their particular intentions. The changes in attitude towards themselves as teachers and towards their teaching were the most significant outcomes.

One teacher stated that the work had provided her with the time to 'think about, question and even change my methods, and the frame of reference in which to make decisions and formulate ideas'. She also stated one year after the research had been completed that she had retained a more generally questioning attitude as a direct result, and that she had changed as a result of what the study had shown her about herself. All transferred what they had learnt into their work with other classes. Informal conversations with all the teachers were held during the two years after the research with them was completed. During the course of these conversations, they often informed the researcher of how the changes they had made in attitude as well as practice were being sustained. They felt that they trusted much more their own ability not only to find, but evaluate and modify their personal solutions to the teaching problems they encountered. In effect, they felt that they had achieved a new critical standard with regard to themselves as teachers. However, all the teachers commented that without the presence of the researcher-consultant, they had been unable or unwilling to find the time and energy to continue with the detailed and systematic process of self-evaluation.

Steve: A Case Study

In the case of one teacher, Steve, evidence of the long-term changes in thinking was collected both during the supported research process, and at intervals up to five years following its completion. His original goal had been not to allow his teaching to be 'dull or unimaginative':

> What I'm looking for . . . is a way of opening up a bit and making things more lively and interesting for them [the pupils] and me, so that I'm better able to get on with them, and the whole experience is more interesting and valuable.

He identified a gap between the values held by the school and those held by the members of the English Department — the 'norm' for students was that the teacher was expert holder of knowledge who viewed the students as passive receivers; and what he and the department valued was 'trying to move towards more active participation, more active learning rather than passive learning'. However, he was also 'torn between wishing for more participation and more liveliness on their [pupils] part, and my consciousness of how much material I want to get through in a given time.' He perceived three major constraints:

1 the demands of the examination syllabus for content coverage;
2 the students' habits and expectations — they were used to adopting a passive role and tended to be unwilling to change;
3 the students' ability — he described many of them as 'stodgy', 'inert', 'fairly passive', and 'not particularly able', and he was pessimistic about their ability to progress autonomously and to be fluent in the spoken or written word. He valued self-confidence, humour, and cheerfulness in pupils; and they in turn saw him as 'friendly', 'encouraging', and 'caring' and 'helpful'.

Steve's planning of his lessons was constrained by his perception that the examination syllabus requirements demanded written work of a particular kind and quantity. These perceived requirements had found expression in the emphasis placed by him on coverage (assimilation) of content selected by him. The result was that he:

1 provided too much information for the pupils to assimilate;
2 made little attempt to discover whether they found the content relevant to their experience;
3 allowed little deviation in terms of pupil talk from the path leading to his own predetermined conclusions.

The students responded by initiating few conversations and by a low level of participation in class discussions. As a result of reflection on his teaching in the first sequence of lessons, he modified his organization, his attitude to content, and his mode of interaction with students in the second. He encouraged exploratory pupil talk through supporting students' ideas generally, and not presenting indigestible amounts of preselected content. They thus moved from being relatively passive receivers of the teacher's knowledge and opinions and finding answers which were 'correct', to being actively involved in the selection and negotiation of content.

In his first written evaluation (a series of chronologically ordered reflections, written three months after our work) he enumerated his thoughts on the value of the process:

> 1 I was interested in class talk — group talk. The video and tapes helped me to realize what goes on and what doesn't go on behind my back. No other method could show me.
> 2 I was taught how to ask questions and structure conversations — I hadn't managed to teach myself this in four years. I was taught by seeing my own stultified conversations with kids.
> 3 I learnt to take it easy in class — not to force all issues and responses into my mould. I got closer to the kids too.
> 4 I found reviewing the video absorbing, reading the transcripts less so. After a while I began to resent spending so much time on it. I began to wonder whether all the time spent was worth what I was gaining. I think it was now — but then I wasn't so sure.

5 Your role — as neutral observer — I accepted and expected. I felt no threat at all, although I was conscious of trying extra hard, being ultra tolerant because there was someone else there.
6 I learnt to revalue the usefulness of resources, particularly teacher produced!
7 It was rewarding to have someone around who had read a lot on our subject and its problems and who could spare the time to have his brains picked over an issue or an author or a book. It helped me take short cut in thinking about issues like 'talk' or group work or resources because there was someone to bounce half-formed ideas off. Every school should have one.

Steve had become aware of the insecurity of his approach. He wrote:

> . . . like all teachers I tended to base my approach on a type of paternalism which says, 'Here is what you don't know yet', and I then have the pleasure of whisking back the curtain to reveal . . . the curriculum . . . Teachers use the content, the knowledge as a fence between themselves and their group and say, in effect, 'If you want to reach me, as a bloke, you've got to get over the fence first'.

He had learnt that he was 'creating fences' and he had identified the causes for this as being 'the sort of personality I have, by producing preselected resources, by prefiguring class discussions, by asking brief, closed questions, by keeping aloof from the kids':

> Your change agency can't change our personalities . . . but what I think it can do is reveal to a teacher the nature of his personality in so far as it does or does not elicit responses and promote a learning environment for his group of kids.

The first round of research made his implicit theories of action explicit. He then set about rebuilding these theories in a second round:

> . . . instead of prepackaged lessons which bolted on to one another in a preordained way, I tried to let the course build up its own tempo. I took things more slowly, invested time in sometimes lengthy rambling chat full of reminiscence and 'trading' of anecdotes and memoirs. This made me feel happier and more secure with the group of people and probably had a similar effect on them . . . Now this seems obvious and basic, but then the most important realizations usually are.

Steve spoke of two positive gains as a result of the research:

> The first one is . . . talk, and I allow far more latitude in a constructive way as far as group and individuals' talk is concerned. And I try and participate in it more, and steer it more . . . The second thing is, the main gain I think, has been the setting of a higher self-standard, I can't think of any other way in which you'd be so compelled to examine yourself and force yourself as high as you possibly can in the classroom. You try it, and if it works, then you've reached a level to which you must always afterwards aspire, and compare whatever else you do with that. I know when I've fallen short a bit, and I usually know why.

Finally, he summarized the value of the research both in terms of its process and product:

> I feel much surer of what the fundamental attributes of a good teacher are in my own mind — without all this navel gazing I would have stayed in my neatly ordered, mechanistic universe for a good while longer. I think I may well have saved myself many errors in approach and the blundering up of a good many blind alleys . . . being a part of this research cost me a lot of time and energy. It was worth it.

Steve's detailed written evaluation of the research contained a clear account of how his attitudes towards it and the researcher-consultant had changed:

> . . . over two years it has progressed from feelings of aloofness, caution and occasional cynicism to . . . real professional regard and genuine interest and concern with every aspect of your study — both in your terms and mine.

He commented on the positive value of self-confrontation and the researcher-consultant's role as 'consciousness raiser' rather than direct 'change agent'.

Some five years later, he wrote about changes that had occurred in his thinking as a result of engaging in the research process. There is little documented evidence of perceived long-term change that has occurred as a result of research or consultancy activities, and so no apology is made for quoting the teacher's unsolicited comments at length:

> My particular concern or perceived need lay in teacher and pupil talk, and it was upon this area that I focused most attention when reviewing the video film of the lessons and in studying tape transcripts. I had prepared a considerable amount of material for discussion, but the talk had not gone well . . . These realizations and others like them grew as the process developed. Having confronted the mismatch between what was desired, the issues were thrown into far sharper focus and it became imperative to abandon the structure I had been relying upon to support 'talk' in my English lessons. In the second sequence I forsook the advance preparation of resources and materials and decided instead to introduce a topic and let the pupils define its direction. The written tasks were self-directed and the talk which led up to them I allowed to be steered by the pupils themselves: they were grouped rather than taught as a whole class and I opted to circulate rather than to control from the 'front' . . . I can attest to the validity of this model of reflection and theory building. There had been a shift in pedagogy which had come about through the critical evaluation of current practice in the light of both personal and public theory. Close reflection upon practice became an eradicable habit. What is significant, however, is the degree and intensity of external support which was required to engender this. There exists no army of researchers who can institute the process on a wide scale. For me this experience accelerated a process which I hope, but cannot be sure, would have taken place anyway. I was enabled to move out rapidly from my 'comfortable routines' and from the 'coping' strategies which often mark the plateau of many teachers at an early stage in their careers. The process gave me renewed access to public theory in the sense that I could use it:

> prior to that I was aware of such theory, but could not employ or affirm it because my personal theory was too tightly in the grip of my current classroom practice. By taking a risk and letting go of accustomed practice, by becoming theoryless for a time, I was able to address and assimilate the public theory to which I aspired.

For this kind of work to develop, channels of communication must be established by the academic community which enable teachers and researchers to engage in a continuing dialogue about the nature of teaching and learning within the classroom. The active support of an outside agent is necessary:

1. To establish and sustain a responsive, mutually acceptable dialogue about classroom events and their social and psychological context.
2. To audit the process rather than the product of possibly biased self-reporting.
3. To create a situation in which the teacher is obliged to reflect systematically on practice. This is unlikely to happen in the crowded school day.
4. To act as a resource which the teacher may use at time appropriate to the needs which he perceives; e.g. to relieve the teacher of the task of data collection.
5. To represent the academic community at the focus of the teacher's professional life. The researcher thus becomes a part of rather than apart from the teacher.

Thus a mutually acceptable language of practice may develop. Problems of transfer (of knowledge), validity and credibility (of research findings), and 'barriers to change' will be minimized. In research such as this the two main principles for intervention theory and change are that:

- the perceived needs of the client(s) are of paramount importance;
- the consultant's role is collaborative and co-equal, but not necessarily neutral.

Partnership Consultancy

Many years ago, Steele (1975) emphasized consultancy as being a process rather than a strict occupational role:

> By the consultancy process, I mean any form of *providing help* on the content, process or structure of a task or series of tasks, where the consultant *is not actually responsible for doing the task* (defined as anything a person, group or organisation is trying to do) itself but is helping those who are. The two critical aspects are that help is being given, and that the helper is not directly responsible within the system (a group or organisation or family) for what is produced . . . Using this definition, consulting is a *function*, not an occupational role per se. (Steele, 1975, pp. 2–3)

This describes well the roles of higher education tutors who lead and participate in school partnerships.

Four primary functions of the consultant are:

- **Teacher role** In this role the consultant will act as knowledge broker by, for example, leading seminars in which issues raised by teachers and data collected from the workplace are discussed, and providing appropriate readings to stimulate discussion.
- **Talisman role** In the role as talisman it is the fact of the consultant's presence that is important. This fact provides a sense of security and legitimacy which allows the clients to feel comfortable enough to experiment in areas where they might not act without support.
- **'Shot-in-the-arm' role** It is important that the regular meetings between teachers from different schools should provide a supportive 'nurturing' atmosphere where trust can be engendered. In order to achieve this the meetings may be held outside school for extended periods. Camaraderie and critical friendship are encouraged through cross-school, small group discussion and inviting other sympathetic outsiders associated with the themes of the network to attend, thus providing added legitimization and intellectual and moral support. This moral support is particularly important as projects develop, when some teachers may feel an increase in work load/anxiety.
- **Clock role/collector** There have been projects where the consultant's most important role seems to be that of a timer or clock for the client system to watch. The regularly scheduled visits to a school (or the thought of it coming soon) serve as a spur to clients to be thinking and experimenting so that they would have something to show the consultant for the time in between the visits. (based on Steele, 1975, pp. 4–6)

Clearly, the building of trust and credibility are as important as the kinds and timings of interventions. Yet it is important to avoid encouraging 'dependency' which acts against capacity-building and, ultimately, extending professional autonomy and self-confidence. Learning partnerships will be temporary, if rich, experiences for the external consultant and the teachers. For example, in exploring the role of the 'temporary' or 'limited term' consultant as part of contracted work with teachers in a primary school which aimed to assist them in reflecting upon and sharing their practices, the university tutor acted as process facilitator, using videotape and stimulated recall techniques. He did not, however, engage in critical dialogue with them about their own teaching, hypothesizing that where external consultants do not have the opportunity to engage in sustained work over an extended period of time (and thus develop roles based on equity of status and the need to exercise a variety of roles as appropriate) it may be better deliberately to avoid taking a critical friend role (Habermas, 1972). Too early an adoption of the role may result in dependency and leave a perceived vacuum for the teacher on withdrawal. The teachers kept journals of their responses to the tutor's role during the work.[2] The

Consultant	Context	Result	Factors to be considered
Listening ear	Short-term 'understanding' consultancy where emphasis is placed on moral support and teacher autonomy	1. Continued independence of the client	1. Development of understanding may be limited 2. The phase of professional development of the client
Critical friend	Longer term 'informed participant' consultancy where emphasis is placed on emotional and intellectual 'equal other' support	1. Short-term interdependence 2. Long-term independence	1. Time and sustained interactivity are needed to build trust and credibility
Expert	A-contextual	1. Dependence on 'superior' 2. Alienation of client	1. Perceived relevance and ownership of agenda and credibility of consultant 2. Perceived power and authority of consultant

Figure 8.2 Researcher-consultant roles (Day, 1987)

hypothesis is expressed in Figure 8.2 in which three typical consultant roles and their likely consequences are represented.

In America, in work of a similar nature, Andrew Gitlin took an 'informed participant' role, as one who 'makes special efforts to facilitate conversations about teachers' ideas, dreams and visions of education, and the relationships between these concepts and their images of a good society' (Goodman, 1994, p. 11). Gitlin (1997) suggests that:

> If robust forms of collaboration are to move beyond contrived approaches that are regulated and compulsory, then the agenda for the learning process needs to be controlled by teachers. The role of the external change agent, in this regard, is both complex and conflicted. One of the benefits of adopting the informed participant role as . . . one who engages participants in discursive practice . . . is that teachers have the opportunity to take leadership roles in furthering this process with members of their [school]. When this occurs the influence of the external change agent can wither away so that long term development projects can continue beyond the commitment of the change agent. (p. 25)

Conclusion: Developing Strategic School–University Partnerships

These examples of partnerships provide further confirmation of research cited in earlier chapters that, although schools are intended to be learning communities, teachers' daily teaching work provides limited opportunities for their own learning.

The intensification (Robertson, 1996), isolation (Lortie, 1975), and busyness (Jackson, 1968; Sharp and Green, 1975) of the environment in which most teachers still work are well documented. Practice makes only practice (Britzman, 1991), and single loop learning (Argyris and Schön, 1974) predominates as a means of control rather than emancipation. Indeed, even where the culture of the school encourages critical reflection through forms of collaboration and critical discourse about teaching, development time during school hours is limited; and the stress of the work itself ensures that beyond that time, energy levels are low for most teachers. Periods of innovation (e.g. decentralization of school management or the imposition of new curricula) may at least temporarily sap the will and professional self-confidence of teachers for whom the safest learning strategy is to minimize risk, 'play safe', and control the pace of change. Added to this is the effect of the personal and professional history and development phase of each participant and the local policy contexts in which schools are embedded. The success of university contributions to individual and organizational development demands considerable understanding of these contexts, and of the cognitive and affective needs of tutors, as well as skill and commitment and, above all, an understanding of the importance of time, reflection, timing and attending to different kinds of development needs.

In providing opportunities for reflection, partnerships between teachers and university colleagues implicitly recognize that teaching is 'profoundly moral activity' (Fenstermacher, 1990, p. 133). Essentially, through the provision of networks, critical friendships, peer coaching, on- and off-site reflection, analysis and planning, such projects assist teachers who have been 'increasingly thrown back on their own reflective resources as a basis for moral judgement':

> Teacher development can help teachers articulate and rehearse resolving these moral dilemmas in their work. By reflecting on their own practice, observing and analysing other teachers' practice or studying case examples of practice, teachers can clarify the dilemmas they face and develop principled, practical and increasingly skilful and thoughtful ways of dealing with them . . . This approach to teacher development elevates the principles of thoughtful, practical judgement above personal prejudice, misleading moral absolutes, or the false certainties of sciences as a guide to action and improvement. (Hargreaves, 1995, p. 261)

A keystone in the success of the partnerships described in this chapter is that they are 'teacher' as well as 'practice' oriented, recognizing the complexities of teacher need and teacher development at different times, in different environments and for different purposes, asserting implicitly that the job of being a teacher and the act of teaching demands thought, commitment, knowledge and passion.

It takes time to change attitudes and practice. Teachers are at different levels of readiness to learn, and the broader culture of the school and national and local policy contexts impact positively or negatively on the ability of teachers to take responsibility for their development. The role of the external interventionist should not be confined to that of a facilitator and course organizer. Listening to teachers' needs and organizing in-service courses and events on this basis only is too limiting. To be effective in the longer term the interventionist needs to be seen to be a part of rather than apart from the local and national broader educational communities. She/he must be able to engage in different kinds of critical dialogue over time in order to: i) promote and sustain a series of reflective conversations about individual and institutional needs within the schools; ii) contribute to the provision of appropriate further professional development events and processes; iii) follow up the effects of these on teachers' thinking and practice and school development; iv) negotiate the boundaries between individually and institutionally identified needs of teachers, schools, policy bodies and universities; and v) engage in ongoing dialogue with other 'external providers' in relation to these.

There is an unresolved issue, however, in relation to the response of university tutors to the reform contexts in which both schools and universities are involved. More than teachers in schools, tutors in universities have long established and strongly defended 'expert' individual and collective identities (Becher, 1989). Changes in the traditional licence of tutors in universities to follow their individual research and knowledge interests by which they identify their substantive 'professional selves' are difficult to legislate (though attempts are being made in America through Professional Development Schools, and in England through School-Centred Initial Teacher Training). Historically, many tutors were appointed precisely because of their uniqueness in terms of research and certainly not because of their human relationship abilities or management qualities, skills or community service ethic. Yet this once institutionally valued 'selfishness' is now less valued by the wider educational community. Tutors are being required to change to a more institutionally defined needs-based agenda which demands collaboration, the learning of new knowledge, and acquisition of new skills in which personal choice must be complementary to collectively identified targets. For many academics 'requirement' means resistance if only for the purposes of self-preservation. More importantly there is a role for management, engaged as they are in strategic thinking to ensure that moral purposes are revisited and that different connections are made which mirror the changed imperatives of teachers and schools within a balance of intelligent service to a number of different communities. Identifying the strengths and limitations of university researchers and teacher educators in relation to school and teacher development needs will be a key strategic factor in initiating and responding to system needs in the future. If the concepts of partnerships between different levels within the system — schools, universities, teacher training and inservice — are to be applied in practice, then each must be developed for diversity and take account of the need for a range of research and development strengths within the university system according to purpose and desired outcomes for the education system as a whole.

The challenge for universities is to engage in strategic planning for initiation and response through which their capacity to respond to schools' agendas as well as to take forward those of the academy will be increased. In developing new kinds of relationships with schools and teachers they will be expressing a service-wide commitment, in which traditional expertise (e.g. in research and knowledge generation) is combined with new expertise in knowledge creation, development and consultancy as part of a more diverse portfolio which connects more closely with the needs of the school community at large. Such a portfolio would demonstrate the moral commitment of university educators to improving teaching and learning in collaboration with schools and teachers.

Notes

1 For a detailed account on evaluation of this in-service programme, see Day (1990).
2 For a detailed account see Day (1987a).
3 See also 'The Challenges of School/University Collaboration', *Theory into Practice*, **35**, 3, Summer 1996. The whole issue is devoted to collaboratively written examples of partnerships in America.

Chapter 9

Networks for Learning: Teacher Development, School Improvement

> Unlike other professions, which are organized to support research activities, teaching is a profession in which it is extraordinarily difficult to find enough time even to collect data and almost impossible to find time to reflect, reread or share with colleagues . . . When groups of teachers come together as researchers, they need sufficient chunks of time in which to work, and they also need sufficient longevity as a group over time . . . When the pace of a community's work is unhurried and when members of the group make a commitment to work through complicated issues over time, then ideas have a chance to incubate and develop, trust builds in the group, and participants feel comfortable raising sensitive issues and risking self revelation. (Cochran-Smith and Lytle, 1996, p. 100)

In 1996, the European Commission published its White Paper, 'Teaching and Learning: Towards the Learning Society', which put forward guidelines for action in the fields of education and training. It suggested the necessity for cooperative partnerships between school and family, school and business, and might have added schools and universities. It proposed that 'the challenge of co-operation between education establishments and enterprises [schools] . . . is to accept . . . [them] . . . as full partners in the training . . . [education] . . . process' (p. 16), and it recommended the notion of 'sustained flexibility' as a necessary condition for success. Writing in a school development context, Michael Huberman (1995a) proposed research-based, cross-school networks, 'with a focus on bridging the gap between peer exchanges, the interventions of external resource people, and the greater likelihood of actual change at the classroom level' (p. 193). Networks are different from partnerships, though they embody the same principles of collaboration and contain many of the same components and ways of working. However, their aim is almost always systemic change and they consist of a number of schools which work together over extended periods of time with the support of staff from universities and other organizations with an interest in promoting improvement efforts. Because they meet over time, this creates opportunities for a wide variety of agreed intervention strategies by university staff and others and for changes in the focus of their work together.

Although only one in a range of professional development opportunities, networks of teachers and other stakeholders which aim to enhance the quality of teaching and learning have become an increasingly important feature of the landscape of professional development. This chapter examines the nature of networks and the precepts and principles of knowledge generation upon which they are based, providing examples of school improvement, learning consortia, communities of practice, and interprofessional partnerships.

Such local, regional, national and international 'Partnerships', 'Joint Ventures' and 'Networks' are proliferating, whether for the purpose of 'improvement' (defined as producing something better than before), or 'development' (defined as fuller working out, stage of advancement, bringing to maturity). That they are potentially powerful is not because they constitute a new form of learning — subject- and phase-specific teachers' networks, school–university partnerships, and networks for the development in action of different ways of teaching, application of curriculum materials and investigating teaching have been around for a long time.[1] Whether initiated by individuals or groups inside or outside schools, a key feature is that all essentially recognize that responsibility for development of the system can no longer be left to others. Networking through partnerships, then, is an important learning mode which can have significant effects upon individual teachers, departments, school communities and universities.

Knowledge Generation

The growth of networks reflects the changes in the understandings of the nature and application of modes of knowledge production in contemporary society identified by Gibbons and colleagues (Gibbons et al., 1994). They describe a traditional means (Mode 1) as that in which, 'problems are set and solved in a context governed by the . . . interests of a specific community' (p. 3). It is characterized by homogeneity, is hierarchical, and tends to preserve its form. It is, in other words, propositional knowledge produced outside the context of use. They identify a transformation in the mode of knowledge production, away from Mode 1 towards Mode 2 knowledge which is created in the context of application. It includes a wider, more temporary and heterogeneous set of practitioners, collaborating on a problem defined in a specific and localized context. The knowledge produced in this context is intended to be useful. It is, 'always produced under an aspect of continuous negotiation and it will not be produced unless and until the interests of the various actors are included' (p. 4).[2] Mode 2 knowledge is still propositional, but Mode 1 problems of relevance, transfer and adoption are minimized. Although the two Modes are distinctive, they do interact. This is the case in relation to a growing number of university–school partnership networks in education. Implicitly, if not explicitly, their participants recognize the limitations of continuing to attempt to hold the traditional (Mode 1) monopoly of knowledge production in universities through institutionalized disciplinary research from outside the school and the benefits of enabling this and knowledge generated from experience to interact. They have recognized that we are now part of a 'vastly expanded knowledge production process' (p. 11) in which everyone is a contributor.

Drucker has pointed out, in writing about teachers as knowledge workers in a knowledge society, that whilst there is much talk about 'entitlement' and 'empowerment' of schools and teachers, we should be talking about 'responsibility' and 'contribution':

> What we should aim at is to make people responsible. What we should ask is not, 'What should you be entitled to?' but 'What should you be responsible for?' The job of management in a knowledge-based organisation is not to make everybody a **boss**. The task is to make everyone a **contributor**. (Drucker, 1994, p. 99)

University departments and individual tutors in many countries have adapted themselves to the new context or indeed played leading roles themselves in establishing the kinds of participatory frameworks which enable this kind of knowledge generation and production. Examples of INSET, Action Research and other partnerships in previous chapters embody the principles and many of the practices of Mode 2 knowledge production but go beyond these, using the move from 'single' to 'double' loop learning in which taken-for-granted contexts, cultural norms and practices are re-examined in collegial settings (Chapter 2 in this volume). In these, and more recently established 'School Improvement' networks and consortia, success is defined not only by the intrinsic or scientific merit of the knowledge produced, but by the specific expectations and results of its application in the context in use.

As 'knowledge workers' whose primary tool is the knowledge inside their heads (Duffy, 1997), teachers need to find ways of expanding their knowledge repertoires. Networks offer potentially powerful opportunities for doing this. Witness, for example, the unsolicited testimony of one mid-career professional:

> The effects of being involved with this project have been far reaching. On a personal level it has given me far greater confidence to tackle 'working with colleagues' since although there is a high personal commitment and ownership, no-one works without support. It is group decisions that are carried through. It has regenerated my feelings about school since it has opened up many opportunities to try different roles. Despite the amount of hard work and persistence which has been required, it has released previously untapped energy levels since the process provides ongoing input . . . The effect . . . on my teaching is to have heightened my awareness of what I had previously treated as a fairly automatic process. I have tried to question why I have done things in a particular way and have been given ideas and strategies to try alternatives. It has created a climate of inquiry and a feeling that solutions can be found through collaboration. The overall effect on my professional life has been to open some windows. I have been prepared to take on greater challenges within school life with increased confidence. (Day, 1997d, pp. 12–13)

This mode of teacher and school development is important, then, not only as a response to structural reform, the pace of change and heightened expectations of school performance in many countries, but also because, at its best, it enables teachers to shape and participate in individual and school developments over time with colleagues from both within and without the school which have benefits for them as individual classroom teachers and for the schools in which they teach. At its best, networking recognizes the need for continuing development that 'fits' individual and organizational need for learning, which moves beyond the privacy that used to characterize teachers' professional lives into forms of collaborative inquiry which are essential to meeting new demands. By definition, networks are also a recognition that learning only from experience will limit development, and that teachers are likely to commit themselves to learning in which they have a stake and which holds personal significance for them. Essentially, then, networks provide 'organisational structures that enable groups of teachers to come together to talk about their work, learn from one another, and address curricular and structural issues' (Cochran-Smith and Lytle, 1996, p. 98). They represent the polar opposite of the 'artisan' (Huberman, 1993a) or 'single loop' (Argyris and Schön, 1974) paradigms of learning alone.

In a recent review of the American literature, Hord (1997) explored the concept and uses of professional learning networks, focusing primarily upon those in which whole schools or departments are involved. Whilst recognizing that such communities of continuous inquiry and improvement are 'embryonic and scattered' (Darling-Hammond, 1996a, p. 10), Hord identified several factors necessary for their development: i) significant contributions made by school principals to provide supportive environments (Leithwood et al., 1997); ii) staff involvement in decision-making, reflective dialogue through shared practice and peer review, and inquiry; and iii) 'undeviating' focus upon student and staff learning (Louis and Kruse, 1995; Brandt, 1992; Sarason, 1990). Although building collaborative learning networks takes time, the literature suggests that there are significant benefits for both staff and students. Among these are:

- reduction in the isolation of teachers;
- increased commitment to the mission and goals of the school and increased vigor in working to strengthen the mission;
- higher likelihood that teachers will be well informed, professionally renewed, and inspired to inspire students;
- significant advances into making teaching adaptations for students, and changes for learners made more quickly than in traditional schools;
- higher likelihood of undertaking fundamental, systemic change. (Hord, 1997, pp. 27–8)

Cycles of Learning

Michael Huberman proposes four progressively more open cycles of learning.

1 *The Closed Individual Cycle* which corresponds most closely to the private learning of teachers in classrooms.

2. *The Open Individual Cycle* in which a teacher seeks assistance from colleagues within school.
3. *The Closed Collective Cycle* in which groups of teachers from several schools with shared interests meet to share experience, discuss issues of teaching and learning. The result is a teacher research community in which teachers move beyond the limitations of development which is based upon their own prior experience by making it public within the group and subjecting it to empathetic critique. Collaborative action research work may well be a significant part of the group's development. The cycle is closed in the sense that there is little call on external expertise. The group, therefore, relies on its collective wisdom which may or may not be sufficient to promote continuing development over time.
4. *Open Collective Cycle* This cycle corresponds most closely to learning partnerships and networks which involve significant others who may not be directly involved in teaching in the classroom, but who may have a variety of skills and propositional knowledge about education which may complement the practical knowledge held by teachers. This 'open collective cycle' model is premised on the assumption that:

> demonstration by experts, systematic observation of teachers undertaking new practices, interventions on the spot in the form of 'coaching' and two-tiered apprenticeship (Schön, 1987) seem to be required for any major shift in the learning environment created by the teacher . . . The same trends appear in the implementation literature (Fullan, 1991). Teachers tend to remain 'stuck' at lower levels of mastery for lack of explicit counsel from external experts or from experienced peers — but from peers who know how to respect and integrate the 'artisanry' of the teacher they are advising. (Huberman, 1995a, p. 206)

The strength of Huberman's illustration of an open collective cycle (see Figure 9.1), which he describes modestly as 'a plausible scenario for the professional development of teachers' (1995a, p. 207), is that it emphasizes that if processes of learning and change are to be successful, there is a need for collaborative work over time which is not restricted to one homogenous group or groups of teachers, but which admits 'outsiders' to its membership in the knowledge that:

- conceptual inputs (knowledge about education) are a necessary part of the process of illuminating, challenging and conceptualizing practical knowledge by providing different perspectives which ultimately enable the 'joint construction of knowledge through conversation' (Cochran-Smith and Lytle, 1996, p. 103);
- didactic inputs — modelling, practice, feedback and coaching (Joyce and Showers, 1988) — enable application and experimentation of learning into practice;
- data collection and analysis are necessary if existing and new practices are to be systematically reviewed.

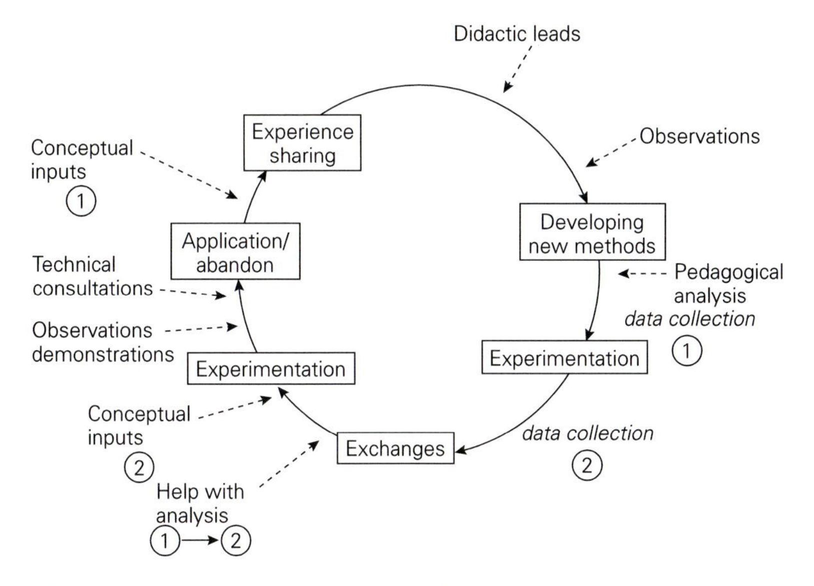

Figure 9.1 Open collective cycle (Huberman, 1995a)

The limitations of Huberman's illustration are that:

- There is an apparent lack of flexibility which seems to limit its fitness for purpose. There is no need for the inputs illustrated by the broken lines in Figure 9.1 to occur at particular points in the cycle, nor is there necessarily a need for them to occur more than once, notwithstanding that they may be different in kind.
- Although beginnings and endings of cycles highlight the need for the achievement of particular agreed goals, there is no discussion of transition between cycles, or the management of that transition.
- Whilst Huberman identifies principles for successful networks, i.e. demonstrating sustained interactivity, commitment to longevity, interlinked projects, strong leadership, supportive infrastructures, and intellectual coherence, he does not say *how* these might be demonstrated in practice.
- Although he acknowledges the need for individual members to have support in their school through ongoing complementary work, he does not attempt to suggest how this might be achieved.
- He does not appear to recognize the time and energy costs for teachers, for, 'While the theory is powerful, the practice is often exhausting and overwhelming' (Trachtman, 1997, p. 192).
- No network is likely to function for long without a leader or leaders who may be process facilitators or coordinators. They will need to be able to call upon and extend the kinds of consultancy roles described in the previous chapter, and be networkers themselves in order to draw upon

appropriate expertise from within and outside the network in order to provide appropriate conceptual and didactic inputs, data collection and analysis, facilitation and technical consultations.

School Improvement

An example of the way in which schools may network through engaging in double loop learning and 'Mode 2' knowledge production is that offered by 'school improvement', defined as:

> . . . a systematic, sustained effort aimed at change in learning conditions and other related internal conditions in one or more schools, with the ultimate aim of accomplishing educational goals more effectively. (van Velzen, Miles, Ekholm, Hameyer and Robin, 1985, p. 48)[3]

The powerful learning and capacity-building effects of involvement in learning networks which not only utilize the knowledge inside teachers' heads but also challenge and extend it are well documented (e.g. Little and McLaughlin, 1991; Bascia, 1991; Carter, 1991; Lord, 1991; Smith, Wiggington, Hocking and Jones, 1991; Fullan, 1993b; Hopkins, West and Ainscow, 1996; Lieberman and Miller, 1992; Louis and Miles, 1990; Elmore, 1992).[4] Networks may focus upon subject-specific enhancement (Lieberman and McLaughlin, 1992); strengthening the schools' capacities to provide quality education for all their pupils (Hopkins et al., 1996); extending the district-wide capacity of staff developers (Sparks and Hirsch, 1997); building community and school partnerships (Stoll and Fink, 1996); and interprofessional collaboration involving e.g. parents, teachers, social workers, psychologists and business (Corrigan, 1997; Day, van Veen and Walraven, 1997). They may be local, national or transnational (Posch and Mair, 1997).

A recent example of *structural networking* between universities, schools and LEAs, has been the emergence in America of Professional Development Schools (PDS). Although by no means uncontroversial,[5] they bring together school teachers and university tutors in a shared responsibility 'for the clinical preparation of new teachers, the professional development of the experienced faculty, the support of research directed at improving practice, and enhanced student learning . . . Work in PDSs is guided by a commitment to a set of principles that include a student-centred approach to teaching and learning; the sharing of responsibilities between the partnering of institutions; the simultaneous renewal of school and university; and a commitment to provide equal opportunity for all participants' (Levine and Trachtman, 1977, pp. 1–2).

Many networks are relatively short-lived, formed in order to achieve a particular task and disbanded once the agreed purposes have been fulfilled. Others, recognizing the more general long-term improvement benefits of heterogeneous partnerships which provide opportunities for on-going development, continue, though membership and specific purposes change. In Canada, the 'Learning Consortium' consists of collaborative teacher education partnerships between school districts (or LEAs) and higher education institutions which contain within them a variety of focused activities relating to school and teacher identified need. Its aim is:

> . . . to improve the quality of education for schools and universities by focusing upon teacher development, school development, and the restructuring of districts and the [university] faculty of education to support improvement on a continuous basis. (Fullan, 1993b, p. 121)

Michael Fullan describes how the 'Learning Consortium' developed between 1988 and 1996:

> While the basic assumptions and objectives were broadly stated, we were committed to launching specific initiatives to realize our aims. We began in 1988 with an emphasis on co-operative learning, a theme that provided a concrete point of departure. By the third year, summer and winter institutes on co-operative learning and follow-through support were well established; a new field-based teacher certification program was in place; and dissemination conferences and inservice were carried out with such collaborative approaches as mentoring, induction, peer coaching, and school improvement planning. The Consortium partners attempted to link these activities by paying attention to such consistent themes as teaching as career-long learning, fostering collaborative cultures and focusing on instruction . . . More recently, the Learning Consortium has begun to incorporate innovative teacher preparation programs as part of its commitment to integrating the teacher education consortium. (Fullan, 1995, p. 262)

Improving the Quality of Education for All

David Hopkins, Mel West and Mel Ainscow, have been working closely with schools from a number of areas in England and elsewhere over a six-year period to strengthen their *capacities to provide quality education*, 'rather than to implement specific curriculum or instructional innovations' (Hopkins et al., 1998a, p. iv). They base their work upon a series of propositions:

- Without a clear focus on the internal conditions of the school, improvement efforts will quickly become marginalised;
- School improvement will not occur unless clear decisions are made about development and maintenance;
- Successful school improvement involves adapting external change for internal purposes;
- School improvement will remain a marginal activity unless it impacts across all levels of the school;
- Data about the school's performance create the energy for development;
- Successful school improvement efforts engender a language about teaching and change. (Hopkins, Ainscow and West, 1997, pp. 263–8)

Like the Learning Consortium, the 'Improving the Quality of Education for All' (IQEA) project is committed to an action inquiry approach through partnership and its external, university-based initiators coordinate the support arrangements, providing training for school coordinators, making regular school visits, contributing to staff training, providing staff development materials, and monitoring the implementation of each school's project (Hopkins et al., 1998a, p. 4).

The IQEA project, then, is 'committed to an approach to educational change that focuses upon raising student achievement through focusing on the teaching–learning process and the conditions which support it' (Hopkins et al., 1997, p. 261). An important distinguishing feature of the project's capacity-building processes is its focus upon extending the range of teaching strategies available to teachers. This is based heavily on work in America which provides 'mounting evidence that . . . the use of appropriate teaching strategies can dramatically increase pupil achievement' (Joyce, Showers and Weil, 1992), and that 'school improvement strategies need to help teachers create a discourse about, and language for, teaching'. Its five principles are:

- School improvement is a process that focuses on enhancing the *quality of students' learning*;
- The vision of the school should be one which embraces *all* members of the school community as both learners and contributors;
- The school will see in external pressures for change important opportunities to secure its *internal priorities*;
- The school will seek to develop structures and create conditions which encourage collaboration and lead to the *empowerment* of individuals and groups;
- The school will seek to promote the view that *monitoring and evaluation of quality* is a responsibility which all members of staff share; (Hopkins et al., 1997, p. 262)

Reflection, inquiry in and out of school, and dialogue are key strategies in work which combines individual and collaborative action research and training sessions. The network coordinators use a variety of interventionist consultancy roles and skills to provide the kinds of conceptual, didactic, data collection and technical inputs described by Huberman (1995a) as being essential to the success of the open collective cycle.

This is an important project because it: i) focuses upon what happens in classrooms; ii) ensures agreed agendas for action and the appropriate training to support these; iii) engages in knowledge generation in the contexts of use; iv) extends development opportunities by recognizing in its design that the heterogeneity, complementarity of knowledge, experience and skills of participants can lead to a synergy; and v) places the participants at the centre of decisions about practice. The model of sustained interactivity does, however, present difficulties and dilemmas, for it requires time, energy and a range of consultancy skills:

> Our commitment to *working with rather than on* schools presents many difficulties and dilemmas. In a more traditional project we might well have chosen to introduce to the schools an established model of development based upon previous research activities. Then, having set the initiative going, our task would have been

> to stand back and record the processes and outcomes of the intervention. In IQEA, we have deliberately chosen to adopt a very different approach, based upon an alternative perspective as to how change can be facilitated. Rather than seeking to impose externally validated models of improvement we are attempting to support schools in creating their own models. Our assumption is that such an approach, that builds upon the biographies and circumstances of particular organisations, is much more likely to bring about and help sustain significant improvements in the quality of schooling. (Hopkins et al., 1998a, p. 5)

Towards Communities of Practice

> If schools are to operate effectively in devolved systems . . . there needs to be a broad community understanding, reflected in system practice and discourse, that much reliance has to be placed on trust in professional judgement at school level. (National Schools Project Report, 1993, p. 13)

In Australia, two national projects — The 'National Schools Network' and the 'Innovative Links Between Schools and Universities' projects (Sachs, 1997; Sachs and Groundwater Smith, 1996) — are school-based initiatives in which teachers and universities are involved in professional development networks which 'break with traditional parochial conceptions of teacher professionalism' (Sachs, 1997), providing opportunities for cross-state and cross-system access to information and best practice. Like IQEA in England and the Learning Consortium in Canada, both projects are based on the notion that there is no single recipe for school improvement and that the development of teacher professionalism and identification of problems and ways of addressing them, whilst best achieved in the local school context, should not be confined to this. Although the aims were to bring about changes in teacher practices, they were not formula driven. Crucially, like the Personal Development Planning Project described in Chapter 5, they assumed a link between the organization and teachers' work; and an interactive, though not always directly complementary connection, between teacher and school development. Importantly, also, the Innovative Links Project which represents 'formal and explicit' partnerships between 14 universities and 100 schools, was designed to move *all* its participants 'beyond their accustomed ways of doing things and their familiar relationships' (Yeatman and Sachs, 1995). Yeatman and Sachs (1995) describe this project as 'new and significant' because:

- teacher professional development has been designed and developed on a whole school basis in ways which break traditional classroom isolation and network teachers into ongoing school-based learning communities and professional conversations;
- it has developed as a formal and explicit relationship between practising teachers and teacher educators in ways which are designed to foster professional development of both these partners; and
- this is a formal partnership between participating schools and universities on a scale of system wide impact and significance. (p. 21)

Collaboration between schools and universities in Australia has led to the development of *communities of practice* in which learning is not in the acquisition of the structure, but in the increased access of learners to participating roles in expert performance (Lave and Wenger, 1991, p. 17):

> A key part of expert performance is the ability to talk about it, to tell stories about it, not as a second order representation of what to do but as an integral part of what it is to be an expert performer. Learning is thus a way of *being* in a particular social world not merely knowing about it or describing it. From this perspective, emphasis is placed upon participation in a community of practitioners, rather than merely the acquisition of a set of skills, or practices deemed to satisfy bureaucratic requirements. (Sachs, 1997, p. 272)

Networks which Turn Disadvantage into Advantage

Networks and communities of practice need not be limited to those in mainstream educational communities. There are a growing number of partnerships which involve parents and social agencies (Frieberg, 1997; Lawson and Briar-Lawson, 1997) and interprofessional partnerships which recognize that no one group of educators alone is able to meet the needs of another. The example in this chapter focuses upon 'at risk' children and young people from disadvantaged communities. The term 'at risk' refers to children and young people who are in danger of failing at school, in their social life, or in making a successful transition to work. Poverty, ethnic status, family circumstance, language, type of school, geography and community are some of the factors which affect educational, social and vocational achievement.

Numerous research studies in many countries show the consequences for society of children and youth who are currently at risk of failure in our schools. In recent years both the number of children and youth who could be considered at risk and their degree of disadvantage have increased. Urban schools experience special challenges in dealing with the diversity of risk and in coping with the problems faced by children and their families, and a growing number are experiencing high dropout rates, student and teacher alienation and underachievement, conditions which are very difficult even for the most effective teachers and schools to influence. Efforts to intervene are complicated by the so-called Matthew effect, i.e. students who are behind at the beginning of school or who learn at a slower rate are likely to show progressive retardation as they continue in school (Reynolds, 1988; Waxman, 1992). Thus, instead of 'blaming the victim' — the child or the student's social and cultural background — it could be argued that school systems, school programmes and organizational and environmental features contribute to students' learning problems (Wang, 1990) and academic failure (Wehlage et al., 1989; Boyd, 1991; Waxman, 1992). Schools that alienate students and teachers, provide low standards and poor quality educational processes, have differential expectations for students, have high non-completion rates, are unresponsive to students, have high truancy and discipline problems, or do not adequately prepare students for the future, may be considered to be 'at risk' (Waxman, 1992).

Reversing the cycle of educational failure for students from at-risk school environments is very difficult, but there is evidence that it can be done. The reality, however, is that most schools are not designed to accommodate the developmental and educational needs of contemporary youth, nor are teachers prepared and trained to relate to these needs. In urban areas especially there has been an increase in absenteeism and truancy, and in dropping out of school. The number of children with recognized special learning needs is rising sharply. Facilities for special target groups, particularly for those ethnic and cultural minority groups in secondary education, are extremely limited. These young people are much more likely to leave school early without a diploma and run a relatively high risk of being unemployed. In some ethnic and cultural minority groups the youth unemployment rate is above 50 per cent. For large numbers of young people, then, education clearly does not perform even its qualification function, and employment prospects, even with qualifications, are diminishing in many countries. The overriding picture is one of worsening pupil problems, burnt-out or disillusioned teachers, and school organizations under pressure. In many cities it is difficult to find qualified teachers that are willing to work in at risk schools (van Veen et al., 1997).

Advancing and sustaining improvement in classrooms in schools in inner-city areas which have high teacher turnover and high absentee rates among students requires that communities of professionals work together and with others, as 'most schools in disadvantaged areas do not have *within them* the capacity for sustainable renewal' (OFSTED, 1993) Barber, Denning, Gough and Johnson (1994) have reviewed urban education initiatives in England; and in America, Lawson and Briar-Lawson (1997) have monitored the growing literature on change initiatives involving schools, families and communities where

> . . . a growing number of teachers are burdened, indeed some overwhelmed, by five interacting challenges:
>
> 1 the growing number of children who enter their classrooms with learning barriers, developmental difficulties and health risk factors
> 2 new requirements for inclusion of special education students in already overcrowded, 'regular' classrooms
> 3 resource shortfalls, outdated teaching–learning materials, deteriorating buildings, and unsafe school environments
> 4 significant changes in teaching–learning strategies, together with new performance-based, accountability requirements
> 5 learning and support needs associated with new computer technologies. (Lawson and Briar-Lawson, 1997, p. 184)

Together, they suggest, these challenges are responsible for the erosion of the development, morale, health and job satisfaction of many teachers which, in turn, lead to 'reductions in the quality of teachers' interactions with students'. In brief, there is a recognition that teachers can no longer do it all and alone. Significantly, they call for an end to the competing 'paradigm wars' or 'schools of thought' which they claim are attempting to influence the direction and process of school improvement, asserting that none have all the answers.

Dean Corrigan extends this theme, calling for a multi-agency, multi-professional approach to creating and sustaining learning opportunities for disadvantaged students, and for children and families to be placed at the centre of improvement efforts. He identifies the kinds of interprofessional partnerships suggested by Nixon and his colleagues in Chapter 1 as being characteristic of the new professionalism.

> In the future, educators will need to learn how to collaborate with professional partners who serve the same clients through other human service professionals such as health care, social work and criminal justice. In addition to preparation in their particular fields of specialization, each of the aforementioned professional partners must possess a common core of knowledge that is derived from the problems faced by their mutual clients and they must have access to the kind of interprofessional education that prepares them to work together across agencies in collaboratively developed family-centered, community-based delivery systems. (Corrigan, 1997, p. 209)

Networks for Learning: Cautionary Notes

Four problematic issues of power, control and autonomy which are central to systemic improvement efforts are: i) collaboration and cooperation; ii) professional autonomy and vested interests; iii) differences between schools and teachers; and iv) roles and relationships between higher education and schools.

Collaboration and Cooperation

Judyth Sachs (1997) writing about the challenge of university–school partnerships, provides a useful distinction between collaboration and cooperation. The former involves joint decision-making, requires time, careful negotiation, trust and effective communication — both parties are learners in an enterprise which focuses upon enhancing professional dialogue. In the latter, role boundaries and power relationships are unquestioned and maintained, and there is little mutual learning in what is essentially the 'expert' provision of professional development which may be more in the interests of those who traditionally hold the knowledge than those who do not.

> When power and prestige are unequal 'collaboration' can easily result in 'co-optation', or even in domination masked by a euphonious label. (Erickson and Christman, 1996, p. 150)

Wagner (1997) analyses three different forms of direct cooperation, 'manifested in exchanges, transactions and agreements negotiated directly between individual educational researchers and schoolteachers or administrators' (p. 14). They are: data-extraction agreements, clinical partnerships, and co-learning agreements. Each of these reflects different conceptions of the researchers' and practitioners' roles.

In data-extraction, the two are clearly bifurcated, with the researcher holding the technical research expertise. In clinical partnerships, there is an understanding that practitioners and researchers can add to knowledge about educational practice by working together, so the two roles are established through negotiation and boundaries are blurred. However, the practitioners remain the object of inquiry. In co-learning agreements, researchers and practitioners regard themselves as 'agents of inquiry *and* as objects of inquiry' (p. 16). Wagner suggests that whilst all three kinds of cooperation are useful in different contexts, it is the last two which offer more possibilities for change, since both acknowledge that practitioner participation in the design and processes of the research is more likely to lead to lasting change (Wagner, 1997).

Professional Autonomy and Vested Interests

> I value highly the tradition of professional autonomy as the basis of educational quality, but it seems that this must now be negotiated at school level. Concessions must be made in individual autonomy in order to provide a basis for collaborative working, for the school staff can no longer be seen as a federal association of teachers and departments: it must be a professional community. And it is with that community their professional autonomy must lie. (Stenhouse, 1975, p. 183)

Open collective cycles of the kind described by Huberman are likely to work best through collaborative partnerships not only between schools or groups of teachers from different schools who act also as change leaders with colleagues in their own schools (as in IQEA) but also between schools and external agencies drawn from, for example, LEAs or universities. There may be, however, different vested interests with different purposes at work.

The kinds of collaboration described in the examples of partnerships and networks in this and the previous chapter are those which are not legislated, nor do they threaten teacher autonomy beyond the making of concessions at school level. On the contrary, in valuing and supporting teachers' choice and participation in their own learning within and without whole school needs, they advance their professionalism. Not all collaboration, however, has this purpose. There has been criticism of some school improvement efforts which have accompanied structural reforms in England, Australia and America, for example, for using words like 'collaboration', 'participation', 'devolution' and 'empowerment' to indicate partnerships between 'managers' and teachers which are in reality a means of ensuring the uncritical implementation of government, state, district or even school policy agendas (Grundy and Bonser, 1997; Smyth, 1991; Ball, 1994; Elliott, 1991, 1996; Gitlin, 1997):

> . . . the language of the new work order is inherently contradictory because, while it preaches organisational democracy and empowerment, it does not really permit workers to question some of the fundamental assumptions underlying the new business of capitalism. (Gee, Hull and Lankshear, 1996, pp. vii–ix)

Such managerially dominated agendas represent a narrow instrumental view of the purposes of education as being to produce economically competitive individuals whilst ignoring the development of 'critical citizenry' (Hursh, 1997). Furthermore, the 'contrived collegiality' in such networks does not attempt to realign power relationships between the key participants which 'delays, distracts, and demeans':

> The inflexibility of mandated collegiality makes it difficult for programs to be adjusted to the purposes and practices of particular school and classroom settings. It overrides teachers' professionalism and the discretionary judgement which comprises it. (Hargreaves, A. 1994, p. 208)

Because most teachers themselves are committed to working for the betterment of their students, they will often go along with system-initiated professional development partnerships and collaborations, however contrived. And, pro-tem, it may be that much is gained. What is important is to be able to distinguish clearly, as in appraisal systems, what underlying view of the purposes of education, teachers, teaching and therefore students is being promoted. The kinds of 'robust' collaboration in the examples of partnership work and networks described in this chapter involve reflective critical inquiry and debate, mutual observation and the confrontation of values and practices over time which are far from being 'politically quiescent' (Hargreaves, A. 1994, p. 195). The developmental journeys taken often create emotional turmoil and ripples of changes which are not always comfortable either for the individual or the group and can, at least temporarily, threaten self-image and self-esteem. This is precisely why the building of joint, authentic purpose, trust and mutual understandings, and the provision of support and continuity of relationships through sustained interactivity are so important for success. Posch's description of the essential features of the range of school networks in different European countries, as 'the autonomous and flexible establishment of relationships to assist responsible action in the face of complexity and uncertainty' (Posch and Mair, 1997, p. 267), provides an apt summary of this position.

Teachers and Schools Are Not the Same

> Over more than a decade of school improvement efforts have taught us that there are some necessary conditions for change.
>
> - The importance of early participation in thinking and planning school improvement efforts;
> - Concrete practical classroom activities;
> - A process labeled Dialog, Decision making and Action;
> - Meetings focus on particular activities for improvement;
> - Teachers can support each other when they are publicly supported by the principal;
> - Teacher expertise can be encouraged through visitations and sharing — but it doesn't just happen; it takes time and much encouragement;

> • Projects are easier to begin when participants volunteer. Volunteers help because they want to and are open to committing themselves to innovation.
>
> . . . in short, when we treat teachers as we would have them treat students, they respond more readily with openness, engagement and commitment. (Lieberman and Miller, 1992, pp. 86–7)

Teachers and schools are not the same, and development is unlikely to follow a linear path. Personal and systematic change are essential companions, but they cannot be realistically expected always to be synchronized, travelling in the same direction at the same time. The time and energy necessary for participation in systematic inquiry work over time will not always be able to be sustained by teachers who have a variety of professional and personal agendas. Systemic school improvement work is one of a range of learning opportunities for teachers. It is neither better nor worse than others, for its effects depend, like those of other forms of continuing professional development, upon the impact it has upon the teacher; and the strength of its impact will depend upon a complex array of variables.

Roles and Relationships between Higher Education and Schools

There remains in the minds of many politicians and teachers a perceived theory–practice, theoretician–practitioner problem; a separateness between those who work in schools and those who work in higher education, between those who are said to practise and those who are said to theorize. Whether we like it or not, this exists partly because of history and partly because of function — after all, few teachers in schools have time built into their work which allows them to reflect, theorize, research and write. It also exists within higher education. Teachers who become teacher educators have for years wrapped around themselves the cloak of busy practicality which has served to comfort and insulate them against change. The separation thus exists because many have implicitly encouraged or colluded in this. There is a consciously calculated protective 'mystique' surrounding 'theory' and 'research'. How, then, are those two groups of relative and alienated strangers going to connect? Certainly there will need to be a more widespread change in attitudes and relationships. Although recent legislative changes in England, Holland, Norway, Sweden and elsewhere in Europe, Australia and North America have provided opportunities (though perhaps not intentionally) for new relationships to be formed between higher education and schools there remains a reticence to do so among many people in both sectors.

Such relationships will involve regular opportunities for the sharing of knowledge, skills and experience enhanced by a range of differentiated short and extended learning opportunities which offer both challenge and support. Teachers, headteachers, external training consultants and academic consultants have key active roles in this, as do collaborative school cultures which build, develop and sustain strategies for support within twin notions of teacher autonomy and collective accountability. Successful partnerships and networks recognize the need for teachers themselves to retain a high degree of control over the direction of their work, increase their participation in shaping the contexts which affect their contributions, whilst at the same time providing access to appropriate critical challenge and support.

Essentially, successful professional learning networks in the future will need to be based upon continuing close knowledge of the factors which constitute 'need' and on skilled intervention support which places need in short- and long-term contexts. Traditional notions of teacher professionalism and educational research will themselves be redefined through a breaking down of individualistic, bifurcated cultures. Government and school policy, through on-going dialogue between stakeholders, may at times match individually defined needs and be supportive of teacher autonomy.

One of the key responsibilities of universities is to connect their own particular interests in teaching and knowledge production with those of the policy, research and 'user' communities they serve on the explicit understanding that whilst the interests of those communities are paramount in forming a learning agenda, they too are open to critique. Work of this kind will be alongside rather than apart from policy-makers, teachers associations, parents, governors, schools, teachers and associated agencies — even those of government — not as 'supplicants' but neither as strangers, seemingly distant from or disinterested in the worlds in which potential partners live. We need to inhabit each other's castles (Somekh, 1994) and to develop dispositions and skills which enable us to do so:

> The competencies we then need as professionals must include the competence to cross borders, cultures and dialects, the learning and translating of multiple languages (the political, the everyday, the academic) and the courage to transgress when faced with social injustices . . . How we practice our authority is then the issue, not what we claim or profess: if we believe in something, then we have to practice it. (Walker, 1996, p. 417)

Successful models of lifelong learning networks between universities, schools and others beyond the 1990s must assert connections between thinking, learning, planning and practice through *self-generated*, supported reflective work at a number of levels. Such work must be perceived as relevant and appropriate to the lifelong cognitive and emotional development needs of all parties. One of the major omissions in the reporting if not the experience of networks for improvement is any systematic interrogation of the effect of the emotional commitment and the underlying moral purposes of the participants upon their success.

Conclusion

In the networking models of professional development described in this chapter, the work does not belong to any one individual or interest group. It is jointly owned by each of the participants. The voices of both are listened to and heeded. Teachers and significant others are actively involved in negotiating processes and outcomes; and the power relationships of cooptation rather than collaboration are avoided (Erickson and Christman, 1996, p. 150). The academy continues to occupy a key independent position from which it has the potential to promote, sustain and extend environments which provide challenge and support through research which both informs and is embedded in development. Teacher educators are, in a sense, interventionists who aim to seek questions which are perceived by teachers and schools as relevant to their needs, to investigate answers to these questions collaboratively and to place the onus for action on the teachers and schools themselves. Professional development is fundamentally about changing thinking and practice — and the contexts in which these occur — in the interests of enhancing the quality of the learning experiences of students and thus providing greater opportunities for greater achievements. Decisions about change in practice must, however, be in the hands of the teachers, just as learning is, ultimately, in the hands of students.

The creation of learning networks of the kind described in this chapter takes time and is not always easy. There will always be individuals and groups whose individual or collective vested self-interest may not be served. In the process, new knowledge and skills will need to be developed and tentative steps to change supported. It will make, as we have seen, new demands on busy professionals. But it is within this shared landscape that the future partnership work of teachers, schools, universities and other agencies in their own and each other's lifelong development can be seen as making sense. It is within this landscape that higher education can play its part in the challenge of supporting the lifelong learning of teachers.

Notes

1 See, for example, the Schools Council funded projects, *Geography for the Young School Leaver*; and the Humanities Projects of the 1970s (Stenhouse, 1980).

2 Gibbons and his colleagues develop the attributes of knowledge production in great detail under the categories of: i) knowledge produced in the context of application; ii) transdisciplinary; iii) heterogeneity and organizational diversity; iv) social accountability and reflexivity; and v) quality control.

3 'School improvement' needs to be distinguished from 'school effectiveness'. Although the latter has been useful in identifying a number of characteristics which so-called effective schools share (see Sammon et al., 1995, p. 8), it has been criticized as embodying a 'set of values which appear to be of a social control ideology' (Elliott, 1996). Elliott criticizes school effectiveness research as mechanistic, being shaped by values of 'hierarchy', 'orderliness', 'uniformity', and 'adherence', and its findings as 'ignoring the complexities of practices in schools', 'failing to describe practices from practitioners' perspectives', and supporting traditional management-dominated hierarchy structures. He cites Perrone's view that the values which underpin notions of effective schools 'entail a view of teachers as technical operatives in a technological system of pupil surveillance and control' (1996, p. 212). He criticizes as reductionist and fundamentalist the nature of school effectiveness research which confuses 'the idea of an *effective school* with that of a *good school*' (p. 213). He criticizes school effectiveness research

findings which do not conceptualize education as a morally complex process which requires teachers to exercise prudent choice (p. 219).

4 Descriptions and analyses of networking between different stakeholders are summarized in, for example, Myers and Stoll (1993); McLaughlin and Oberman (1996); Sparks and Hirsh (1997); Hollingsworth (1997); Lieberman and Miller (1992); Lieberman and McLaughlin (1992); Stringfield and Teddlie (1988); Glickman (1990); Stringfield (1995); McLaughlin and Talbert (1993).

5 See Labaree and Pallas (1996) for a detailed critique of the assumptions which lie behind PDSs and the potential negative impact on the university researcher's work.

Chapter 10

The Role of Teachers in a Learning Society

Students spend only 12 per cent of their lives in schools and so schools are only one of a number of potential settings for education. Nevertheless, they are arguably the most crucial in the formation of attitudes towards learning and much — perhaps too much — is expected of them and their teachers.

> They have been given an impossible task by an over-expectant society. They have had donated to them, almost by default, the responsibility of widening their role in society. They have not been given the necessary resources and the authority to fulfil that role, either through the constant training and retraining of teachers, or through the increased funding which might enable them to compete with the professional media men . . . Further, as is typical in times of stress and change . . . [schools] are pressured to adopt ever more rigid structures and curricula more appropriate to a full-employment, industrial, mid-20th (or even 19th) century environment, rather than to the new and urgent paradigm of change, information technology, lifelong learning and the post-industrial order. (Longworth and Davies, 1996, p. 40)

Both the assignment to schools of responsibilities for basic and lifelong 'citizenship' education and the causal link between education, training and employment implied in much of the lifelong learning rhetoric do not match the current action of governments who have been accused of 'trying to construct a new [learning] society with the intellectual equivalent of straw rather than bricks' (Coffield, 1996, p. 1). This final chapter examines the influences of a changing world upon schools and the kinds of investment needed in teachers if they are to fulfil the expectations placed upon them in the twenty-first century.

The Director of the ESRC's research programme into 'The Learning Society' in England, suggests that the creation of a learning society needs to be built upon a theory of learning which encompasses 'not only the cognitive processes within the needs of individuals but also the social relationships and arrangements which stimulate learning', recognizing that learning is a shared responsibility by 'all the social partners — government, employers, trade unions *and* individuals' (Coffield, 1996, p. 9).

Handy (1989) has predicted for the job market in the next century in which:

> It will increasingly be the individual's responsibility to make sure that the opportunities on offer add up to a sensible career path . . . Education in those

> circumstances becomes an investment, experience an asset, provided that it is wide and not shallow. (p. 127)

However, Coffield (1996) identifies the emphasis upon the role of the individual as the key to competitiveness as 'the weakest aspect' of British and European policies on education, training and employment:

> . . . it is possible that millions of British citizens will individually make rational decisions to train and retrain and yet no adequate national policy on education and employment and no marked improvement in national prosperity will result. (Coffield, 1996, p. 6)

The Changing World

It is a truism to state that the circumstances of the students whom teachers teach are changing. For example, in England it has been predicted that by the first decade of the new century, some 45 per cent of children are likely to have experienced some form of non-conjugal household structure by the time they reach 16 years of age (Walker, 1995). The standard household of husband, wife and children is now a minority formation — 31 per cent of children are now born outside marriage. Children who experience family disruption are more likely to suffer social, educational and health problems than a comparable sample whose families remain intact (Cockett and Tripp, 1994). Children of lone parents (19 per cent in UK) are particularly at risk of poverty and this creates additional stresses. Children watch considerable amounts of TV and video, often unsupervised. They may appear to be more sophisticated, especially in relation to technology, but they are also more vulnerable, uncertain of their values, and, paradoxically, may lack motivation, self-esteem and self-confidence in school-centred learning. They need teachers who understand them, who are able to provide a secure environment, who provide critical, caring access to knowledge.

Schools are not only places within which teachers have responsibilities for mediating values derived from students' life experience. They also exist within competing socio-economic values and contexts and contribute to them. On this theme, an annual report of the ILO, a United Nations agency, suggested that part of the problem in Europe, where the unemployment rate is at 10 per cent, is that international market pressures are forcing rapid changes in the structure of industrial economies which are now having to move from producing 'low value-added goods and services into high-technology and high-quality service industries'. In America, for example, one effect has been 'to displace low-skill workers and increase the demands for highly skilled ones'. The analyst concludes that if this trend is followed in Europe:

> . . . the only way we can sustain, or even improve, the relatively high living standards that most people in the developed world enjoy is if we are educated, trained

> and motivated to produce the high quality goods and services that justify such standards. (McRae, 1995, p. 4)

The need for more highly educated, motivated employees who are able to use more autonomy and apply skills in combination with flexible technology and work processes to produce more per worker is recognized, too, in America where the move from the specialist to the adaptable generalist is well under way:

> Employers want employees with solid academic basics, but they want the applied versions of the three Rs. Applied reading, writing and maths are substantially different from the versions taught in schools. In addition, employers want a set of behavioural skills that are not taught at all in traditional academic curricula, such as problem solving, communication skills, interpersonal skills and leadership. (Carnevale, 1994)

The collective and individual kinds of experiences that students are likely to bring with them into school — with which teachers will have to work if they are to gain the commitment and motivation necessary for the development of these kinds of skills and qualities in the crowded and not always predictable world of many poorly resourced schools and classrooms — need to be understood by teachers in order to prepare them for the opportunities, responsibilities and experiences of adult life.

Both outside and inside school, we are witnessing a continuing exponential expansion of telecommunications. This information and communication technology will provide students — indeed all of us — with more opportunities to learn through CD Roms, virtual reality, and interactive technologies which will enable people from different parts of the world to talk to each other simultaneously, to surf on the INTERNET, to cruise on the superhighway, to dance to the tune of Cyberspace. Yet this new technology may become a vehicle for containment and control in which not all students have access and where schools do not develop multiple forms of teaching and learning.

In British Columbia, Canada, the Sullivan Commission's 'Year 2000 Framework for Learning' report concluded that:

> In view of the new social and economic realities *all* students, regardless of their immediate plans following school, will need to develop a flexibility and versatility undreamed of by previous generations. Increasingly, they will need to be able to employ critical and creative thinking skills to solve problems and make decisions, to be technologically literate as well as literate in the traditional sense, and to be good communicators. Equally, they will need to have well developed interpersonal skills and be able to work cooperatively with others. Finally, they will need to be lifelong learners. (Canadian Ministry of Education, 1991, p. 2)

This vision of schooling takes account of the changing nature of society and is much closer to the needs articulated by business. It implies a need for teachers who are adaptable, for their teaching to be of a consistently high quality and for their roles to change if they are to contribute to the endeavour of lifelong learning for the twenty-first century which is so regularly espoused by governments and employers as being essential.

In many countries, despite the rhetoric, investment in formal education which is designed to meet the needs of the individual, the economy and society in the twenty-first century is too little and, more seriously, continues to be inappropriate and misdirected. Current conditions of service in teaching still do not attract the best minds. The innovation overload which schools in many countries have experienced over the last two decades has frayed the spirit and energy of many of the most committed. Attempts to establish 'national standards' in England, America and elsewhere is yet another means of measuring teachers without providing complementary development opportunities, and, however well-intentioned, is unlikely to win back lost self-esteem or confidence. All the indicators point to fewer applications for teaching and more early retirements, often through disillusionment and stress-related illness. How, then, can we seriously discuss investment in lifelong learning when the system for creating, maintaining and developing its foundations is itself unhealthy, and reform programmes themselves are so out-of-step with the needs of the workplace?

Investing in Schools

> Almost all parties . . . agree that schools could be better than they are. The question is: Better at what? For some, the problem is rooted in the failure of the schools to teach the 'basic skills' to all children . . . for others . . . the problem goes well beyond the failure of the schools to teach all children to read, write, and cipher. The fundamental problem is that schools do not prepare all children to function effectively in the world of ideas. The schools do not prepare all children to think critically and creatively. The schools do not prepare children to be lifelong learners. In brief, schools do not prepare the young for life in an information-based, knowledge-work society — the society in which. . . . children now live and in which they will be required to function as adults. (Schlechty, 1990, p. xvii)

For a love of lifelong learning to grow, every school must be a learning community which, regardless of the age, ability or curriculum content promotes three essential purposes. They must:

1 *Help each individual to achieve*. This means that time must be liberated for teachers to create the conditions which will allow for the growth of self-esteem, the nurturing of motivation and the challenge of sustained commitment. Schools must be able to respond to the needs of the young and to provide for many a secure haven in which uninterrupted learning and achievement can occur. Children are growing up in a changing and fragmented world in which home relationships are being redefined, once certain values challenged and long-term employment in one occupation unlikely.

2 *Build a broad, rather than narrow, knowledge base.* The European Commission White Paper, 'Teaching and Learning: Towards the Learning Society' (1996) regards the 'wherewithal to grasp the meanings of things, to understand and to create' as an essential function of schools in order to prepare students for adjustment to the economic and employment situation; and what science is now confirming about Gardner's identification of multiple intelligences provides welcome support for those who believe that schools need to subscribe to a broader view of intelligence.[1] Those who charge schools to continue to fixate on promoting academic ability are missing the point. Cognitive and emotional intelligences are not opposing competences, but complementary and interactive. Both must be attended, particularly in the years of formal schooling. The development of 'emotional intelligence' is particularly important in a world in which little is certain anymore, because:

> IQ offers little to explain the different destinies of people who start out with roughly equal promise, schooling and opportunity . . . academic intelligence offers virtually no preparation for the turmoil — or opportunities — that life's vicissitudes bring. (Goleman, 1995, pp. 35–6)

Knowing your emotions, the ability to manage and motivate oneself and handle relationships are essential companions to knowledge. Together these would seem to be necessary qualities for survival in the twenty-first century.

3. *Be a part of rather than apart from the society*

> If the student's potential is to be fulfilled, then the school must provide the framework for learning. (Dalin and Rust, 1996, p. 79)

An increasing number of writers are making the link between schools — their cultures, purposes and processes — and the contexts in which their students live and work, understanding that schools stand 'at the crucial interface between past and future, charged both with the conservation of culture and with its radical renewal' (Beare and Slaughter, 1993, p. 15) in a world which holds ever more uncertain prospects for many students:

> As the overlapping waves of social, technical, political, economic, cultural and environmental change have washed over us, so the strictures, the continuities, expectations, values and meanings which once sustained the cultural landscape have weakened or dissolved entirely . . . If schools are to play a more culturally constructive role than they are doing at present, their work requires some broadly defined social purpose, something that goes beyond purely personal, economic and short-term considerations which derive solely from what has gone before . . . In short, educators need a credible vision of a future that works and that reconnects each individual with the wider world. (Beare and Slaughter, 1993, p. 16)

These three purposes of schools are foundation stones in the development of a lifelong learning society. They combine support and challenge for each individual according to need and context with a practical awareness of the demands engendered by: i) the impact of the information society (the continuing explosion of information and communications technology is already creating a need for guidance in selection and use — for information is not knowledge, and knowledge is not wisdom); ii) internationalization (with its erosion of barriers between labour markets); and iii) the scientific and technical world. Schools have a vital role to play in countering the real and imagined insecurities and challenges created by these three major 'upheaval' factors.

It is not so much that one particular vision is needed, but Beare and Slaughter (1993), Dalin and Rust (1996), Handy (1993) and others are signalling changes in the social position and role of the school. Schools need to be *in* rather than *of* what we now recognize as the knowledge society. They need to live and communicate a vision of future society based upon an understanding of the worlds in which their students live, their learning needs and the demands of society and the world of work; and they need to be filled with teachers who are learners, who encourage children to want to learn, to treat the world as a land with limitless horizons, to achieve.

> In the knowledge society people have to learn how to learn . . . subjects may matter less than the students' capacity to continue to learn and their motivation to do so. Post-capitalist society requires lifelong learning. For this we need a discipline of learning. But lifelong learning also requires that learning be alluring, indeed, that it become a high satisfaction in itself if not something the individual craves. (Drucker, 1994, p. 183)

Teachers and schools will need to move further along the 'partnership' road with informal and formal learning contracts not only with individual pupils and parents and local communities, but with businesses, as they increasingly become a more integral part of open systems of learning (Drucker, 1994, p. 186). Government reforms which focus upon reshaping the governance and structures of schools as a means of increasing their effectiveness rather than addressing how learning capacities of students and teachers may be enhanced are as naive as the belief that the provision of computers for all will itself result in a new commitment to learning by students.

The Leadership Factor

Good schools and good teachers seem to be able to assimilate externally imposed change into their own visions for students. In America, Beck and Murphy (1996) observed a successful elementary school that was site-managed over an extended period of time. They concluded that student learning, transformed teaching, and increasing parental involvement were due principally to four imperatives:

1. The imperative to promote learning — especially, but not exclusively — for students;
2. The imperative for persons to assume leadership roles and to focus energies and resources of stakeholders in productive ways;
3. The imperative to cultivate a sense of community within the school and to link the school with the larger community in mutually beneficial ways;
4. The imperative to support efforts to build the capacity of administrators, teachers, and parents so that they are better able to support student learning. (Beck and Murphy, 1996, p. 118)

These imperatives are not unlike those of Rosenholtz (1989) and Nias (1989), though expressed differently. Success in meeting them demands not only knowledgeable, skilful teachers, but teachers who are committed to their students and each other. Values, beliefs, perceptions and behaviours cannot be changed by directives, but can be cultivated, nurtured and encouraged within communities which create and sustain conditions that allow teachers concerned about providing students with powerful learning opportunities to act on their commitments. These conditions include:

- support for risk taking;
- freedom from excessive bureaucratic constraints;
- time, money and administrative support for substantive professional development. (Beck and Murphy, 1996, p. 123)

The conditions will themselves be underpinned by values. Jerry Patterson, Superintendent of Schools in Wisconsin, provides his own vision of 'tomorrow's schools' by contrasting today's and tomorrow's values in five key areas:

Value 1 Openness to Participation

Today's Value: Our organization values employees listening to the organization's leaders and doing what the leaders tell them to do.

Tomorrow's Value: Our organization values employees actively participating in any discussion or decision affecting them.

Value 2 Openness to Diversity

Today's Value: Our organization values employees falling in line with the overall organization direction.

Tomorrow's Value: Our organization values diversity in perspectives leading to a deeper understanding of organizational reality and an enriched knowledge base for decision making.

Value 3 Openness to Conflict

Today's Value: Our organization values employees communicating a climate of group harmony and happiness.

Tomorrow's Value: Our organization values employees resolving conflict in a healthy way that leads to stronger solutions for complex issues.

Value 4 Openness to Reflection

Today's Value: Our organization values employees conveying a climate of decisiveness. Firm decisions are made and implemented without looking back.

Tomorrow's Value: Our organization values employees reflecting on their own and others' thinking in order to achieve better organizational decisions.

Value 5 Openness to Mistakes

Today's Value: Our organization values employees concentrating on making no mistakes and working as efficiently as possible.

Tomorrow's Value: Our organization values employees acknowledging mistakes and learning from them.

(Patterson, 1993, p. 7)

Although written in the context of school leadership, these values might equally be expressed in classrooms where learning is recognized as being complex and non-linear and where teachers and students are learners and leaders.

Investing in Teachers

> Nothing will ever replace the centrally important role of the teacher in the learning process. The personal relationship between the teacher and the learner will remain at the centre of the pedagogical mission for awakening, initiating, guiding, motivating and transmitting wisdom and tacit knowledge such as moral values, personal and interpersonal development. However, the role of the teacher will change fundamentally for we are moving from a teaching to a learning model. (European Round Table of Industrialists, 1997, p. 9)

Whether learning takes place inside or outside a school building, good teachers who are knowledgeable about learners and learning, who themselves are committed to learning, and who can provide the right frameworks for learning by knowing what questions to ask will always be needed. They are now not only being called upon to provide the knowledge necessary for enabling students to achieve in examinations but also to equip each one to confront problems 'for which specialists have only partial solutions or no solution at all' (Dalin and Rust, 1996, p. 79).

In writing about his vision of the current transformation of society, Peter Drucker (1993) points to the importance of schools and teachers in providing a foundation of values and practices for lifelong learning through skilfully promoting student motivation and achievement. Yet, they have 'rarely been allowed to focus on the strengths of students and to challenge them', (p. 184) more often having to help them to do 'a little less poorly' what they are not particularly good at. The widespread availability of new technologies will, he claims, 'free teachers from spending most, if not all, their time on routine learning, on remedial learning, on repetitive learning' (p. 185), and enable them to focus upon individual learning, discovering the students' strengths, and focusing them on achievement. Learning which combines knowledge with understanding requires that teachers work with *surface learning* (knowledge components or facts) and *deep learning* (connections, relationships, holistic understanding) (Svingby, 1993). Free-standing facts are necessary but they are meaningless unless understood in authentic contexts.

> Standards of learning ought to be measured in terms of their capacity to help learners to engage in deep learning. A primary task of the school is to develop instructional programmes, curriculum resources and organisational structures that are geared to focus the school on competence regarding deep learning . . . Schools must, among other things, help children and youth to learn to think. (Dalin and Rust, 1996, p. 89)

Changed circumstances and increasing expectations mean that teachers now need not only to be knowledge brokers but 'learning counsellors'[2] in settings in which the distinction between student and teacher will become blurred.

> Students with extensive resources will engage in teacher roles, and teachers also will be students, in that they will engage in lifelong education and training . . . teachers will serve as role models in the school where understanding will be more important than knowledge, where personality development will be essential and where the whole person will stand in the centre . . . The message to teachers is that the 'answer' is no longer the key in the learning process. The key is the 'question'. Teachers will no longer be expected to have the one and only right answer. They will be expected to stimulate the curiosity of each child, to focus on the basic issues and to help each child to discover and to work systematically. (Dalin and Rust, 1996, p. 145)

What must be faced, however, is that teachers will have 'differing degrees of comfort' (Caine and Caine, 1997, p. 214) with the kinds of interactive, multilayered roles and relationships required in classrooms where 'learning to learn' is as important as 'learning to achieve'. Long ago, for example, Argyris and Schön (1974) distinguished between two models of teacher behaviour. In Model 1, teachers unilaterally design the teaching environment and control it, whereas in Model 2, they '. . . design situations or environments where participants can be originators and can experience high personal causation. . . . tasks are controlled jointly . . . protection of self is a joint enterprise and oriented towards growth' (cited in Caine and Caine, 1997, p. 216). In classrooms of the twenty-first century, it is likely that teachers will need to play an even greater variety of roles and employ a greater range of teaching approaches according to need.

Teachers, like their students, actively construct ways of knowing which act as maps of their worlds. Just as classrooms must be learning environments in which pupils receive, respond to and actively participate in generating knowledge, so professional development opportunities must provide a range of learning experiences which encourage teachers to reflect upon and inquire into their thinking and practice through interaction between their own and others' experience, so that they are able to embrace the challenge of new teaching roles and see these as challenges rather than burdens to be borne.

> If the school wants to enhance lifelong learning, teachers will have to adopt new roles; they will no longer be the dispenser of factual information or theoretical or practical knowledge but will be 'facilitators of learning' — those who 'help' young people to discover or acquire knowledge, attitudes, skills and aptitudes or competencies. They will stimulate within pupils critical attitudes and those [pro]-active learning styles which are the basis of the lifelong learning process. Teachers should be lifelong learners themselves and this should be an element of the open professionalism of the teacher. (Beernaert, 1994, p. 6)

Teachers' abilities to meet the challenges of learning for and in the twenty-first century will be conditioned not only by the environments in which they work, but also their own world views. Caine and Caine (1997) identified four core qualities:

- A sense of self-efficacy grounded in authenticity;
- The ability to build relationships that facilitate self-organisation;
- The ability to see connections between subjects, discipline and life;
- The capacity to engage in self-reflection, to grow and adapt. (p. 221)

Yet the greatest problems for teachers in engaging in the kinds of sustained interactivity necessary for meeting the learning and achievement needs of individual students continue to be time, disposition and support. It is these themes which have dominated the chapters in this book and which make up the complex and shifting landscapes in which the meaning of teacher development is located. Most schools are not yet places where adults as well as children are encouraged to learn.

Despite the growing rhetoric of the importance of 'lifelong learning', it does not appear yet that the necessary connection between the quality of teachers' motivations, commitments and vision of learning for their students and their planning, participation and monitoring of their own learning over a career has been made. Indeed, for many teachers the last 20 years have been years of survival rather than development. As social and economic changes have placed new demands upon and created new expectations from schools, hardly a year has passed without some reform being mooted, negotiated or imposed in the name of raising standards, increasing 'user' participation and pupil entitlement. Traditional relationships have been dismembered as national governments have pursued simultaneously 'loose tight' policies of centralization and decentralization. Though the nature of government intervention in different countries has varied, the universal effects have been similar.[3] Teachers have had to bear an increased workload and work longer hours. Many inner-city teachers remain overwhelmed by the alienation of students, manifested in, at best, passive tolerance and, at worst, behavioural difficulties, unsupportive parents, minimal resources, little community respect, and the sheer effort of survival. Elsewhere, the constant measuring of outputs is complemented by a paucity of opportunity for sustained teacher development. There is so little time and energy for establishing the learning partnerships, and emphasis on the knowledge, qualities and skills of students so clearly demanded by employers. Even if there were, the preparation of teachers at all levels remains dominated by technicist 'training' models.

The economic and social arguments for improving the capacity of individuals to learn are now beginning to be more clearly articulated (Gibbs, 1996, p. 9). For example, the influence of teachers upon students in the early years and the association between pre-school education and educational attainments in reading and mathematics and social (behavioural) outcomes, on their attitudes to learning, self-esteem and task orientation have been well documented (Sylva, 1996, p. 19), as have the benefits accrued to students from good teachers and good schools in all phases of education. On the downside, however, there is evidence that many students do not relate well to the school curriculum or to 'traditional' teaching and learning roles, and 'drop out' either metaphorically or in fact. The costs of secondary school dropout in Canada, for example, have been estimated at, 'more than $4 billion over the working lifetimes of the nearly 137000 youths' (Lafleur, 1992, p. 2). Low educational achievement correlates also with lower work and life chances for the individual. Conditions for teaching and learning are less than ideal in most schools.

Developing the Professional Self

In a wide-ranging investigation into the state of education and its possible futures, the National Commission on Education in England (1993) investigated seven key 'goals': i) effective schooling; ii) schools, society and citizenship; iii) the teaching profession and quality; iv) higher and further education; v) preparing for work today and tomorrow; vi) better ways of learning; and vii) resources.[4] It put forward seven goals for achievement in the years ahead. Three of these relate directly to the theme of this chapter:

> *Goal No 3*: Every pupil in every lesson has the right to good teaching and adequate support facilities . . . Every pupil is entitled to be taught every lesson by a highly professional teacher competent to teach that lesson. (p. 44)
>
> *Goal No 4*: Everyone must be entitled to learn throughout life and be encouraged in practice to do so . . . Learning does not stop at 16, at 18, at 21 or at any other age. Everyone must have the entitlement to go on learning whether for employment purposes or to fulfil other personal goals. There must be real opportunity to use the entitlement, and incentive and encouragement to do so. (p. 45)
>
> *Goal No 5*: The management of education and training must be integrated, and those with a stake in them must have this recognised . . . All those with a major stake in the system must have a place in its management, and accountability at each level is essential. (p. 45)

The National Commission on Education concluded with a vision of the teacher in the twenty-first century:

> In our vision, a teacher in the 21st century will be an authority and enthusiast in the knowledge, ideas, skills, understanding and values to be presented to pupils.

> The teacher will be an expert on effective learning, with knowledge of a range of classroom methods that can be intelligently applied and an understanding of appropriate organisational and management styles, conditions, and resources. The teacher will have the capacity to think deeply about educational aims and values, and thereby critically about educational programmes. The teacher will be willing to motivate and encourage each and every pupil, assessing progress and learning needs in their widest sense, even when this involves them in areas outside formal education. The teacher will in the first instance be an educator, not only of the 'subject' being taught but also aiming to extend the intellectual, imaginative, inquiring and critical powers of his or her pupils, and to encourage them to question their wider personal and social values. (p. 197)

Neither the assignment by others nor the claim of 'professional' by self is enough. Behaving and developing as a professional demands a lifelong commitment to learning, preferably with, but if necessary without, the support of the organization. In the twenty-first century, participation in one's own development over a career is a basic requirement for everyone who wishes to be recognized and behave as a professional. Lifelong learning is a particular responsibility for teachers in schools which themselves aspire to become and improve as learning organizations in which teachers are the leading learners:

> In a community of learners, the most important role of teacher . . . is that of leading learner: one who engages in the central enterprise of the schoolhouse by displaying and modelling the behaviour we expect and hope students will acquire. As one bumper sticker puts it so well: 'You can't lead where you won't go' . . . an elementary school teacher put it even better: 'Learning is not something like chicken pox, a childhood disease that makes you itch for a while, and then leaves you immune for the rest of your life.' (Barth, 1996, p. 29)

In the context of both external demands for improvement and internal professional responsibility, a number of needs of teachers as professionals may be identified:

- the need to maintain purpose and vision;
- the need to model lifelong learning;
- the need to revisit the routines of their work which restrict development;
- the need to be professionally, morally and contractually accountable;
- the need to work collaboratively in building and maintaining learning cultures with pupils, colleagues, parents and community.

Traditional concepts of and approaches to professional development are limiting in their ability to connect with individual and system needs because they are not based upon an understanding of the complexities of teachers' lives and conditions of work nor upon an understanding of how teachers learn and why they change (or do not change), and thus how schools also develop. They do not place the individual learner at the centre of their agenda and so cannot properly serve the needs of person or system in any other than a fragmented way. They rarely contain within them a vision of the challenges which face teachers, schools and students in the new economically and socially turbulent worlds in which they are growing up. They espouse the importance of building and sustaining teacher morale and the centrality of high-quality teaching in school improvement efforts, but rarely demonstrate them in practice.

It is clear from research and experience that teachers' learning is affected by:

- work experiences;
- life histories;
- career phase;
- external social and political conditions and contexts;
- school cultures;
- leadership and peer support;
- opportunities for reflection;
- authentic dialogue between individual and system;
- the quality of the learning experiences;
- the relevance of the learning experience to intellectual and emotional needs;
- their confidence in participation in need identification practices and their contexts;
- their ownership of their learning.

A lifelong commitment to learning, and to modelling learning, demands that, even in the knowledge that it will be discontinuous and not always comfortable, it is planned, recorded, and reviewed alone and in consultation with others. It is only by this kind of attentiveness and caring that teachers themselves will continue to learn and develop; it is only through teacher development that the quality of students' learning opportunities can be assured. The aim of continuing professional development is deceptively simple. It is to act as a means of reviewing and, where appropriate, improving teachers' commitment to teaching and their abilities to provide the best possible learning and achievement opportunities for students. The practice of CPD is, however, complex.

Although much learning occurs naturally through experience, this alone is not sufficient for development which needs:

- to connect with requirements at critical moments in teachers' development lives;
- to enable self-confrontation through reflection which raises questions about purposes, practices and contexts;
- extended critical engagement with peers and others;
- to connect educational knowledge with knowledge about education through partnerships and networks which bring together a range of stakeholders;
- to be a part of an ongoing dialogue between teacher and the school which recognizes that the needs of system and individual may not always coincide but will always serve one another;
- to reflect participation in a range of different kinds of learning opportunities over time appropriate to need;

- to be focused upon classroom and school management, subject knowledge, broader intellectual, emotional commitment and vision needs;
- to be based upon a personal development plan owned and used as a review and planning means by each teacher over a career.

As with children, so with teachers, the key to successful learning is motivation which cannot be achieved by means of tight, centralized control. Personal commitment and involvement are likely to be limited when teachers must follow dictums devised by others (Rubin, 1989).

There are three investment strategies which, if followed, are likely to produce dividends of enormous proportions for all with a stake in our educational future.

1. Investing in the Whole Teacher: Teaching Skills Are Not Enough

It has been argued that improving teachers' skills is the only way to bring about the better standards of learning the nation requires, that the time has come to 'shift the focus of policy from the structure and regulation of education, to teaching and learning itself', so that 'teachers might be supported in acquiring and maintaining, the most refined, advanced skills in pedagogy' (Barber, 1994). Whilst no one could fail to support this sensible plea, to focus upon developing teaching methods alone as a means of achieving learning and to promote one over another, is to miss the point that professional development must be concerned with teachers' whole selves since it is these which bring significance to the meaning of the teaching act and the learning which results. Policy should be designed to nurture, cherish and enhance and, where necessary, restore the sense of moral purpose which is at the core of all good teaching.

A sense of vision is particularly important for teachers and schools, because, in the years up to and into the twenty-first century they will be expected to make a difference and be seen to make a difference in the learning lives of children and young people, in changing circumstances.

Governments will continue to rely upon education as a means of increasing their economic competitiveness. My vision for the twenty-first century is that good teaching will be recognized as work which involves both the head and the heart, that it is in the first instance an interpersonal activity, 'directed at shaping and influencing (not moulding), by means of a range of pedagogical skills what people become as persons through whatever it is that is taught' (Sockett, 1993, p. 13). It is, of course, important that teachers of the twenty-first century are able to use a range of pedagogical skills which fit their purposes. However, the application of pedagogical skills needs to be a consequence of the exercise of pedagogical judgment which is informed by reflection in, on and about the purposes, contexts, processes and outcomes of teaching and learning. There must be a public recognition that effective learning involves, essentially, an 'interactive chemistry' between learner and teacher which depends as much on process as content, and is an expression of visions and values and perceptions as much as competences and knowledge. Ethics and values, therefore, must play an explicit role alongside rational concerns. The diminishing sense of agency or control that many teachers report must be replaced by a sense of accountability with trust.

2. *Investing in Learning Partnerships: Changing Roles*

One of the biggest challenges for teachers is that which is posed by the telecommunications revolution which will inevitably enlarge the role of the individual with more access to information and greater ability to communicate to anyone, anywhere, anytime. As a result, it is reasonable to predict that the boundaries between in-school and out-of-school learning will become more blurred — they already are — and teachers' roles as 'expert knowledge holders' will be eroded. Instead they will become knowledge brokers, learning counsellors skilled in learning processes; for whilst technologies escalate our hopes for a better life, we regularly find ourselves unable to harness their potential. Their application in school depends upon resources way beyond those presently in place, and, more importantly, upon the understandings and skills of teachers to facilitate and problematize their use and mediate the information they convey.

There are three issues which must be addressed alongside the growing use of the new technologies. First, though much of student learning through information technology will not require the use of social skills, it may be enhanced by it. Students will continue to need to test and consolidate their learning by reflecting upon and exchanging ideas, ideals and opinions with other pupils. There is some evidence that even now, in primary schools, one-to-one teacher–child interactions are brief and, for most children, infrequent, and collaborative work rare. The teacher's role will, therefore, be as process facilitator and interventionist rather than content expert. Second, the new technologies emphasize that learning is not only the result of school experience but of other influences — the home, the media, and friends. Whilst technologies facilitate and enhance the provision of education, 'the educator's role is to preserve the human component because human interaction is the key to the successful application of communication technologies to the delivery of lifelong learning' (Stanford, 1994). Third, the information received will need to be subject to critical appraisal. Teachers are in a key position as 'learning counsellors'. Schooling will, perforce, become more of a partnership and 'learning contracts' between teachers, pupils and parents, established on a more explicit basis. *Learning, if not teaching, will become everyone's business.*

3. *Investing in Continuing Professional Development: Making a Difference*

Investing in education means investing in the continuing professional development of teachers. All students are entitled to be taught by good teachers qualified to teach the subject in question; and the success, quality and enjoyment of what goes on in schools depends above all on the heads and teaching staff. Yet, so far, the bulk of CPD continues to focus upon 'keeping teachers updated about recent reforms, in particular the curriculum', and has 'hindered personal development and the continuing development of teaching practices and strategies' (NCE, 1993, p. 219).

Nor does it enhance their career-long commitment. In Luxembourg, the ETUCE (European Assembly of Teacher Trade Unions) found that

> Static or linear conceptions of teacher education must be replaced by a holistic understanding of the inter-relatedness of teachers' personal and professional development with research and development, school improvement and the changing social and political aspirations for the education service and by an appreciation that a dynamic system will challenge existing organisational structures and power bases and require responsiveness to the needs of the practitioners. (1994, 7.12)

Such an holistic understanding implies that opportunities for professional learning and development must be available, and fully resourced, which recognize that for teachers, as for students and other adults of the twenty-first century, learning is a lifelong business.

This book has sought to present the continuing professional development of teachers as an endeavour worthy of investment. It is: i) essential to the learning, well-being and achievements of students and schools; ii) vital to the maintenance and development of their own commitment and expertise; and iii) a major responsibility of teachers and employers. In examining the personal, professional, and policy contexts in which teachers work, it has investigated the complexities of learning and development and, in doing so, identified a variety of ways in which teachers learn, why they develop (or do not develop), in what circumstances, and what kinds of intervention are appropriate in support of learning.

To develop schools we must be prepared to develop teachers. A first step in this process is to help teachers remind themselves that they do have a crucial role to play in making a difference to the lives of students. Also, because their roles will continue to change, teachers need to have their own individual learning curricula as a means of generating and regenerating the understandings, critical thinking skills, emotional intelligence, craft skills and intellectual flexibility demanded as they prepare pupils for uncertain worlds in which neither the corporate learning process nor the individual one is optional.

Teachers are potentially the single most important asset in the achievement of the vision of a learning society. It is the kinds and quality of the training and development opportunities throughout their careers and the culture in which they work which will influence their own promotion of lifelong learning values and their ability to help students to learn how to learn to succeed. They are at the 'cutting edge'. It is they who hold the key to students' growing or diminishing self-esteem, achievement, and visions of present and future possibilities for learning through their own commitment, knowledge and skills.

A vision of lifelong learning demands emotionally intelligent teachers who are educated to think, reflect, evaluate, look for and provide opportunities for the development of individual achievement which challenge and support each student in their care. It demands a reversal of the stripping of the learning opportunities and resourcing of schools and the self-esteem of those who work in them. It demands a focus, over time, in those whose stake is demonstrably in the present and future lifelong health of the nation. For the rhetoric to match the reality, it demands investment in teachers.

Notes

1. For detailed considerations of this see, for example, Beare and Slaughter (1993); Drucker (1994); and Dalin and Rust (1996).
2. This is a term coined by Longworth and Davies (1996). Among the skills they suggest that teachers will need are: how to guide the learner through myriad pathways to learning sources; how to motivate learning; how to develop and maintain databases; how to set individualized learning models; how to develop and administer targeted evaluation techniques and personal progress modules; how to use distance learning technologies; how to set up personal profiling systems; where the best educational courses on a variety of topics can be found, locally, nationally and internationally (p. 140).
3. We should not assume that the emphasis on teaching a subject-based National Curriculum which is monitored and tested at regular intervals in English schools, necessarily applies to other countries. It does not. In Norway, for example, Reform 94 offers six goals for schooling: i) a person seeking for meaning; ii) a creative person; iii) a working person; iv) an enlightened person; v) a cooperating person; vi) an environmentally sensitive person. In New Zealand, the 'new' curriculum consists of essential learning areas — mathematics, science, technology, the Arts, Health and Physical Well-being, combined with essential skills, principles and attitudes and values (in Dalin and Rust, 1996, pp. 154–6).
4. The National Commission on Education was an independent body, funded by the Paul Hamlyn Foundation, and not associated with any political party. It was established in 1991 for the purpose of identifying and examining key issues facing education and training over the next 25 years.

References

ACHILLES, C.M., NYE, B.A., ZAHARIAS, J.B. and FULTON, B.D. (1993a) 'The Lasting Benefits Study (LBS) in Grades 4 and 5 (1990–1991): A legacy from Tennessee's four year (K-3) class size study (1985–1989), *Project STAR*', Paper presented at North Carolina Association for Research in Education, Greensboro, North Carolina.

ACHILLES, C.M., NYE, B.A., ZAHARIAS, J.B., FULTON, B.D. and BINGHAM, S. (1993b) 'Prevention or remediation? Is small class a reasonable treatment for either?' Paper given to National Conference of Professors of Educational Administration, Palm Springs, Ca.

ACKER, S. (1990) 'Managing the drama: The headteachers' work in an urban primary school', *Sociological Review*, **38**, pp. 247–71.

AINSCOW, M., HOPKINS, D., SOUTHWORTH, G. and WEST, M. (1994) *Creating the Conditions for School Improvement*, London, David Fulton Publishers.

ALEXANDER, R. (1996) *Other Primary Schools and Ours: Hazards of International Comparison*, Coventry, University of Warwick.

ALEXANDER, R., ROSE, J. and WOODHEAD, C. (1992) *Curriculum Organisation and Classroom Practice in Primary Schools: A Discussion Paper*, London, DES.

APPLE, M.W. (1989) 'Critical introduction: Ideology and the state in educational policy', in DALE, R. (ed.) *The State and Education Policy*, Milton Keynes, Open University Press.

APPLE, M.W. (1992) *Teachers and Texts: A Political Economy of Class and Gender Relations in Education*, New York, Routledge.

ARGYRIS, C. and SCHÖN, D.A. (1974) *Theory in Practice: Increasing Professional Effectiveness*, New York, Jossey-Bass.

ASHTON, P. and WEBB, R. (1986) *Making the Difference*, New York, Longman.

AYERS, W. (1990) 'Small heroes: In and out of school with 10 year old city kids', *Cambridge Journal of Education*, **20**, 3, pp. 269–76.

BAIN, H. and ACHILLES, C.M. (1986) Interesting developments on class size, *Phi Delta Kappan*, **67**, 9, pp. 662–5.

BALL, S. (1987) *The Micro-Politics of the School: Towards a Theory of School Organisation*, London, Methuen.

BALL, S. (1994) *Education Reform: A Critical and Post-structural Approach*, Buckingham, Open University Press.

BALL, S. and GOODSON, I. (eds) (1985) *Teachers' Lives and Careers*, Lewes, Falmer Press.

BANDURA, A. (1997) *Self-Efficacy: The Exercise of Control*, New York, Freeman.

BARBER, M. (1994) 'Power and control in education 1994–2004', *British Journal of Educational Studies*, **XXXXII**, No 4, pp. 348–62.

BARBER, M., DENNING, T., GOUGH, G. and JOHNSON, M. (1994) *Urban Education Initiatives: The National Pattern. A Report for the Office for Standards in Education*, Keele University, OFSTED.

BARNETT, R. (1994) *The Limits of Competence: Knowledge, Higher Education and Society*, Society for Research in Higher Education and Open University Press, p. 159.

BARTH, R. (1990) *Improving Schools from Within: Teachers, Parents and Principals Can Make a Difference*, San Francisco, Jossey-Bass.

BARTH, R. (1996) *Building a Community of Learners*, South Bay School Leadership Team Development Seminar Series: Seminar 10, California, California School Leadership Centre.

BASCIA, N. (1991) 'The trust agreement projects: Establishing local professional cultures for teachers', Paper presented at the Annual Meeting of the American Educational Research Association, April, Chicago.

BASSEY, M. (1995) 'When do numbers get too great?', *Times Educational Supplement*, May 12 1995.

BEARE, H. and SLAUGHTER, R. (1993) *Education for the Twenty-First Century*, London, Routledge.

BECHER, A. (1989) *Academic Tribes and Territories*, Buckingham, Society for Research into Higher Education and Open University Press.

BECK, L.G. and MURPHY, J. (1993) *Understanding the Principalship: Metaphorical Themes 1920s–1990s*, New York, Teachers College Press.

BECK, L.G. and MURPHY, J. (1996) *The Four Imperatives of a Successful School*, Thousand Oaks, CA, Corwin Press Inc.

BEER, M., EISENSTAT, R. and SPECTOR, B. (1990) *The Critical Path to Corporate Renewal*, Boston, MA, Harvard Business School Press.

BEERNAERT, Y. (1994) *Lifelong Learning as a Contribution to Quality Education in Europe*, Brussels, European Lifelong Learning Monograph.

BEERNAERT, Y. (1997) 'European educational projects as a contribution to lifelong learning', *Context*, **16**, pp. 6–8.

BELENKEY, M.F., CLINCKY, B.M., GOLDBERGER, N.R. and TARALE, J.M. (1986) *Women's Ways of Knowing*, New York, Basic Books.

BENNER, P. (1984) *From Novice to Expert: Excellence and Power in Clinical Nursing Practice*, California, Addison-Wesley Publishing Co.

BENNETT, N. (1994) *Class Size in Primary Schools: Perceptions of Headteachers, Chairs of Governors, Teachers and Parents*, School of Education, University of Exeter.

BENNIS, W. and NANUS, B. (1985) *Leaders: The Strategies for Taking Charge*, New York, Harper and Row.

BIOTT, C. (1991) 'Imposed support for teachers' learning: Implementation or development partnerships?', in BIOTT, C. and NIAS, J. (eds) *Working and Learning Together for Change*, Buckingham, Open University Press, pp. 3–18.

BLASE, J. and ANDERSON, G. (1995) *The Micropolitics of Educational Leadership: From Control to Empowerment*, London, Cassell.

BLASE, J., DEDRICK, C. and STRATHE, M. (1986) 'Leadership behaviour of school principals in relation to teacher stress, satisfaction, and performance', *Journal of Humanistic Education and Development*, **24**, 4, pp. 159–71.

BOLAM, R. (1986) 'Conceptualizing in-service', in HOPKINS, D. (ed.) *Inservice Training and Educational Development: An International Survey*, Beckenham, Croom Helm.

BOLAM, R. (1990) 'Recent developments in England and Wales', in JOYCE, B. (ed.) *Changing School Culture through Staff Development, The 1990* ASCD *Yearbook*, pp. 147–67, ASCD, 1250, N Pitt Street, Alexandria, Virginia, USA.

BOWE, R. and BALL, S. (1992) *Reforming Education and Changing Schools: Case Studies in Policy Sociology*, London, Routledge.

BOYD, W.L. (1991) 'What makes ghetto schools succeed or fail?', *Teachers College Record*, **92**, pp. 331–62.

BOYLE, M.L. (1996) 'Post-welfarism and the reconstruction of teachers' work', Presentation at the BERA Annual Conference, University of Lancaster 13 September, 1996.

BRADLEY, H. (1991) *Staff Development*, London, Falmer Press.

BRADLEY, H. and HOWARD, J. (1992) 'Patterns of employment and development of teachers after INSET courses', Report to Department of Education, Cambridge Institute of Education.

BRANDT, R. (1992) 'On building learning communities: A conversation with Hank Levin', *Educational Leadership*, **50**, 1, pp. 19–23.

BRANDT, R. (1996) 'On a new direction for teacher evaluation: A conversation with Tom McGreal', *Educational Leadership*, **53**, 6, pp. 30–3.

BREDESON, P.V. (1989) 'An analysis of the metaphorical perspectives of school principals', in BURDEN, J.L. (ed.) *School Leadership: A Contemporary Reader*, Newbury Park, CA, Sage Publications Inc., pp. 297–317.

BRITZMAN, D.P. (1986) 'Cultural myths in the making of a teacher: Biography and the social structure in teacher education', *Harvard Educational Review*, **56**, 4, pp. 442–45.

BRITZMAN, D.P. (1991) *Practice Makes Practice: A Critical Study of Learning to Teach*, Albany, State University Press.

BROOKFIELD, S. (1987) *Developing Critical Thinkers: Challenging Adults to Explore Alternative Ways of Thinking and Acting*, New York, Teachers College Press.

BROWN, S. and MCINTYRE, D. (1986) 'How do teachers think about their craft?' in BEN-PERETZ, M., BROMME, R. and HALKES, R. (eds) *Advances of Research on Teacher Thinking*, Lisse, Swets and Zeitlinger.

BULLOUGH, R.V. and GITLIN, A.D. (1994) 'Challenging teacher education as training: Four propositions', *Journal of Education for Teaching*, **20**, 1, pp. 67–81.

BURBULES, N.C. (1985) Education under siege, *Educational Theory*, **36**, pp. 301–13.

BURGESS, R.G. (1988) 'A headteacher at work during the teachers' dispute', Paper presented at the Histories and Ethnographies of Teachers' Conference, St Hilda's College, Oxford, 12–14 September, 1988.

Butt, R. (1984) 'Arguments for using biography in understanding teacher thinking', in Halkes, R. and Olson, J.K. (eds) *Teacher Thinking: A New Perspective on Persisting Problems in Education*, Lisse, Swets and Zeitlinger B.V.

Butt, R. and Raymond, D. (1987) 'Arguments for using qualitative approaches in understanding teacher thinking: The case for biography', *Journal of Curriculum Theorizing*, **7**, 1, pp. 62–93.

Caine, R.N. and Caine, G. (1997) *Education on the Edge of Possibility*, Association for Supervision and Curriculum Development, Alexandria, Virginia.

Calderhead, J. (1989) 'Reflective teaching and teacher education', *Teaching and Teacher Education*, **5**, 1, pp. 43–51.

Calderhead, J. (1993) 'The contribution of research on teachers' thinking to the professional development of teachers', in Day, C., Calderhead, J. and Denicolo, P. (eds) *Research on Teacher Thinking: Understanding Professional Development*, London, Falmer Press.

Caldwell, B.J. and Spinks, J.M. (1988) *The Self-Managing School*, London, Falmer Press.

Callahan, R.E. (1962) *Education and the Cult of Efficiency*, Chicago, University of Chicago Press.

Campbell, R. and Neill, S. (1993) *Four Years On: The Future of Curriculum Reform at Key Stage 1*, London, ATL.

Campbell, R. and Neill, S. (1994a) *Secondary Teachers at Work*, London, Routledge.

Campbell, R. and Neill, S. (1994b) *Primary Teachers at Work*, London, Routledge.

Campbell, R. and Neill, S. (1994c) *Curriculum Reform at Key Stage 1: Teacher Commitment and Policy Failure*, Harlow, ATL/Longman.

Carlgren, I. (1990) '*Relations between thinking and acting in teachers' innovative work*', in Day, C., Pope, M. and Denicolo, P. (eds). *Insights into Teachers' Thinking and Practice*, London, Falmer Press.

Carlgren, I. and Lindblad, S. (1991) 'On teachers' practical reasoning and professional knowledge: Considering conceptions of context in teachers' thinking', *Teaching and Teacher Education*, **7**, 5/6, pp. 507–16.

Carnevale, A.P. (1994) Quality Education: School Reform for the New American Economy. Keynote Lecture, 1st Global Conference on Lifelong Learning, Rome, Italy.

Carr, W. and Kemmis, S. (1986) *Becoming Critical: Education, Knowledge and Action Research*, London, Falmer Press.

Carter, B. (1991) 'The Stanford/schools collaborative: Building an inquiring community of practitioners and researchers', Paper presented at the Annual Meeting of the American Educational Research Association, April, Chicago.

Christensen, J.C., Burke, P., Fessler, R. and Hagstrom, D. (1983) 'Stages of teachers' careers: Implications for staff development', cited in Oja, S.N. (1989) 'Teachers: Ages and stages of adult development', Holly, L. and McLaughlin, C.S. (eds) *Perspectives on Teacher Professional Development*, London, Falmer Press.

Clandinin, D.J. (1986) *Classroom Practices: Teacher Images in Action*, London, Falmer Press.

CLANDININ, D.J. and CONNELLY, F.M. (1984a) 'Teachers' personal practical knowledge', in HALKES, R. and OLSON, J.K. (eds) (1984) *Teacher Thinking: A New Perspective on Persisting Problems in Education*, Heirewig, Holland, Swets.

CLANDININ, J. and CONNELLY, M. (1984b) 'Teachers' personal practical knowledge: Image and narrative unity', Unpublished paper.

CLANDININ, D.J. and CONNELLY, F.M. (1985) 'Teachers' personal practical knowledge: Calendars, cycles, habits and rhythms and the aesthetics of the classroom', Paper presented at the University of Calgary — OISE Conference on Teachers' Personal Practical Knowledge, Toronto.

CLANDININ, D.J. and CONNELLY, F.M. (1987) 'What is "personal" in studies of the personality?', *Journal of Curriculum Studies*, 19, 6.

CLANDININ, D.J. and CONNELLY, F.M. (1995) 'Teachers' professional knowledge landscapes: Teacher stories–Stories of teachers–School stories–Stories of schools', *Educational Researcher*, **25**, 3, pp. 24–30.

CLARK, C.M. and YINGER, R.J. (1977) 'Research on teacher thinking', *Curriculum Inquiry*, **7**, 4, pp. 279–305.

CLAXTON, G. (1997) *Hare Brain, Tortoise Mind: Why Intelligence Increases When You Think Less*, London, Fourth Estate.

COCHRAN-SMITH, M. and LYTLE, S.L. (1996) 'Communities for teacher research: Fringe or forefront?', in MCLAUGHLIN, M.W. and OBERMAN, I. (eds) *Teacher Learning: New Policies, New Practices*, New York, Teachers College Press, pp. 92–114.

COCKETT, M. and TRIPP, J. (1994) *Rowntree Trust Report*, London: Joseph Rowntree Trust.

COFFIELD, F. (1996) 'A tale of three little pigs: Building the learning society with straw', Paper presentation to the European Educational Research Association Conference, Seville, Spain, September 27–30th, 1996.

COLE, A.L. (1997) 'Impediments to reflective practice', *Teachers and Teaching: Theory and Practice*, **3**, 1, March, 1997, pp. 7–27.

CONNELLY, F.M. and CLANDININ, D.J. (1988) *Teachers as Curriculum Planners: Narratives of Experience*, New York, Teachers College Press.

CONNELLY, F.M. and CLANDININ, D.J. (1990) 'Stories of experience and narrative inquiry', *Educational Researcher*, **19**, 5, pp. 2–14.

CONNELLY, F.M. and CLANDININ, D.J. (1995) 'Narrative and education', *Teachers and Teaching: theory and Practice*, **1**, 1, pp. 73–85.

CONNELLY, M.F. and DIENES, B. (1982) 'The teachers' role in curriculum planning: A case study', in LEITHWOOD, K. (ed.) *Studies in Curriculum Decision-Making*, Toronto, OISE.

COOPER, C. and KELLY, M. (1993) 'Occupational stress in headteachers: A national UK study', *British Journal of Educational Psychology*, **63**, pp. 130–143.

COOPER, H.M. (1989) 'Does reducing student-to-instructor ratios affect achievement?' *Educational Psychologist*, **24**, 1, pp. 78–98.

COOPER, M. (1982) 'The study of professionalism in teaching', Paper presented at the Annual Meeting of the American Educational Research Association, April, New York.

Cope, P., Inglis, B., Riddell, S. and Sulhunt, O. (1992) 'The value of in-service degrees: Teachers' long-term perceptions of their impact', *British Educational Research Journal*, **18**, 3, pp. 297–307.

Copeland, W.D., Birmingham, C., De La Cruz, E. and Recht, B. (1991) 'The reflective practitioner in teaching: Toward a research agenda', Paper presented at Annual Conference of the American Educational Research Association, April 3–7, 1991, Chicago.

Corrigan, D. (1997) 'Creating collaborative systems: Implications for inter-professional partnerships in teacher education', in Day, C., van Veen, D. and Walraven, G. (eds) *Children and Youth at Risk and Urban Education: Research, Policy and Practice*, Leuven-Apeldoorn, Garant Publishers, pp. 209–34.

Cowan, B. and Wright, N. (1990) 'Two million days lost', *Education*, 2 February, pp. 117–18.

Crawford, K. (1995) 'What do Vygotskian approaches to psychology have to offer action research?', *Educational Action Research*, **3**, 2, pp. 239–48.

Crowther, F. and Postle, G. (1991) *The Praxis of Professional Development: Setting Directions for Brisbane Catholic Education*, Brisbane, Brisbane Catholic Education Centre.

Cuban, L. (1992) 'Managing dilemmas while building professional communities', *Educational Researcher*, **211**, pp. 4–11.

Dadds, M. (1993) 'The feeling of thinking in professional self-study', *Educational Action Research Journal*, **1**, 2, pp. 287–304.

Dadds, M. (1995) *Passionate Enquiry and School Development: A Story about Teacher Action Research*, London, Falmer Press.

Dalin, P. and Rust, V.D. (1996) *Towards Schooling for the Twenty First Century*, London, Cassell.

Daresh, J.C. (1987) 'The highest hurdles of the first year principal', Paper presented at the Annual Meeting of the American Educational Research Association, April 20–24, Washington, D.C.

Darling-Hammond, L. (1990) 'Teacher professionalism: Why and how?', in Lieberman, A. (ed.) *Schools as Collaborative Cultures: Creating the Future Now*, London, Falmer Press.

Darling-Hammond, L. (1993) 'Reframing the school reform agenda: Developing capacity for school transformation', *Phi Delta Kappan*, **74**, 10, pp. 752–61.

Darling-Hammond, L. (1996a) 'The quiet revolution: Rethinking teacher development', *Educational Leadership*, **53**, 6, pp. 4–10.

Darling-Hammond, L. (1996b) 'The right to learn and the advancement of teaching: Research, policy and practice for democratic education', *Educational Researcher*, **25**, 6, pp. 5–17.

Davies, L. (1978) 'The view from the girls', *Educational Review*, **30**, 2.

Davies, L. (1987) 'The role of the primary school head', *Educational Management and Administration*, **15**, pp. 43–7.

Day, C. (1981) 'Classroom-based in-service teacher education: The development and evaluation of a client-centred model', Occasional Paper 9, Brighton, University of Sussex Education Area.

DAY, C. (1985) 'Professional learning and researcher intervention: An action research perspective', *British Educational Research Journal*, **11**, 2, pp. 133–51.

DAY, C. (1987a) 'Sharing practice through consultancy: Individual and whole school staff development in a primary school', *Curriculum Perspectives*, **7**, 1, May, 1987, pp. 7–15.

DAY, C. (1987b) 'Professional learning through collaborative in-service activity', in SMYTH, J. (ed.) *Educating Teachers: Changing the Nature of Pedagogical Knowledge*, London, Falmer Press.

DAY, C. (1989) 'Issues in the management of appraisal for professional development', *Westminster Studies in Education*, **12**, pp. 3–15.

DAY, C. (1991) 'Roles and relationships in qualitative research', *Teaching and Teacher Education*, **7**, 5/6, pp. 537–47.

DAY, C. (1990) 'In-service as consultancy: The evaluation of a management programme for primary school curriculum leaders', in AUBREY, C. (ed.) *Consultancy in the United Kingdom*, London, Falmer Press.

DAY, C. (1993a) 'The development of teachers' thinking and practice: Does choice in itself lead to empowerment', in BUSHER, H. and SMITH, M. (eds) *Managing Educational Institutions: Reviewing Development and Learning*, BEMAS.

DAY, C. (1993b) 'Reflection: A necessary but not sufficient condition for professional development', *British Educational Research Journal*, **19**, 1, pp. 83–93.

DAY, C. (1993c) 'The importance of learning biography in supporting teacher development: An empirical study', in DAY, C., CALDERHEAD, J. and DENICOLO, P. (eds) *Research on Teacher Thinking: Understanding Professional Development*, London, Falmer Press, pp. 221–32.

DAY, C. (1993d) 'Personal development planning: Towards a lifelong development model of teacher growth', Paper presented to Annual Conference of the British Educational Research Association, 10–13 September 1993, University of Liverpool.

DAY, C. (1994a) 'Planning for the professional development of teachers and schools: A principled approach', in SIMPSON, T.A. (ed.) *Teacher Educators' Handbook*, Queensland University of Technology, Australia.

DAY, C. (1994b) 'Personal development planning: A different kind of competency', *British Journal of In-service Education*, **20**, 3, pp. 287–301.

DAY, C. (1996) 'Professional learning and school development in action: A personal development planning project', in MCBRIDE, R. (ed.) *Teacher Education Policy*, London, Falmer Press.

DAY, C. (1997a) 'Being a professional in schools and universities: Limits, purposes and possibilities for development', *British Educational Research Journal*, **23**, 2, pp. 193–208.

DAY, C. (1997b) 'Working with the different selves of teachers: Beyond comfortable collaboration', in HOLLINGSWORTH, S. (ed.) *International Action Research: A Casebook for Educational Reform*, London, Falmer Press.

DAY, C. (1997c) 'In-service teacher education in europe: Conditions and themes for development in the 21st century', *Journal of In-service Education*, **23**, 1, pp. 39–54.

DAY, C. (1997d) 'Stories of change and development in England: Trick or treat?', Paper presented to the 6th Norwegian National Conference on Educational Research, University of Oslo, May 1997.

DAY, C. and BAKIOGLU, A. (1996) 'Development and disenchantment in the professional lives of headteachers', in GOODSON, I.F. and HARGREAVES, A. (eds) *Teachers Professional Lives*, London, Falmer Press.

DAY, C. and HADFIELD, M. (1996) 'Metaphors for movement: Accounts of professional development', in KOMPF, M., BOAK, R.T., BOND, W.R. and DWOREK, D.H. (eds) *Changing Research and Practice: Teachers' Professionalism, Identities and Knowledge*, London, Falmer Press.

DAY, C., HALL, C., GAMMAGE, P. and COLES, M. (1981) *Leadership and Curriculum in the Primary School: The Roles of Senior and Middle Management*, London, Paul Chapman Ltd.

DAY, C. and PENNINGTON, A. (1993) 'Conceptualizing professional development planning: A multi-dimensional model', in GILROY, P. and SMITH, M. (eds) *International Analyses of Teacher Education, JET Papers One*, Abingdon, England, Carfax Publishing Co.

DAY, C., TOLLEY, H., HADFIELD, M., WATLING, R. and PARKINS, E. (1996) *Class Size Research and the Quality of Education: A Critical Survey of the Literature*, Haywards Heath, The National Association of Headteachers.

DAY, C., VAN VEEN, D. and WALRAVEN, G. (eds) (1997) *Children and Youth at Risk and Urban Education: Research, Policy and Practice*, Apeldoorn: Garant Publishers.

DEAL, T. and KENNEDY, A. (1984) *Corporate Cultures: The Rites and Rituals of Corporate Life*, Reading, MA, Addison-Wesley.

DENICOLO, P. and POPE, M. (1990) *Adults Learning — Teachers Thinking*, in DAY, C., POPE, M. and DENICOLO, P. (eds) (1990) *Insights into Teachers' Thinking and Practice*, London, Falmer Press.

DEWEY, J. (1938) *Experience and Education*, New York, Collier Books.

DORMER, J. and FOSTER, M. (1995) *Staff Development Services in Devon: An Evaluative Study*, Exeter, Devon Education Staff Development Unit, Devon County Council.

DOYLE, W. (1977) 'Learning the classroom environment: An ecological analysis', *Journal of Teacher Education*, **28**, 6, pp. 51–5.

DOYLE, W. and PONDER, G. (1977) 'The practicality ethic and teacher decision making', *Interchange*, **8**, pp. 1–12.

DREYFUS, H.L. and DREYFUS, S.E. (1977) 'Uses and abuses of multi-attribute and multi-aspect model of decision-making'. Unpublished manuscript, Department of Industrial Engineering and Operations Research, Berkeley, University of California.

DREYFUS, H.L. and DREYFUS, S.E. (1986) *Mind Over Machine: The Power of Human Intuition and Expertise in the Era of the Computer*, New York, The Free Press.

DRUCKER, P.F. (1994) *Post-Capitalist Society*, Oxford, Butterworth-Heinemann.

DUFFY, F.M. (1997) 'Supervising schooling, not teachers', *Educational Leadership*, **54**, 8, May, pp. 78–83.

DUFFY, G. (1977) 'A study of teachers' conceptions of reading', Paper presented to the National Reading Conference, New Orleans.

EAST SUSSEX ACCOUNTABILITY PROJECT (1979) 'Accountability in the middle years of schooling: An analysis of policy options', in MCCORMICK, R. (ed.) (1982) *Calling Education to Account*, London, Open University/Heinemann Educational.

EBBUTT, D. (1985) 'Educational action research: Some general concerns and specific quibbles', in BURGESS, R. (ed.) *Issues in Educational Research*, London, Falmer Press, pp. 152–74.

Education, **11**, 6, pp. 611–25.

EDWARDS, A. and BRUNTON, D. (1993) 'Supporting reflection in teachers' learning', in CALDERHEAD, C. and GATES, P. (eds) (1993) *Conceptualizing Reflection in Teacher Development*, London, Falmer Press, pp. 154–66.

EGAN, G. (1982) *The Skilled Helper*, Monterey, CA, Brooks/Cole.

EISNER, E. (1979) *The Educational Imagination*, West Drayton, Collier-Macmillan.

ELBAZ, F. (1983) *Teacher Thinking: A Study of Practical Knowledge*, London, Croom Helm.

ELBAZ, F. (1990) 'The evolution of research on teacher thinking', in DAY, C., POPE, M. and DENICOLO, P. (eds) *Insights into Teachers' Thinking and Practice*, London, Falmer Press.

ELBAZ, F. (1991) 'Research on teachers' knowledge: The evolution of a discourse', *Journal of Curriculum Studies*, **23**, 1, Jan–Feb, pp. 1–19.

ELBAZ, F. (1992) 'Hope, attentiveness and caring for difference: The moral voice', *Teaching and Teacher Education*, **8**, 5/6, pp. 421–32.

ELLIOTT, J. (1977) 'Conceptualizing relationships between researcher/evaluation procedures and in-service teacher education', *British Journal of In-Service Education*, **4**, 1 and 2, pp. 102–115.

ELLIOTT, J. (1982) 'Institutionalising action research in schools', in ELLIOTT, J. and WHITEHEAD, D. (eds) *Action Research for Professional Development and Improvement of Schooling*, **5**, Cambridge, CARN Publications.

ELLIOTT, J. (1984) 'Improving the quality of teaching through action research', *Forum*, **216**, 3.

ELLIOTT, J. (1988) 'Why put case study at the heart of the police training curriculum?', in SOUTHGATE, P. (ed.) *New Directions in Police Training*, London, HMSO, pp. 148–69.

ELLIOTT, J. (1991) *Action Research for Educational Change*, Buckingham, Open University Press.

ELLIOTT, J. (1993) 'What have we learned from action research in school-based evaluation?' *Educational Action Research*, **1**, 1, pp. 175–86.

ELLIOTT, J. (1994) 'Research on teachers' knowledge and action research', *Educational Action Research*, **2**, 1, pp. 133–37.

ELLIOTT, J. (1996) 'School effectiveness research and its critics: Alternative visions of schooling', *Cambridge Journal of Education*, **26**, 2, pp. 199–224.

ELMORE, R. (1992) 'Why restructuring alone won't improve teaching', *Educational Leadership*, April 1992, pp. 44–9.

Eraut, M. (1978) 'Accountability at school level — some options and their implications', in Becher, A. and Maclure, S. (eds) *Accountability in Education*, Windsor, NFER.

Eraut, M. (1985) 'Knowledge creation and knowledge use in professional contexts', *Studies in Higher Education*, **10**, 2, pp. 117–33.

Eraut, M. (1987) 'Inservice teacher education', in Dunkin, M.J. (ed.) *The International Encyclopedia of Teaching and Teacher Education*, Oxford, Pergamon Press, pp. 730–43.

Eraut, M. (1989) 'Teacher appraisal and/or teacher development: Friends or foes?', in Simons, H. and Elliott, J. (eds) *Rethinking Appraisal and Assessment*, Milton Keynes, Open University Press.

Eraut, M.E. (1991) 'Indicators and accountability at school and classroom level', Paper for General Assembly on International Education Indicators, OECD/CERI.

Eraut, M.E. (1993) 'Developing professional knowledge within client-centred orientation', Unpublished paper, University of Sussex.

Eraut, M.E. (1994) *Developing Professional Knowledge and Competence*, London, Falmer Press.

Eraut, M. (1995) 'Developing professional knowledge and competence', in Guskey, T.R. and Huberman, M. (eds) *Professional Development in Education: New Paradigms and Practices*, Columbia University, Teachers College Press.

Eraut, M.E. (1995) 'Schon shock: A case for reframing reflection-in-action?', *Teachers and Teaching: Theory and Practice*, **1**, March, 1995, pp. 9–22.

Eraut, M.E. (1996) 'Professional knowledge in teacher education', In Nuutinen-P (ed.) University of Joensu, Bulletin of the Faculty of Education, No. 64, pp. 1–27.

Eraut, M.E. (1998) 'Concepts of competence', Unpublished.

Eraut, M., Alderton, J., Cole, G. and Senker, P. (1997a) 'Learning from other people at work', in Coffield, F. (ed.) *Skill Formation*, Policy Press.

Eraut, M., Alderton, J., Cole, G. and Senker, P. (1997b) 'The impact of the manager on learning in the workplace', Paper presentation at BERA Conference, York, England, September, 1997.

Eraut, M., Alderton, J., Cole, G. and Senker, P. (1998) *Development of Knowledge and Skills in Employment*, Research Report No. 5, University of Sussex, Institute of Education.

Eraut, M., Barton, J. and Canning, A. (1978) 'Some teacher perspectives on accountability', SSRC Working Paper, University of Sussex School Accountability Project.

Eraut, M., Pennycuick, D. and Radnor, H. (1987) *Local Evaluation of INSET: A Metaevaluation of TRIST Evaluations*, NCDSMT, Bristol.

Erickson, F. and Christman, J.B. (1996) 'Taking stock/making change: Stories of collaboration in local school reform', *Theory into Practice*, Summer, 1996, **35**, 3, pp. 149–57.

Esteve, J. (1989) 'Teacher burnout and teacher stress', in Cole, M. and Walker, S. (eds) (1989) *Teaching and Stress*, Oxford, Aldern Press, pp. 4–25.

Etzioni, A. (ed.) (1969) *The Semi-Professions and Their Organisation*, New York, Free Press.

European Assembly of Teacher Trade Unions (1994) *Teacher Education*, Document 4c (point 5c), Luxembourg, Centre Jean Monnet.

European Round Table of Industrialists (1997) *Investing in Knowledge: The Integration of Technology in European Education*, ERT, Avenue Henri Jaspar, 113, B-1060, Brussels.

European Commission White Paper/Commission of the European Communities (1996) *Teaching and Learning: Towards the Learning Society*, Brussels.

Evans, J. and Penney, D. (1994) 'Whatever happened to good advice? Service and inspection after the Education Reform Act', *British Educational Research Journal*, **20**, 5, pp. 519–33.

Fang, Z. (1996) 'A review of research on teacher beliefs and practices', *Educational Research*, **38**, 1, Spring, 1996, pp. 47–65.

Farber, B. (1991) *Crisis in Education*, San Francisco, Jossey-Bass.

Feiman-Nemser, S. (1990) 'Teacher preparation: Structural and conceptual alternatives', in Houston, W.R. (ed.) *Handbook of Research on Teacher Education*, New York, Macmillan Publishing Co., pp. 212–33.

Fenstermacher, G. (1990) 'Some moral considerations on teaching as a profession', in Goodlad, J., Soder, R. and Sirotnik, K. (eds) *The Moral Dimensions of Teaching*, San Francisco, Jossey-Bass, pp. 130–51.

Fernandez, R.R. and Timpane, P.M. (1995) *Bursting at the Seams: Report of the Citizens' Commission on Planning for Enrollment Growth*, US Department of Education.

Fessler, R. (1985) 'A model for teacher professional growth and development', in Burke, P. and Heideman, R. (eds) *Career Long Teacher Education*, Springfield, Illinois, Charles C Thomas.

Fessler, R. (1995) 'Dynamics of career stages', in Guskey, T.R. and Huberman, M. (eds) *Professional Development in Education: New Paradigms and Practices*, New York, Teachers College Press.

Fessler, R. and Christensen, J. (1992) *The Teacher Career Cycle: Understanding and Guiding the Professional Development of Teachers*, Boston, Allyn and Bacon.

Fineman, S. (1993) 'Organisations as emotional arenas', in Fineman, S. (ed.) *Emotion in Organisations*, London, Sage, pp. 9–10.

Flinders, D. (1988) 'Teacher isolation and the new reform', *Journal of Curriculum and Supervision*, **5**, 4, pp. 17–29.

Fraser, B.J. (1991) *Educational Leadership*, **4**, 8, May 1997, p. 46.

Fraser, B.J. (1991) 'Two decades of classroom environment research', in Fraser, B.J. and Walberg, H.J. (eds) *Educational Environments: Evaluation, Antecedents and Consequences*, Oxford, Pergamon Press.

Freire, P. (1996) *Letters to Cristine*, New York, Routledge.

French, N.K. (1993) 'Elementary teacher stress and class size', *Journal of Research and Development in Education*, **26**, 2, 66–73.

FRIEBERG, H.J. (1997) 'The life-cycle of improving American inner-city elementary schools: Implications for policy and practice', in DAY, C., VAN VEEN, D. and WALRAVEN, G. (eds) *Children and Youth at Risk and Urban Education: Research, Policy and Practice*, Leuven-Apeldoorn, Garant Publishers, pp. 167–80.

FRIED, R.L. (1995) *The Passionate Teacher*, Boston, Beacon Press.

FUCHS, E. (1973) 'How teachers learn to help children fail', in KEDDIE, N. (ed.) *Tinker . . . Tailor . . . The Myth of Cultural Deprivation*, pp. 75–85, London, Penguin.

FULLAN, M.G. (1982) *The Meaning of Educational Change*, New York, Teachers College Press.

FULLAN, M.G. (1992) *Successful School Improvement*, Buckingham, Open University Press.

FULLAN, M. (1993a) 'Why teachers must become change agents', *Educational Leadership*, **50**, 6, March 1993, pp. 12–17.

FULLAN, M. (1993b) *Change Forces: Probing the Depths of Educational Reform*, London, The Falmer Press.

FULLAN, M.G. (1995) 'The limits and the potential of professional development', in GUSKEY, T.R. and HUBERMAN, M. (eds) *Op.cit.*, pp. 253–268.

FULLAN, M. and HARGREAVES, A. (1992) *What's Worth Fighting For in Your School?* Buckingham, Open University Press.

FULLAN, M. WITH STIEGELBAUER, S. (1991) *The New Meaning of Educational Change*, London, Cassell.

FULLER, F. (1970) *Personalized Education for Teachers: One Application of the Teacher Concerns Model*, Austin, Texas, University of Texas, Research and Development Center for Teacher Education.

GALLY, J. (1986) 'The structure of administrative behaviour: An international dimension in educational administration', Paper presented at the Annual Meeting of the American Educational Research Association, April, San Francisco.

GALTON, M., HARGREAVES, L. and PELL, A. (1996) *Class Size, Teaching and Pupil Achievement*, Hamilton House, National Union of Teachers.

GANNAWAY, H. (1976) 'Making sense of school', in DELAMONT, S. and STUBBS, M. (eds) *Explorations in Classroom Observation*, London, J. Wiley and Sons.

GARDNER, H. (1983) *Frames of Mind: The Theory of Multiple Intelligences*, New York, Basic Books.

GARDNER, H. and HATCH, T. (1989) 'Multiple intelligences go to school', *Educational Researcher*, **18**, 8.

GEE, J., HULL, G. and LANKSHEAR, C. (1996) *The New Work Order: Behind the Language of the New Capitalism*, Sydney, Allen and Unwin.

GIBBONS, M., LIMOGES, C., NOWOTNY, H., SCHWARTZMAN, S., SCOTT, P. and TROW, M. (1994) *The New Production of Knowledge: The Dynamics of Science and Research in Contemporary Societies*, London, Sage Publications.

GIBBS, B. (1996) 'Going it alone', in R.S.A. (1996) *For Life: A Vision of Learning in the 21st Century*, London, Royal Society for the encouragement of Arts, Manufacturers and Commerce, pp. 8–10.

GILROY, P. and DAY, C. (1993) 'The erosion of INSET in England and Wales: Analysis and proposals for a redefinition', *Journal of Education for Teaching*, **19**, 2, pp. 151–57.

GITLIN, A. (1997) 'Collaboration and progressive school reform', Paper presented at the 6th Norwegian National Conference on Educational Research, University of Oslo, May 1997.

GLASS, G.V. and SMITH, M.L. (1978) *Meta Analysis of Research on the Relationship of Class Size and Achievement*, San Francisco, LA: Far West Lab for R and D. Cited in COOPER, H.M. (1989) 'Does reducing student-to-instructor ratios affect achievement?', *Educational Psychologist*, **24**, 1, pp. 79–98.

GLICKMAN, C. (1990) 'Pushing School reforms to a new edge: The seven ironies of school empowerment', *Phi Delta Kappan*, pp. 68–75.

GOLEMAN, D. (1995) *Emotional Intelligence*, New York, Bantam Books.

GOODMAN, J. (1994) 'External change agents and grassroots school reform: Reflections from the field', *Journal of Curriculum and Supervision*, **9**, 2, pp. 113–35.

GOODLAD, J.I., SODER, R. and SIROTNIK, K.A. (eds) (1990) *The Moral Dimensions of Teaching*, San Francisco, Jossey-Bass.

GOODSON, I.F. (ed.) (1992) *Studying Teachers' Lives*, London, Routledge.

GOODSON, I.F. and HARGREAVES, A. (eds) (1996) *Teachers' Professional Lives*, London: Falmer Press.

GORE, J.M. and ZEICHNER, K. (1991) 'Action research and reflective teaching in preservice education: A case study from the US', *Teaching and Teacher Education*, **7**, pp. 119–36.

GORE, J.M. and ZEICHNER, K.M. (1995) 'Connecting action research to genuine teacher development', in SMYTH, J. (ed.) *Critical Discourses on Teacher Development*, London, Cassell.

GRACE, G. (1995) *School Leadership: Beyond Education Management*, London, Falmer Press.

GRAY, J. and WILCOX, B. (1995) *Good School, Bad School: Evaluating Performance and Encouraging Improvement*, Buckingham, Open University Press.

GRIMMETT, P.L. and ERICKSON, G.L. (1988) *Reflection in Teacher Education*, New York, Teachers College Press.

GRIMMETT, P., MACKINNON, A., ERICKSON, G. and RIECKEN, T. (1990) 'Reflective practice in teacher education', in CLIFT, R.T., HOUSTON, W.R. and PUGACH, M. (eds) *Encouraging Reflective Practice: An Analysis of Issues and Programs*, New York, Teachers College Press, pp. 20–38.

GROUNDWATER-SMITH, S. (1998) 'Putting teacher professional judgement to work', *Educational Action Research*, **6**, 1, pp. 21–8.

GRUNDY, S. (1994) 'Action research at the school level', *Educational Action Research*, **2**, 1, pp. 23–38.

GRUNDY, S. and BONSER, S. (1977) 'A new work order in Australian schools? Investigations from down under', Paper presented at the 6th National Conference on Educational Research, University of Oslo, Norway, 20–22 May.

GUDMUNDSDOTTIR, S. (1990) 'Curriculum stories: Four case studies of social studies teaching', in Day, C., Pope, M. and Denicolo, P. (eds) (1993) *Insights into Teachers' Thinking and Practice*, London, The Falmer Press.

Guskey, T.R. and Huberman, M. (eds) (1995) *Professional Development in Education: New Paradigms and Practices*, Columbia University, Teachers College Press.

Habermas, J. (1972) *Knowledge and Human Interest*, London, Heinemann.

Hallinger, P. and Murphy, J. (1985) 'Defining an organizational mission in schools', Paper presented at the Annual Meeting of the American Educational Research Association, April, Chicago.

Handal, G. (1991) 'Promoting the articulation of tacit knowledge through the counselling of practitioners', in Letiche, H.K., van der Wolf, J.C. and Plooij, F.X. (eds) *The Practitioner's Power of Choice In Staff Development and In-Service Training*, Amsterdam/Lisse, Swets and Zeitlinger B.V.

Hammersley, M. (1993) 'On the teacher as researcher', *Educational Action Research*, **1**, 3, pp. 425–46.

Handal, G. and Lauvas, P. (1987) *Promoting Reflective Teaching*, Milton Keynes, UK, Open University Press.

Handy, C. (1989) *The Age of Unreason*, London, Business Books Ltd.

Hargreaves, A. (1992) Cultures of Teaching: A Focus for Change. In Hargreaves, A. and Fullan, M.G. (eds) (1992) *Understanding Teacher Development*. Columbia University: Teachers College Press.

Hargreaves, A. (1993) 'Dissonant voices, dissipated lives: Teachers and the multiple realities of restructuring', Paper presented to the Fifth Conference of the International Study Association on Teacher Thinking, Gothenburg, Sweden, 12–17 August 1993.

Hargreaves, A. (1994) *Changing Teachers, Changing Times: Teachers' Work and Culture in the Postmodern Age*, New York, Teachers College Press.

Hargreaves, A. (1995) *Development and desire: A Postmodern Perspective*, in Guskey, T. and Huberman, M. (eds) pp. 9–34.

Hargreaves, A. (1997a) 'Revisiting voice', *Educational Researcher*, **25**, 1, Jan/Feb 1996, pp. 12–19.

Hargreaves, A. (1997b) 'Rethinking educational change: Going deeper and wider in the quest for success', in Hargreaves, A. (ed.) *Rethinking Educational Change with Heart and Mind*, 1997 ASCD Yearbook, Alexandria VA, Association for Supervision and Curriculum Development, pp. 1–26.

Hargreaves, A. (1998) 'Feeling like a teacher: The emotions of teaching and educational change', *Phi Delta Kappan* (in press).

Hargreaves, A. and Earl, L. (1990) *Rights of Passage*, Toronto: Ontario Institute for Studies in Education.

Hargreaves, D.H. (1972) *Interpersonal Relations and Education*, London, Routledge and Kegan Paul Ltd.

Hargreaves, D. (1982) *The Challenge of the Comprehensive School*, London, Routledge and Kegan Paul.

Hargreaves, D. (1994) 'The new professionalism: The synthesis of professional and institutional development', *Teaching and Teacher Education*, **10**, 4, pp. 423–38.

HARLAND, J. and KINDER, K. (1997) 'Teachers' continuing professional development: Framing a model of outcomes', *Journal of In-service Education*, **23**, 1, 1997, pp. 71–84.

HARLAND, J., KINDER, K. and KEYS, W. (1993) *Restructuring INSET: Privatisation and Its Alternatives*, Slough, NFER.

HARRIS, A. (1996) 'Teaching as a profession: Response to Eric Hoyle', in WATSON, K., MODGIL, C. and MODGIL, S. (eds) *Teachers, Teacher Education and Training*, London, Cassell, pp. 55–7.

HARTLEY, D. (1986) 'Instructional isomorphism and the management of consent in education', *Journal of Educational Policy*, **1**, 2, pp. 229–37.

HARTLEY, D. (1989) 'Beyond collaboration: The management of professional development policy in Scotland, 1979–1989', *Journal of Education for Teaching*, **15**, 3, pp. 211–23.

HATTON, N. and SMITH, D. (1995) 'Facilitating reflection: Issues and research', *Forum of Education*, **50**, 1, April, 1995, pp. 49–65.

HAWLEY, C.A. and HAWLEY, W.D. (1997) *Peabody Journal of Education*, **72**, 1, pp. 234–45.

HELSBY, G. (1995) 'Teachers' construction of professionalism in England in the 1990s', *Journal of Education for Teaching*, **21**, 3, pp. 317–32.

HELSBY, G. (1996) 'Defining and developing professionalism in English secondary schools', *Journal of Education for Teaching*, **22**, 2, p. 141.

HELSBY, G. (1997) 'Multiple truths and contested realities: The changing faces of teacher professionalism in England', Paper presentation to 6th Norwegian National Conference on Educational Research, University of Oslo, May 20–22.

HELSBY, G. and KNIGHT, P. (1997) 'Continuing professional development and the national curriculum', in HELSBY, G. and MCCULLOCH, G. (eds) *Teachers and the National Curriculum*, London, Cassell.

HELSBY, G., KNIGHT, P., MCCULLOCH, G., SAUNDERS, M. and WARBURTON, T. (1997) 'Professionalism in crisis', A Report to Participants on the Professional Cultures of Teachers Research Project, Lancaster University, January 1997.

HELSBY, G. and MCCULLOCH, G. (1996) 'Teacher-professionalism and curriculum control', in GOODSON, I.F. and HARGREAVES, A. (eds) (1996) *Teachers Professional Lives*, London, Falmer Press.

HELSBY, G. and MCCULLOCH, G. (1997) *Teachers and the National Curriculum*, London, Cassell.

HENDERSON, E.S. and PERRY, G.W. (1981) *Change and Development in Schools*, Maidenhead, McGraw-Hill.

HOCHSCHILD, A.R. (1993) *The Managed Heart: Commercialization of Human Feeling*, Berkeley, University of California Press, p. 7.

HOLLINGSWORTH, S. (ed.) (1997) *International Action Research: A Casebook for Educational Reform*, London, Falmer Press.

HOLLY, M.L. (1989) *Writing to Grow: Keeping a Personal-Professional Journal*, Oxford, Heinemann Educational Books.

Holly, M.L. (1991) 'Personal and professional learning: On teaching and self-knowledge', Paper presented to the Collaborative Action Research Network Conference, April 1991, University of Nottingham, England.

Hopkins, D. (1986) *Inservice Training and Educational Development: An International Survey*, Beckenham: Croom Helm.

Hopkins, D. (1989) 'Identifying INSET needs: A school improvement perspective', in McBride, R. (ed.) *The In-Service Training of Teachers*, Lewes, The Falmer Press.

Hopkins, D. (1996) 'Towards a theory of school improvement', in Gray, J., Reynolds, D. and Fitz-Gibbon, C. (eds) *Merging Traditions: The Future of Research on School Effectiveness and School Improvement*, London, Cassell.

Hopkins, D., Ainscow, M. and West, M. (1994) *School Improvement in an Era of Change*, London, Cassell.

Hopkins, D., Ainscow, M. and West, M. (1997) 'School improvement — propositions for action', in Harris, A., Bennett, N. and Preedy, M. (eds) *Organisational Effectiveness and Improvemet in Education*, Buckingham, Open University Press, pp. 261–70.

Hopkins, D., West, M. and Ainscow, M. (1998a) *Improving the Quality of Education for All*, London, David Fulton Publishers.

Hopkins, D., West, M. and Beresford, J. (1998b) 'Conditions for school and classroom development', *Teachers and Teaching: Theory and Practice*, **4**, 1, pp. 115–42.

Hord, S.M. (1997) *Professional Learning Communities: Communities of Continuous Inquiry and Improvement*, Austin, Texas, Southwest Educational Development Laboratory.

Hoy, K. and Brown, B.L. (1988) 'Leadership behaviour of principals and the zone of acceptance of elementary teachers', *Journal of Educational Administration*, **26**, 1, pp. 22–38.

Hoyle, E. (1980) 'Professionalization and de-professionalisation in education', in Hoyle, E. and Megarry, J. (eds) *World Yearbook of Education 1980: The Professional Development of Teachers*, London, Kogan Page.

Hoyle, E. (1986) *The Politics of School Management*, Sevenoaks, Hodder and Stoughton Educational.

Huberman, M. (1989) 'The professional life cycle of teachers', *Teachers' College Record*, **91**, 1, Fall 1989, pp. 31–57.

Huberman, M. (1992) 'Critical introduction', in Fullan, M.G. (ed.) *Successful School Improvement*, Buckingham, Open University Press.

Huberman, M. (1993a) 'The model of the independent artisan in teachers' professional relations, in Little, J.W. and McLaughlin, M.W. (eds) *Teachers' Work: Individuals, Colleagues and Contexts*, New York, Teachers' College Press, pp. 11–50.

Huberman, M. (1993b) 'Changing minds: The dissemination of research and its effects on practice and theory', in Day, C., Calderhead, J. and Denicolo, P. (eds) *Research on Teacher Thinking: Understanding Professional Development*, London, Falmer Press, pp. 34–52.

HUBERMAN, M. (1995a) 'Networks that alter teaching', *Teachers and Teaching: Theory and Practice*, **1**, 2, pp. 193–221.

HUBERMAN, M. (1995b) 'Professional careers and professional development and some intersections', in GUSKEY, T. and HUBERMAN, M. (eds) (1995) *Professional Development in Education: New Perspectives and Practices*, New York, Teachers College Press.

HUBERMAN, M. (1995c) *The Lives of Teachers*, London, Cassell.

HUGHES, M. (1985) 'Leadership in professionally staffed organisations', in HUGHES, M., RIBBINS, P. and THOMAS, H. (1985) *Managing Education*, London, Cassell.

HULING, L., TRANG, M. and CORRELL, L. (1981) 'Interactive research and development: A promising strategy for teacher education', *Journal of Teacher Education*, **32**, pp. 13–14.

HURSH, D. (1997) 'Critical collaborative action research in politically contested times', in HOLLINGSWORTH, S. (ed.) *International Action Research: A Casebook for Educational Reform*, London, Falmer Press, pp. 124–34.

IMANTS, J.G.M. and DE BRABANDER, C.J. (1996) 'Teachers' and principals' sense of efficacy in elementary schools', *Teaching and Teacher Education*, **12**, 2, pp. 179–96.

INDEPENDENT Newspaper, 12.6.97.

INGVARSON, L. and GREENWAY, P.A. (1984) 'Portrayals of teacher development', *Australian Journal of Education*, **28**, 1, pp. 45–65.

JACKSON, P.W. (1968) *Life in Classrooms*, New York, Holt, Rinehart and Winston.

JACKSON, P.W. (1971) 'Old dogs and new tricks: Observations on the continuing education of teachers', in RUBIN, L.J. (ed.) *Improving In-service Education: Proposals and Procedures for Change*, Boston, Allyn and Bacon.

JACKSON, P.W., BOOSTROM, R.E. and HANSEN, D.T. (1993) *The Moral Life of Schools*, San Francisco, Jossey-Bass.

JANSEN, B., REEHORST, E. and DELHAAS, R. (1995) 'Action research networking and environmental education in the Netherlands: A challenging and successful action research strategy for educational renewal', *Educational Action Research*, **3**, 2, pp. 195–210.

JERSILD, A.T. (1995) *When Teachers Face Themselves*, New York, Teachers College Press.

JOHNSON, J. (1990) 'What are teacher perceptions of teaching in different classroom contexts? Project STAR: Tennessee State Department of Education', Paper presented at the annual meeting of the American Educational Research Association, Boston, Ma.

JOHNSTON, S. (1994) 'Is action research a "natural" process for teachers?', *Educational Action Research Journal*, **2**, 1, pp. 39–48.

JOYCE, B.R. and SHOWERS, B. (1980) 'Improving in-service training: The messages of research', *Educational Leadership*, **37**, 5, February, pp. 379–85.

JOYCE, B. and SHOWERS, B. (1982) 'The coaching of teaching', *Educational Leadership*, **40**, 2, pp. 4–10.

JOYCE, B. and SHOWERS, B. (1988) *Student Achievement through Staff Development*, New York, Longman.

Joyce, B., Showers, B. and Weil, M. (1992) *Models of Teaching, 4th edition*, Englewood Cliffs, NJ, Prentice-Hall.

Keddie, N. (1971) 'Classroom knowledge', in Young, M.F.D. (ed.) *Knowledge and Control*, London, Collier-Macmillan.

Kelchtermans, G. (1993) 'Getting the story, understanding the lives: From career stories to teachers' professional development', *Teaching and Teacher Education*, **9**, 5/6, pp. 443–56.

Kinder, K., Harland, J. and Wootten, M. (1991) *The Impact of School-Focused INSET on Classroom Practice*, Slough, NFER.

Klein, K. (1985) 'The research on class size', *Phi Delta Kappan*, **66**, pp. 578–80.

Klette, K. (1998) 'Working time blues: On how Norwegian teachers experience restructuring in education', Paper presented to Annual Meeting of the American Educational Research Association, 13–17 April, San Diego, CA.

Knowles, J.G. (1993) 'Life-history accounts as mirrors: A practical avenue for the conceptualization of reflection in teacher education', in Calderhead, J. and Gates, P. (eds) *Conceptualizing Reflection in Teacher Development*, London, Falmer Press, pp. 70–92.

Knowles, M.S. (1984) *The Adult Learner: A Neglected Species*, (3rd edition) Houston, Gulf.

Kohn, M.N. and Kottcamp, R.B. (1993) *Teachers: The Missing Voice in Education*, Albany, SUNY.

Kolb, D.A. (1984) *Experiential Learning: Experience as a Source of Learning and Development*, Englewood Cliffs, NJ, Prentice Hall.

Korthagen, F.A.J. and Wubbels, T. (1995) 'Characteristics of Reflective Practitioners: Towards an operationalization of the concept of reflection', *Teachers and Teaching: Theory and Practice*, **1**, 1, March, pp. 51–72.

Kremer-Hayon, L. and Fessler, R. (1991) 'The inner world of school principals: Reflections on career life stages', Paper presented at Fourth International Conference of the International Study Association on Teacher Thinking, 23–27 September, University of Surrey, England.

Labaree, D.F. (1995) 'The lowly status of teacher education in the United States: The impact of markets and the implications for reform', in Shimahara, N.K. and Holowinsky, I.Z. (eds) *Teacher Education in Industrialized Nations: Issues in Changing Social Contexts*, New York, Garland Publishing Inc.

Labaree, D.F. and Pallas, A.M. (1996) Rejoinder: The Holmes Groups Mystifying Response. *Educational Researcher*, Vol. 25, No. 5, June/July 1996, pp. 28–31.

Lacey, C. (1977) *The Socialisation of Teachers*, London, Methuen.

Lafleur, B. (1992) 'Dropping out: The cost to Canada, Conference Board of Canada', cited in Ball, C. (1996) A learning society: A vision and a plan to change the learning culture in the United Kingdom, in Royal Society of Arts (1996) *For life: a vision for learning in the 21st century*, London, RSA.

Lakoff, G. and Johnston, M. (1980) *Metaphors We Live By*, Chicago, University of Chicago Press.

Larsson, M.S. (1977) *The Rise of Professionalism: A Sociological Analysis*, Berkeley, CA, University of California Press.

LAVE, J. and WENGER, E. (1991) *Situated Learning: Legitimate Peripheral Participation*, Cambridge, Cambridge University Press.

LAWSON, H.A. and BRIAR-LAWSON, K. (1997) 'Toward family-supportive community schools', in DAY, C., VAN VEEN, D. and WALRAVEN, G. (eds) *Children and Youth at Risk and Urban Education: Research, Policy and Practice*, Leuven-Apeldoorn, Garant Publishers, pp. 181–208.

LECOMPTE, M.D. and DWORKIN, A.G. (1992) *Giving Up on School: Student Dropouts and Teacher Burnouts*, Newbury Park, CA, Corwin Press.

LEITHWOOD, K. (1990) 'The principal's role in teacher development', in JOYCE, B. (ed.) *Changing School through Staff Development*, Alexandria, VA, Association for Supervision and Curriculum Development.

LEITHWOOD, K., BEGLEY, P.T. and COUSINS, J.B. (1992) *Developing Expert Leadership for Future Schools*, London, Falmer Press.

LEITHWOOD, K. and JANTZI, D. (1990) 'Transformational leadership: How principals can help reform school cultures', Paper presented at the Annual Meeting of the American Educational Research Association, Boston.

LEITHWOOD, K., LEONARD, L. and SHARRATT, L. (1997) 'Conditions fostering organisational learning in schools', Paper presented at the Annual Meeting of the International Congress on School Effectiveness and Improvement, Memphis, Tennessee.

LEITHWOOD, K.A. and MONTGOMERY, D.J. (1984) 'Obstacles preventing principals from becoming more effective', *Education and Urban Society*, **17**, 1, pp. 73–88.

LEVINE, M. and TRACHTMAN, R. (eds) (1997) *Making Professional Development Schools Work*, New York, Teachers College Press.

LEVINSON, D.J., DARROW, C., KLEIN, E.B., LEVINSON, M. and MCKEE, B. (1978) *The Seasons of a Man's Life*, New York, Knopf.

LIEBERMAN, A. (1990) *Schools as Collaborative Cultures: Creating the Future Now*, New York, Falmer Press.

LIEBERMAN, A. (1992) 'School/University collaboration: A view from the inside', *Phi Delta Kappan*, **74**, 2, pp. 147–56.

LIEBERMAN, A. (1996) 'Practices that support teacher development: Transforming conceptions of professional learning', in MCLAUGHLIN, M.W. and OBERMAN, I. (eds) (1996) *Teacher Learning: New Policies, New Practices*, New York, Teachers College Press.

LIEBERMAN, A. and MCLAUGHLIN, M.W. (1992) 'Networks for educational change: Powerful and problematic', *Phi Delta Kappan*, **73**, 9, pp. 673–7.

LIEBERMAN, A. and MILLER, L. (1992) *Teachers — Their World and Their Work: Implications for School Improvement*, Columbia University, Teachers College Press.

LIGHTFOOT, S.L. (1983) 'The lives of teachers', in SHULMAN, L.S. and SYKES, G. (eds) *Handbook of Teaching and Policy*, pp. 241–60, New York, Longman.

LISTON, D. and ZEICHNER, K. (1991) *Teacher Education and the Social Conditions of Schooling*, New York, Routledge and Chapman Hill.

LITTLE, J.W. (1982) 'Norms of collegiality and experimentation: Workplace conditions of school success', *American Educational Research Journal*, **19**, pp. 325–40.

LITTLE, J.W. (1990) 'The persistence of privacy: Autonomy and initiative in teachers' professional relations', *Teachers' College Record*, **91**, pp. 509–56.

LITTLE, J.W. (1992) 'Opening the black box of professional community', in LIEBERMAN, A. (ed.) *The Changing Context of Teaching*, Chicago, University of Chicago Press, pp. 157–78.

LITTLE, J.W. (1993) 'Teachers' professional development in a climate of educational reform', *Educational Evaluation and Policy Analysis*, Summer 1993, **15**, 2, pp. 129–51.

LITTLE, J.W. and MCLAUGHLIN, M.W. (1991) *Urban Math Collaboratives: As the Teachers Tell It*, Stanford CA, Centre for Research on the Context of Teaching.

LOGAN, L. and SACHS, J. (1988) *Checklist for Designing and Evaluating Inservice Education Proposals*, St Lucia, Department of Education, University of Queensland.

LOGAN, L. and SACHS, J. (1991) 'Which teacher development project?', *School Organisation*, **11**, 3, pp. 303–11.

LONGWORTH, K. and DAVIES, W.K. (1996) *Lifelong Learning: New Vision, New Implications, New Roles for People, Organisations, Nations and Communities in the 21st Century*, London, Kogan Page.

LORD, B. (1991) 'Subject area collaboratives, teacher professionalism and staff development', Paper presented at the Annual Meeting of the American Educational Research Association, April, Chicago.

LORTIE, D. (1975) *Schoolteacher*, Chicago, University of Chicago Press.

LOUIS, K.S. (1992) 'Restructuring and the problem of teachers' work', in LIEBERMAN, A. (ed.) *Yearbook of the National Society for the Study of Education*, Chicago, NSSE, University of Chicago Press.

LOUIS, K.S. (1994) 'Beyond "managed change": Rethinking how schools improve', *School Effectiveness and Improvement*, **5**, 1, pp. 2–24.

LOUIS, K.S. and KRUSE, S.D. (1995) *Professionalism and Community: Perspectives on Reforming Urban Schools*, Thousand Oaks, CA, Corwin Press.

LOUIS, K. and MILES, M.B. (1990) *Improving the Urban High School: What Works and Why*, New York, Teachers College Press.

LUBBEN, F., CAMPBELL, B. and DLAMINI, B. (1995) *In-Service Support for a Technological Approach to Science Education*, London, Oversees Development Administration.

MACLEAN, R. (1992) *Teachers' Careers and Promotion Patterns: A Sociological Analysis*, London, Falmer Press.

MAKINS, V. (1969) 'Child's eye view of teacher', *Times Educational Supplement*, 19 and 26 September.

MANCINI, V., WUEST, D., VANTINE, K. and CLARK, E. (1984) 'Use of instruction in interaction analysis on burned out teachers: Its effects on teaching behaviours, level of burnout and academic learning time', *Journal of Teachers in Physical Education*, **3**, 2, pp. 29–46.

MANTHEI, R., GILMORE, A., TUCK, B. and ADAIR, V. (1996) 'Teacher stress in intermediate schools', *Educational Research*, **38**, 1, 3–19.

MARSICK, V.J. and WATKINS, K. (1990) *Informal and Incidental Learning in the Workplace*, New York, Routledge.

MCCORMICK, R. and JAMES, M. (1983) *Curriculum Evaluation in Schools*, London, Croom Helm.

MCCUTCHEON, G. and JUNG, B. (1990) 'Alternative perspectives on action research', *Theory into Practice*, **29**, pp. 144–51.

MCKERNAN, J. (1988) Teacher as researcher: Paradigm and praxis, *Contemporary Education*, **59**, pp. 154–58.

MCKERNAN, J. (1994) 'Teaching educational action research: A tale of three cities', *Educational Action Research*, **2**, pp. 95–112.

MCLAUGHLIN, M.W. (1993) 'What matters most in teachers' workplace context?', in LITTLE, J.W. and MCLAUGHLIN, M.W. (eds) *Teachers' Work: Individuals, Colleagues and Contexts*, New York, Teachers College Press, pp. 73–103.

MCLAUGHLIN, M.W. and OBERMAN, I. (eds) (1996) *Teacher Learning: New Policies, New Practices*, Columbia University, Teachers College Press.

MCLAUGHLIN, M.W. and TALBERT, J.E. (1993) *Contexts That Matter for Teaching and Learning*, Stanford, Center for Research on the Context of Secondary School Teaching, Stanford University.

MCRAE, H. (1995) *The Privilege of Unemployment*, Independent on Sunday, 26 February, p. 4.

MCTAGGART, R. (1989) 'Bureaucratic rationality and the self-educating profession: The problem of teacher privatism', *Journal of Curriculum Studies*, **21**, 4, pp. 345–61.

MCTAGGART, R. (1991) 'Principles for participatory action research', *Adult Education Quarterly*, **41**, pp. 168–87.

MILLETT, A. (1996) 'Quality teaching — a national priority', Plenary Address at the North of England Education Conference, Gateshead, Jan 5th, 1996.

MINISTRY OF EDUCATION (1991) *Year 2000: A Framework for Learning: Enabling Learners*, Report of the Sullivan Commission, British Columbia, Canada.

MINTZBERG, H. (1994) *The Rise and Fall of Strategic Planning*, New York, Free Press.

MOLLER, J. (1997) 'The work of school principals in context: Conflicting expectations, demands and desires', Paper presented at the 6th Norwegian National Conference on Educational Research, May 20–22, Oslo, Norway.

MORTIMORE, P., SAMMONS, P., STOLL, L., LEWIS, D. and ECOB, R. (1994) 'Key factors for effective junior schooling', in POLLARD, A. and BOURNE, J. (eds) *Teaching and Learning in the Primary School*, London, Routledge.

MOSTELLER, F. (1995) 'The Tennessee study of class size in the early school grades', *The Future of Children*, **5**, 2.

MUNBY, H. and RUSSELL, T. (1990) 'Metaphor in the study of teachers' professional knowledge', *Theory into Practice*, **29**, 2, pp. 116–21.

MYERS, K. and STOLL, L. (1993) 'Mapping the movement', *Education*, 16 July.

NFIE (1996) *Teachers Take Charge of Their Learning: Transforming Professional Development for Student Success*, Washington, DC, NFIE.

NASH, R. (1976) 'Pupils' expectations of their teachers', in DELAMONT, S. and STUBBS, M. (eds) *Explorations in Classroom Observation*, London, J. Wiley and Sons.

NATIONAL COMMISSION ON EDUCATION (1993) *Learning to Succeed: Report of the Paul Hamlyn Foundation*, London, Heinemann.

NATIONAL CONFEDERATION OF PARENT TEACHER ASSOCIATIONS (1996) 'The state of schools in England and Wales', Survey by the National Confederation of Parent Teacher Associations.

NATIONAL SCHOOLS PROJECT REPORT OF THE NATIONAL EXTERNAL REVIEW PANEL (1993) p. 13, in SACHS, J. (1997) 'Reclaiming teacher professionalism: An Australian perspective', Paper presented at the 6th Norwegian National Conference on Educational Research, University of Oslo, May.

NELSON, M.H. (1993) 'Teachers' stories: An analysis of the themes', in DAY, C., CALDERHEAD, J. and DENICOLO, P. (eds) *Research on Teacher Thinking: Understanding Professional Development*, London, Falmer Press, pp. 151–66.

NEWMAN, K. (1979) 'Middle-aged, experienced teachers' perceptions of their career development', Paper presented at the Annual Meeting of the American Educational Research Association, April, San Francisco.

NEWMAN, K., BURDEN, P. and APPLEGATE, J. (1980) 'Helping teachers examine their long range development', in HOLLY, M.L. and MCLAUGHLIN, C.S. (eds) *Perspectives on Teacher Professional Development*, London, The Falmer Press.

NEWTON, D.P. and NEWTON, L.D. (1994) 'A survey of the use made of non-contact days: The infamous five', *British Journal in In-service Education*, **20**, 3, pp. 387–96.

NIAS, J. (1989) *Primary Teachers Talking. A Study of Teaching as Work*, London, Routledge.

NIAS, J., SOUTHWORTH, G. and CAMPBELL, P. (1992) *Whole School Curriculum Development in the Primary School*, London, Cassell.

NIAS, J., SOUTHWORTH, G.W. and YEOMANS, R. (1989) *Staff Relationships in the Primary School: A Study of School Culture*, London, Cassell.

NIXON, J., MARTIN, J., MCKEOWN, P. and RANSON, S. (1997) 'Towards a learning profession: Changing codes of occupational practice within the new management of education', *British Journal of Sociology of Education*, **18**, 1, pp. 5–28.

NODDINGS, N. (1984) *Awakening the Inner Eye: Intuition in Education*, New York, Teachers College, Columbia University.

NODDINGS, N. (1987) 'Fidelity in teaching, teacher education, and research for teaching', *Harvard Educational Review*, **56**, 4, pp. 496–510.

NODDINGS, N. (1992) *The Challenge to Care in Schools*, New York, Teachers College Press.

NODDINGS, N. and WITHERELL, C. (1991) 'Themes remembered and foreseen', in WITHERELL, C. and NODDINGS, N. (eds) *Stories Lives Tell: Narrative and Dialogue in Education*, New York, Teachers College Press.

NOLDER, R. (1992) 'Towards a model of accelerated professional development', *British Journal of In-Service Education*, **18**, 1, pp. 35–41.

O'DONOHUE, T.A., BROOKER, R. and ASPLAND, T. (1993) 'Harnessing teachers' dilemmas for professional development: A Queensland initiative', *British Journal of In-Service Education*, **19**, 2, Summer 1993, pp. 14–20.

O'HANLON, C. (1992) 'Reflection in or on action', in LEINO, A.L., HELLGREN, P. and HAMALAINEN, K. (eds) *Integration of Technology and Reflection in Teaching*, ATEE Conference Proceedings, University of Helsinki, pp. 274–83.

O'HANLON, C. (1996) 'Is there a difference between action research and quality development? Within or beyond the constraints?', in O'HANLON, C. (ed.) *Professional Development through Action Research in Educational Settings*, London, Falmer Press.

OECD (1989) 'The condition of teaching: General report', Restricted Draft, Paris. Quoted in SIKES, P.J. (1992) 'Imposed change and the experienced teacher', in FULLAN, M. and HARGREAVES, A. (eds) (1992) *Teacher Development and Educational Change*, London, The Falmer Press.

OFSTED (1993) *Access and Achievement in Urban Education*, London, HMSO.

OFSTED (1996) *The Appraisal of Teachers 1991–6*, London, OFSTED Publications.

OJA, S.N. (1989) Teachers: Ages and stages of adult development, in HOLLY, M.L. and MCLAUGHLIN, C.S. (1989) (eds) *Perspectives on Teacher Professional Development*, Lewes, The Falmer Press.

OSTERMAN, K.F. and KOTTKAMP, R.B. (1993) *Reflective Practice for Education: Improving Schools through Professional Development*, Newbury Park, CA, Corwin Press.

OZGA, J. (1995) 'Deskilling a profession: Professionalism, deprofessionalisation and the new managerialism', in BUSHER, H. and SARAN, R. (eds) *Managing Teachers as Professionals in Schools*, London, Kogan Page, pp. 21–37.

OZGA, J. and LAWN, M. (1988) 'Interpreting the labour process of teaching', *British Journal of Sociology of Education*, **9**, pp. 323–36.

PAJARES, F. (1996) 'Self-efficacy beliefs in academic settings', *Review of Educational Research*, **66**, 4, pp. 543–78.

PARKAY, F.W., CURRIE, G. and RHODES, J.W. (1992) 'Professional socialisation: A longitudinal study of twelve high school principals', *Educational Administration Quarterly*, **28**, 1, pp. 43–75.

PARTNERSHIP ACT (1890) *Halsbury Statutes*, Vol. 32, Sec. 1(1), p. 782/3.

PASCALE, P. (1990) *Managing on the Edge*, New York, Touchstone.

PATTERSON, J.L. (1993) *Leadership for Tomorrow's Schools*, Alexandria, Virginia, Association for Supervision and Curriculum Development.

PETERS, R.S. (1966) *Ethics and Education*, London, Allen and Unwin.

PETERSON, W. (1964) 'Age, teacher's role and the institutional setting', in BIDDLE, B. and ELENA, W. (eds) *Contemporary research on teacher effectiveness*, New York, Holt, Rinehart and Winston, pp. 264–315.

POLANYI, M. (1967) *The Tacit Dimension*, Garden City, New York, Doubleday.

POLLARD, A., BROADFOOT, A., CROSS, P., OSBORN, M. and ABBOT, D. (1994) *Changing English Primary Schools: The impact of the Education Reform Act at Key Stage One*, London, Cassell.

Popkewitz. T. (1996) 'Rethinking decentralization and state/civil society distinctions: The state as a problematic for governing', *Journal of Education Policy*, **11**, 1, pp. 27–51.

Posch, P. and Mair, M.G. (1997) 'Dynamic networking and community collaboration: The cultural scope of education action research', in Hollingsworth, S. (ed.) *International Action Research: A Casebook for Educational Research*, London, Falmer Press, pp. 261–74.

Postman, N. (1992) *Technopoly*, New York, Knopf.

Prick, L. (1986) *Career Development and Satisfaction among Secondary School Teachers*, Amsterdam, Vrije Universiteit.

Purkey, W. and Smith, M.S. (1982) 'Synthesis of research on effective schools', *Educational Leadership*, **40**, 3, pp. 64–9.

Raudenbush, S.W., Rowan, B. and Cheong, Y.F. (1992) 'Contextual effects on the self-perceived efficacy of high school teachers', *Sociology of Education*, **65**, 1, pp. 150–67.

Reeves, J., Mahony, P. and Leif-Moos (1997) 'Headship: Issues of career', *Teacher Development*, **1**, 1, pp. 43–56.

Rényi, J. (1998) 'Building learning into the teaching job', *Educational Leadership*, **55**, 5, February 1998, pp. 70–4.

Reynolds, D. (1988) 'The consultant sociologist: A method for linking sociology of education and teachers', in Woods, P. and Pollard, A. (eds) *Sociology and Teaching: A New Challenge for the Sociology of Education*, Beckenham: Croom Helm, pp. 158–75.

Reynolds, D. and Farrell, S. (1996) *Worlds Apart? A Review of International Surveys of Educational Achievement Involving England*, University of Newcastle, Newcastle.

Reynolds, M.C. (1989) 'Students with special needs', in Reynolds, M.C. (ed.) *Knowledge Base of the Beginning Teacher*, Oxford, Pergamon.

Riseborough, G.F. (1981) 'Teacher careers and comprehensive schooling: An empirical study', *Sociology*, **15**, 3, pp. 352–81.

Rivera-Batiz, F.L. and Marti, L. (1995) *A School System at Risk: A Study of the Consequences of Overcrowding in New York City Schools*, New York, IUME Research Report No. 95–1.

Robertson, M. (1992) 'Teacher development and gender equity', in Hargreaves, A. and Fullan, M. (eds) *Understanding Teacher Development*, London, Cassell.

Robertson, S.L. (1996) 'Teachers' work, restructuring and postfordism: Constructing the new "professionalism"', in Goodson, I.F. and Hargreaves, A. (eds) *Teachers' Professional Lives*, London, Falmer Press.

Robinson, G.E. (1990) 'Synthesis of research on the effects of class size', *Educational Leadership*, April, pp. 80–90.

Rosenholtz, S. (1989) *Teachers' Workplace: The Social Organisation of Schools*, New York, Longman.

Rossman, G.B., Corbett, H.D. and Firestone, W.A. (1988) *Change and Effectiveness in Schools: A Cultural Perspective*, New York, Suny Press.

RUBIN, L. (1989) 'The thinking teacher: Cultivating pedagogical intelligence', *Journal of Teacher Education*, **40**, 6, pp. 31–4.

RUDDUCK, J. (1988) 'The ownership of change as a basis for teachers' professional learning', in CALDERHEAD, J. (ed.) (1988) *Teachers' Professional Learning*, London, Falmer Press.

RUDDUCK, J. (1991) *Innovation and Change*, Buckingham, Open University Press.

RUDDUCK, J. (ed.) (1995) *An Education that Empowers: A Collection of Lectures in Memory of Lawrence Stenhouse*, Clevedon, Multilingual Matters.

RUDDUCK, J. (1997) 'Professional development and school improvement: Reviewing the concept of partnership', Address to the International Study Association on Teachers' Thinking Conference, Kiel, Germany, October 1–5.

RUDDUCK, J., DAY, J. and WALLACE, G. (1997) 'Students' perspectives on school improvement', in HARGREAVES, A. (ed.) *Rethinking Educational Change with Heart and Mind*, 1997 ASCD Yearbook, Alexandria Vit, ASCD, pp. 73–91.

RYAN, K. (1987) 'The moral education of teachers', in RYAN, K. and MCLEAN, G.F. (eds) *Character Development in Schools and Beyond*, Westport CT, Praeger, pp. 358–80.

RYLE, G. (1949) *The Concept of Mind*, London, Hutchinson.

SACHS, J. (1997a) 'Reclaiming the agenda of teacher professionalism: An Australian experience', *Journal of Education for Teaching*, **23**, 3, pp. 263–75.

SACHS, J. and GROUNDWATER-SMITH, S. (1996) Celebrating teacher professional knowledge: School reform and teachers' professional judgement. Paper presented to 'Re-engineering Education for Change' Conference, UNESCO and Asia Pacific Centre for Educational Innovation and Development, Bangkok.

SACHS, J. and LOGAN, L. (1990) 'Control or development? A study of inservice education', *Journal of Curriculum Studies*, **22**, 5, pp. 473–81.

SALOVEY, P. and MAYER, J.D. (1990) 'Emotional intelligence', *Imagination, Cognition, and Personality*, **9**, pp. 185–211.

SAMMONS, P., HILLMAN, J. and MORTIMORE, P. (1995) 'Key characteristics of effective schools: A review of school effectiveness research', A report by the Institute of Education for the Office for Standards in Education (OFSTED), London University, International School Effectiveness and Improvement Centre.

SANDER, T. (ed.) (1994) *Current Changes and Challenges in European Teacher Education: European Yearbook of Comparative Studies in Teacher Education — 1994*, Belgium, Nijs-Herent.

SARASON, S.B. (1990) *The Predictable Failure of Educational Reform*, San Francisco, Jossey-Bass.

SCHEIN, E.H. (1985) *Organisational Cutlure and Leadership: A Dynamic View*, San Francisco, Jossey-Bass.

SCHLECHTY, P.C. (1990) *Schools for the 21st Century: Leadership Imperatives for Educational Reform*, San Francisco, Jossey-Bass.

SCHMUCK, R.A. and SCHMUCK, P.A. (1974) *A Humanistic Psychology of Education*, Mayfield, National Press Books.

SCHÖN, D.A. (1971) *Beyond the Stable State: Public and Private Learning in a Changing Society*, Harmondsworth, England, Penguin Books Ltd.

SCHÖN, D.A. (1983) *The Reflective Practitioner: How Professionals Think in Action*, New York, Basic Books.

SCHÖN, D.A. (1987) *Educating the Reflective Practitioner: Toward a New Design for Teaching and Learning in the Professions*, New York, Basic Books.

SCHÖN, D.A. (1991) *The Reflective Turn: Case Studies in Reflective Practice*, New York, Teachers College Press.

SENGE, P.M. (1990) *The Fifth Discipline*, New York, Currency/Doubleday.

SERGIOVANNI, T.J. (1984) 'Leadership and excellence in schooling', *Educational Leadership*, **41**, 5, pp. 4–13.

SERGIOVANNI, T.J. (1992) *Moral Leadership*, San Francisco, Jossey-Bass.

SERGIOVANNI, T.J. (1995) *The Principalship: A Reflective Practice Perspective*, Boston, Allyn and Bacon.

SHARMAN, R.G. (1987) 'Organisational supports for implementing an instructional innovation', *The Alberta Journal of Educational Research*, **33**, 4, pp. 236–46.

SHARP, R. and GREEN, A. (1975) *Education and Social Control: A Study in Progressive Primary Education*, London, Routledge and Kegan Paul Ltd.

SHIMAHARA, K. (1997) 'Professional development: The Japanese view of teaching as craft', Paper presented to the 6th Norwegian National Conference on Educational Research, University of Oslo, May 20–22nd.

SHULMAN, L. (1987) 'Knowledge and teaching: Foundations of the new reform', *Harvard Educational Review*, **57**, 1, pp. 1–22.

SIKES, P.J. (1992) 'Imposed change and the experienced teacher', in FULLAN, M. and HARGREAVES, A. (eds) (1992) *Teacher Development and Educational Change*, London, The Falmer Press.

SIKES, P.J., MEASOR, L. and WOODS, P. (1985) *Teacher Careers: Crises and Continuities*, London, Falmer Press.

SLAVIN, R.E. (1989) 'Class size and student achievement: Small effects of small classes', *Educational Psychologist*, **24**, 1, pp. 99–110.

SLAVIN, R.E. (1990) 'Class size and student achievement: Is smaller better?', *Contemporary Education*, **62**, 1, pp. 6–12.

SLAVIN, R.E. (1994) 'School and classroom organization in beginning reading: Class size, aides and instructional grouping', in SLAVIN, R.E., KARWEIT, N. and WASIK, B.A. *Preventing Early Reading Failure: Research, Policy and Practice*, Boston, Allyn and Bacon.

SMITH, G.A. (1995) 'Living with Oregon's measure 5: The costs of property tax relief in two suburban elementary schools', *Phi Delta Kappan*, **76**, 6, pp. 452–61.

SMITH, H., WIGGINTON, E., with HOCKING, K. and JONES, R.E. (1991) 'Foxfire teacher networks', in LIEBERMAN, A. and MILLER, L. (eds) *Staff Development for Education in the '90s*, New York, Teachers College Press, pp. 193–220.

SMYLIE, M. (1995) 'Teacher learning in the workplace: Implications for school reform', in GUSKEY, T.R. and HUBERMAN, M. (eds) *Professional Development in Education: New Paradigms and Practices*, New York, Teachers College Press.

SMYTH, J. (1991) *Teachers as Collaborative Learners*, Milton Keynes, Open University Press.

SOCKETT, H. (1989a) 'Research, practice and professional aspiration within teaching', *Journal of Curriculum Studies*, **21**, 2, pp. 97–112.

SOCKETT, H. (1989b) 'A moral epistemology of practice', *Cambridge Journal of Education*, **19**, 1, pp. 33–41.

SOCKETT, H. (1993) *The Moral Base for Teacher Professionalism*, New York, Teachers College Press.

SOMEKH, B. (1988) 'Action research and collaborative school development', in MCBRIDGE, R. (ed.) *The In-service Training of Teachers*, London, The Falmer Press, p. 164.

SOMEKH, B. (1994) 'Inhabiting each other's castles: Towards knowledge and initial growth through collaboration', *Educational Action Research*, **2**, 3, pp. 357–82.

SOUTHWORTH, G. (1993) 'School leadership and school development: Reflections from research', *School Organisation*, **13**, 1, pp. 73–87.

SPARKS, D. and HIRSCH, S. (1997) *A New Vision for Staff Development*, Alexandria, Virginia, Association for Supervision and Curriculum Development.

STAESSENS, K. and VANDENBURGHE, R. (1994) 'Vision as a core component in school culture', *Journal of Curriculum Studies*, **26**, 2, pp. 187–200.

STALLINGS, J. (1979) 'Follow through: A model for in-service teacher training', *Curriculum Inquiry*, **9**, pp. 163–81.

STALLINGS, J.A. (1989) 'School achievement effects and staff development: What are some critical factors?', Paper presented at the Annual Meeting of the American Educational Research Association, San Francisco.

STANFORD, B. (1994) 'Using technology for lifelong learning — strategies for relevance in flexible and distance learning', Keynote Lecture, 1st Global Conference on Lifelong Learning, Rome.

STARRATT, R. (1991) 'Building an ethical school: A theory for practice in educational leadership', *Educational Administration Quarterly*, **27**, 2, pp. 185–202.

STEADMAN, S., ERAUT, M., FIELDING, M. and HORTON, A. (1995) *Making School-based INSET Effective*, Research Report No. 2, University of Sussex Institute of Education.

STEELE, F. (1975) *Consulting for Organisational Change*, University of Amherst, Massachusetts Press.

STENHOUSE, L.A. (1975) *An Introduction to Curriculum Research and Development*, London, Heinemann Educational Books Ltd.

STENHOUSE, L. (1979) 'Research as a basis for teaching', in STENHOUSE, L. (1983) *Authority, Education and Emancipation*, p. 163.

STENHOUSE, L. (ed.) (1980) *Curriculum Research and Development in Action*, London, Heinemann Educational Books.

STERNBERG, R.J. (1985) *Beyond IQ*, New York, Cambridge University Press.

STERNBERG, R.J. and HORVATH, J.A. (1995) 'A prototype view of expert teaching', *Educational Researcher*, **24**, pp. 9–17.

STIEGELBAUER, S. (1992) 'Why we want to be teachers', Paper presented at the Annual Meeting of the American Educational Research Association, San Francisco.

STOLL, L. and FINK, D. (1996) *Changing Our Schools: Linking School-Effectiveness and School Improvement*, Buckingham, Open University Press.

STRINGFIELD, S. (1995) 'Attempting to enhance student learning through innovative programs: The case for schools evolving into high reliability organizations', *School Effectiveness and School Improvement*, **6**, 1, pp. 67–96.

STRINGFIELD, S. and TEDDLIE, C. (1998) 'A time to summarize: The Louisiana School Effectiveness Study', *Educational Leadership*, **46**, 2, pp. 43–9.

STRONACH, I. and MACLURE, M. (1996) 'Mobilising meaning, demobilising critique? Dilemmas in the deconstruction of educational discourse', *Cultural Studies*, **1**, pp. 257–74.

SUGRUE, C. (1996) *Complexities of Teaching: Child-centred Perspectives*, London, Falmer Press.

SVINGBY, G. (1993) Effektive kunnskaper, *Bedre skole*, 2 cited in DALIN and RUST (1996) *Towards Schooling for the Twenty First Century*, London, Cassell.

SYLVA, K. (1996) 'Right from the start: The importance of pre-school education and learning', in ROYAL SOCIETY OF ARTS (1996) *For Life: A Vision for Learning in the 21st Century*, London, RSA.

TALBERT, J.E. and MCLAUGLIN, M. (1994) 'Teacher professionalism in local school contexts', *American Journal of Education*, **102**, pp. 123–53.

TAMPOE, M. (1998) *Liberating Leadership*, London, The Industrial Society.

TAYLOR, F.W. (1911) *The Principles of Scientific Management*, New York, Harper.

TAYLOR, P.H. (1962) 'Children's evaluations of the characteristics of the good teacher', *British Journal of Educational Psychology*, **32**.

TEDESCO, J.C. (1997) 'Enhancing the role of teachers', in DAY, C., VAN VEEN, D. and WONG-KOOI SIM (eds) *Teachers and Teaching: International Perspectives on School Reform and Teacher Education*, Leuven/Apeldoorn, Garant.

TRACHTMAN, L. (1997) 'The stories of insiders', in LEVINE, M. and TRACHTMAN, R. (eds) *Making Professional Development Schools Work*, New York, Teachers College Press, pp. 185–93.

TRAVERS, C.J. and COOPER, C.L. (1996) *Teachers Under Pressure: Stress in the Teaching Profession*, London, Routledge.

TRIGGS, E. and FRANCIS, H. (1990) *The Value to Education of Long (Award Bearing) Courses for Serving Teachers*, Report of a Leverhulme Project, 1988–9, Institute of Education, University of London.

TRIPP, D. (1993) *Critical Incidents in Teaching: Developing Professional Judgement*, London, Routledge.

TROMAN, G. (1996a) 'The rise of the new professionals? The restructuring of primary teachers' work and professionalism', *British Journal of Sociology of Education*, **17**, 4, pp. 473–87.

TROMAN, G. (1996b) 'Headteachers, collaborative, school cultures, and school improvement: A changing relationship?', *Educational Action Research*, **4**, 1, pp. 119–44.

UNESCO (1996) *Enhancing the role of teachers in a changing world*, ED/BIE/CONFINTED 45/Info 10 Paper Presented by Educational International to

UNESCO, International Conference on Education, Forty-fifth Session, Geneva 30 Sept–5 October.

USHER, R. (1993) 'Experiential learning or learning from experience: Does it make a difference? In BOUD, D., COHEN, R. and WALKER, D. (eds) (1993) *Using Experience for Learning*, Buckingham, Open University Press.

VAN MANEN, M. (1977) 'Linking ways of knowing with ways of being practical', *Curriculum Inquiry*, **6**, 3, pp. 205–28.

VAN MANEN, M. (1995) 'On the epistemology of reflective practice', *Teachers and Teaching: Theory and Practice*, **1**, 1, pp. 33–50.

VAN VEEN, D., DAY, C. and WALRAVEN, G. (1997) 'Youngsters at risk and urban education: Problems and the role of research', in DAY, D., VAN VEEN, D. and WALRAVEN, G. (eds) *Children and Youth at Risk and Urban Education: Research, Policy and Practice*, Apeldoorm: Grant Publishers, pp. 9–16.

VAN VELZEN, W., MILES, W., EKHOLM, M.B., HAMEYER, U. and ROBIN, D. (eds) (1985) *Making School Improvement Work: A Conceptual Guide to Practice*, Leuven, Acco.

VONK, J.H.C. (1995) 'Teacher education and reform in Western Europe: Socio-political contexts and actual reforms', in SHIMAHARA, N.K. and HOLOWINSKY, I.Z. (eds) *Teacher Education in Industrialized Nations: Issues in Changing Social Contexts*, New York, Garland Publishing Inc., pp. 225–312.

WAGNER, J. (1997) 'The unavoidable intervention of educational research: A framework for reconsidering researcher–practitioner co-operation', *Educational Researcher*, **26**, 7, pp. 13–22.

WALBERG, H.J. (1991) 'Educational productivity and talent development', in FRASER, B.J. and WALBERG, H.J. (eds) *Educational Environments: Evaluation, Antecedents and Consequences*, Oxford, Pergamon Press.

WALBERG, H.J. (1991) *Educational Leadership*, **54**, 8, May 1997, p. 46.

WALKER, J. (1995) 'Parenting in the 1990s', *RSA Journal*, **CXLIII** (5456), pp. 29–41.

WALKER, M. (1996) 'Subaltern Professionals: Acting in pursuit of social justice', *Educational Action Research*, **4**, 3, pp. 407–25.

WANG, M. (1990) 'Programs that promote educational equity', in BAPTISTE, H.P., WAXMAN, H.C., WALKER DE FELIX, J. and ANDERSON, J.E. (eds) *Leadership, Equity and School Effectiveness*, Newbury Park, CA, Corwin Press.

WATTS, H. (1981) 'Can you feed a frog on tadpole food?' *Insight*, *Journal of the National Conference of Teachers' Centres Leaders*, **4**, 2, pp. 32–40.

WATTS, J. (1980) 'Sharing it out: The role of the head in participatory government', in BUSH, T. et al. (eds) *Approaches to School Management*, London, Harper and Row.

WAXMAN, H.C. (1992) 'Reversing the cycle of educational failure for students in at-risk environments', in WAXMAN, H.C., WALKER DE FELIX, J., ANDERSON, J.E. and BAPTISTE, H.P. (1992) *Students at Risk in At-Risk Schools. Improving Environments for Learning*, Newbury Park, CA, Corwin Press.

WEBB, K. and BLOND, J. (1995) 'Teacher knowledge: The relationship between caring and knowing', *Teaching and Teacher Education*, **II**, 6, pp. 611–25.

WEHLAGE, G.G., RUTTER, R.A., SMITH, G.A., LESKO, N. and FERNANDEZ, R.R. (1989) *Reducing the Risk: Schools as Communities of Support*, London, Falmer Press.

WELLINGTON, B. and AUSTIN, P. (1996) 'Orientations to reflective practice', *Educational Research*, **38**, 3, pp. 307–16.

WESTOBY, A. (ed.) (1988) *Culture and Power in Educational Organisations*, Milton Keynes, Open University Press.

WHITAKER, P. (1997) *Primary Schools and the Future: Celebrations, Challenges and Choices*, Buckingham, Open University Press.

WILCOX, B. and GRAY, J. (1996) *Inspecting Schools: Holding Schools to Account and Helping Schools to Improve*, Buckingham, Open University Press.

WINTER, R. (1989) 'Problems in teacher appraisal — an action-research solution', in ELLIOTT, J. and SIMONS, H. (eds) (1989) *Rethinking Appraisal and Assessment*, Milton Keynes, Open University Press.

WISE, A.E., DARLING-HAMMOND, L., MCLAUGHLIN, M.W. and BERNSTEIN, H.T. (1984) *Teacher Evaluation: A Study of Effective Practice*, Santa Monica, Calif. Rand Corporation, June.

WOODS, P. (1993) *Critical Events in Teaching and Learning*, London, Falmer Press.

WOODS, P. (1994) 'Adaptation and self-determination in English primary schools', *Oxford Review of Education*, **20**, 4, pp. 387–410.

WORD, E., ACHILLES, C.M., BAIN, H., FOLGER, J., JOHNSTON, J. and LINTZ, N. (1990) 'Project STAR final executive summary: Kindergarten through third grade results (1985–89)', *Contemporary Education*, **62**, 1, pp. 13–16, NCDS.

WRAGG, E.C., WIKELEY, F.J., WRAGG, C.M. and HAYNES, G.S. (1996) *Teacher Appraisal Observed*, London, Routledge.

WRIGHT, N. and BOTTERY, M. (1996) 'Choice of INSET in the LEA, GM and Independent sectors: Is a market at work?', *British Journal of In-service Education*, **22**, pp. 151–73.

YEATMAN, A. and SACHS, J. (1995) *Making the Links: A Formative Evaluation of the First Year of the Innovative Links between Universities and Schools for Teacher Development*, Perth, WA, Murdoch University.

YINGER, R. (1979) 'Routines in teacher planning', *Theory in Practice*, **18**.

YINGER, R. (1987) 'Learning the language of practice', *Curriculum Inquiry*, **17**, 3, pp. 293–318.

ZEICHNER, K. (1993) 'Action research: Personal renewal and social reconstruction', *Educational Action Research*, **1**, 2, pp. 199–220.

ZEICHNER, K.M. (1995) 'Beyond the divide of teacher research and academic research', *Teachers and Teaching: Theory and Practice*, **1**, 2, pp. 153–72.

ZEICHNER, K.M. and LISTON, D.P. (1996) *Reflective Teaching: An Introduction*, New Jersey, Laurence Erlbaum Associates.

Index